GEOFFREY BAKER AND BRUNO FUNARO

SHOPPING CENTERS
DESIGN AND OPERATION

PROGRESSIVE ARCHITECTURE LIBRARY

REINHOLD PUBLISHING CORPORATION
330 West Forty-second Street, New York, U.S.A.

Printed in U.S.A. by L. Middleditch Co.
Binding by Russell-Rutter Co., Inc.
Composition by Nu-Type Service

ORDER OF CONTENTS

SHOPPING CENTERS, WHY, HOW, AND WHERE?

INCREASE IN BUYING POWER. CHANGE IN RETAILING PATTERN
SHIFTING OF POPULATION. INCREASED USE OF AUTOS, BUSES
ORGANIZATION OF A PLANNED CENTER
WHAT ABOUT DOWNTOWN?

Two stores side by side have always, under a free enterprise system, done more than twice the business of a single store. Every merchant in the world realizes the value of this cumulative pull; it is implicit in every Main Street, every Fifth Avenue, every crossroads store group. However, the shopping centers with which we are chiefly concerned in this book, represent a new species — a compound of the department store, the rural general store, the downtown shopping block, and a traditional street market.

This new type of store group will usually be under single ownership, a dominating fact which more often than not will show itself through a certain architectural unity which ties the stores together. Each tenant will have been selected by the owner of the center to fit into a pre-ordained pattern of merchandising. Together this group of tenants will be able to supply all of a shopper's day-to-day needs; larger centers are designed to satisfy once-a-year needs too, purchases which used to require a trip downtown. The typical customer in this new type of shopping center will be driving a private car. Instead of occupying a ground area of approximately 3 sq. ft., as a pedestrian, the auto-shopper requires an area of approximately 300 sq. ft., before dismounting. The area allocated for parking will exceed the actual floor area of the stores by as much as 3:1. In the future this disproportion may increase even further, for automobiles in the United States are at present increasing, percentage-wise, at a faster rate than people. The historical opportunity which causes this new type of shopping center to

emerge is, naturally, a complex of facts. We shall discuss here only those four which seem to us most influential: increase in buying power, changes in retailing pattern, shifting of population, increased use of automobiles and buses. Each is related to and influenced by every other; to divide an environment into four sections is merely for convenient analysis and indexing.

Increase in Buying Power

Since 1940, even when the decreased purchasing power of the dollar is taken into account, there has been a sizeable increase in the amount of money available for spending in retail stores.

The population has increased by approximately 20 millions. The number of wage-earners has increased, proportionately, even further; there are now 14 million more than there were in 1940 — they are making more money. Average wages for industrial workers have increased from $25.20 per week in 1940 to over $60.00 per week today.

These increases have been by no means offset by a large decrease in the purchasing power of the dollar. Disposable personal income, after payment of taxes, *with all figures converted to a uniform 1948 dollar**, has risen from an average per capita figure of $979 in 1940 to $1,314 in 1950.

Moreover, because of rent control, a greater proportion of this income has been available for retail purchases. This is clearly shown by a comparison of the Retail Price Index, compiled by the U.S. Office of Business Economics, with the

Consumers' Price Index, compiled by the U.S. Bureau of Labor Statistics. The former shows the expenditures by moderate-income families in metropolitan areas, but does not include rent. It increased 90% between 1940 and 1950. The Consumers' Price Index, on the other hand, which does include rent, increased only 73% during these ten years.

The continued leveling of incomes has also worked to the advantage of retail store sales. Comparing gross family incomes in 1929 and 1949, we find that the lowest group, with incomes up to $2,400, included 42% of all U.S. families in 1929; in 1949 this group formed only 29% of the total. Very high income families also decreased, from 9% to 4% of the total. The middle income group, on the other hand, increased from 48% to 66% of all the families in the U.S.†

Change in retailing pattern

In the depression-haunted Thirties, when crops were being plowed under and little pigs being slaughtered, in tentative efforts to master the economics of abundance, expansion was a less urgent problem than economy. Store building lagged, but operating efficiency increased. The most spectacular evidence is the supermarket which, in less than ten years, transformed the food retailing pattern.

---

*"Compass Points of Business", November 1950. Dun & Bradstreet Inc.

†1929 figures prepared by Prof. Paul Nystrom of Columbia University, brought up to 1949 by Prof. Paul D. Converse of the University of Illinois, and quoted in *Business Week*, June 24, 1950.

The housewife was lured by cheap prices to do the work formerly done by clerks and delivery vans. Self-service had arrived. Now 80% of shoppers prefer it. But because this implies a trip to the store (usually in the family automobile) they buy groceries less often. And more than 50% of these canny housewives, to the grocer's despair, do almost all their weekly food shopping on Friday or Saturday, thus causing a recurrent and wasteful peak, which cannot be flattened out even by promoting "specials" on other days. Nevertheless the self-service supermarket is now coming into its own; in 1950 it was found that one out of every three had been built since 1947. Distribution costs have been drastically cut; and other types of retail store are beginning to take advantage of the grocers' experience with self-service.

Automatic merchandising (see page 8), already well-established for handling cigarettes, candy and soft drinks, is now being tested by department stores for many other of the smaller, standardized items. Malcolm P. McNair, Filene Professor of Retailing at Harvard University, says that "it is an outworn myth that all women look on shopping as a major sport to be indulged in as often and as long as possible. . . . The sales counter with a row of sales people all at fixed stations behind the counter is today entirely obsolete. . . . Practically every survey made shows large chunks of sales people's time spent merely in idleness. . . . If razor blades, toothpaste and men's shorts are purchased in much the same hasty pickup fashion as cigarettes, why shouldn't large quantities of them be sold through vending machines?"

The automatic vending machine may also be used to great advantage (as it has already been in Europe) for after-hours selling, when the rest of the store is closed. The machine may also take over small but necessary departments which do not normally do enough business to justify the salary of a whole-time sales clerk; or it may be used to help out in other departments which are just too big to be run by a single sales clerk, but not quite big enough to justify two; unlike a human, the machine can be fitted to perform as half a clerk and cost less.

Supermarkets, having flirted with such complex mechanical servants as Clarence Saunders' "Keydoozle", or the Skillman Collecting Machine (see pages 8 and 9), are still frightened that any mechanical failure of such servants after their introduction may be more damaging to confidence than the more customary human failures of the clerk.

Customers have already been trained to do their own collecting, so mechanical improvements are at present being applied rather to the handling of merchandise from the time it reaches the store by truck until it is put on the self-service display stands, to the devising of faster, more economical accounting, and to some improved method of transporting bags of groceries from the check-out gates to the shopper's car. For this last stage in the self-service routine underground belt conveyors leading from the stores to some central pick-up station in the parking field seem to have hopeful possibilities (see page 34). Some self-service supermarkets are now offering home delivery, at a small extra charge.

Self-service was but one of the merchandising economies which spread through the food business during the depression Thirties (and because the greatest proportion of every family's retail spending goes for food, changes in the pattern of distribution in the food business are of vital importance both to the consumer and to other retail business). The second economy was a general increase in scale. The big chain grocers eliminated their smaller units and increased the size of their larger stores. 100 x 100 ft. has now become a minimum supermarket size. In the early Thirties it would have been almost a maximum size.

The A & P in 1927 had 15,566 stores. Annual sales per store averaged $48,690. By 1941 the number had been cut to 6,042; sales per store had jumped to $237,537. Today they have only 4,682 stores, yet sales per store now average more than $500,000.

As the larger supermarkets (both chain and independent) continue to gain in sales volume, and the smaller ones to lose, this trend toward consolidation and a general increase in scale is continuing. Food retailing being a highly competitive business, the profit margins remain very small. On 1949 sales of $2.9 billion the A & P net profit was only $33.3 million (i.e. only 1.1% of sales). For comparison's sake it may be mentioned that the profit figure for General Motors—the only company in the world selling more goods than the A & P—during the same period was 11.5% of sales.

To offset the low profit margins on food, the supermarkets are exploiting their immense customer traffic to the full by spreading into other household goods which yield a higher profit. There has been a steady increase in the number of stores stocking drugs, toiletries, ice cream, and household sundries such as light bulbs, brooms and cooking pans, even though there are hardware, drug, and variety stores in the immediate neighborhood. In outlying rural areas the general store is taking on some of the self-service features of the supermarket.

Shifting of Population

Stores follow people; and people have been on the move. The census figures reveal the surge and drift, from the farms (where machines are replacing hands) to the cities (where higher wages and more amenities are alluring), from the city (where accommodation is hard to find) to the suburbs (where the air is clean, and the grass is green, and the taxes seem so low), and from East to West across the continent (to the traditional land of promise).

Industrial expansion in the West and Southwest was particularly violent during World War II. Towns of 10,000, even 20,000 people were flung up within a couple of years, and usually far from existing downtown shopping centers. Planning new store groups to serve these new communities should have been a comparatively simple matter. Here were "captive" consumers; there were no competing stores within convenient distance, particularly when gas was rationed.

Design-wise many of these centers, like those in the Government-sponsored Greenbelt towns ten years earlier, are of great interest (see pages 128 and 236). They have strongly influenced the design of more recent, privately promoted centers. But their economic experience is worth very little, for, encased in their own community, they are isolated from the unforeseeable stresses and shifts of competitive business centers with a less controlled environment.

More realistic estimates of the number, sizes and types of store required for a given community may now be arrived at through the experience of economic analysts working for private promoters. Of far wider importance in developing new shopping centers during the last few years, since World War II, has been the spontaneous movement from the city to the suburbs. The result is that more than half the total U.S. population now lives in 168 "standard metropolitan areas" (the central city and its suburbs).

A few 1950 census figures will show most dramatically how it is the suburbs rather than the central city which have shown lively growth during the last ten years. In the New York and Northeastern New Jersey metropolitan area the population increase was 4.7% inside the central city, 22.6% outside. In Chicago the increase was 6.2% inside, 30.8% outside. In Washington, D. C., the disparity is more striking still: 20.3% inside the city, 116.4% in the surrounding suburbs.

The great housing developments that have sprung up to shelter these millions of families trying to escape the overcrowding, dirt, congestion, and high rents of the central city, these straggling blocks of garden apartments and these rows of single-family houses are often on large tracts of land far removed from any old-established village center.

Such isolation is, indeed, almost axiomatic. For these families are leaving the city to find open space, even perhaps a little land for truck gardening, at least enough ground for a vegetable garden. These families are willing to make do without some of the city conveniences, in return for lower taxes. They seldom realize that their coming, and particularly the cost of their children's schooling, will almost immediately set the tax rate to jumping. The wide extension of utilities and good state roads, automatic household equipment of every kind and, above all, the tremendous increase in the number of private cars and in their annual average use, as reflected by mileage — all these have made suburban, and even rural living, tolerably comfortable for the most confirmed city dweller. Only during a storm, with electric wires down, roads blocked, and the telephone out of commission, does one of these new city exiles begin to realize

what country life can be in an unmodernized, back-country farmhouse. Yet, strangely enough it is a misty golden picture of such a rural past—Thoreau via Bromfield—which joins in a Trinity with better public schools and lower taxes to encourage the young city family in its original exodus to the suburbs.

This surburban development pays very little heed to existing administrative boundaries. Rapid transit lines and highways become the most important directional guides of city growth. Inchoate lumps of housing are scattered across the countryside according to the possibilities of real estate profit, and with small regard for over-all planning.

Occasionally a single development will be large enough to exist as a community in its own right, Levittown, for example, or Park Forest (see pages 258 and 267). Or some Federal government agency, or a large private industry may create a new town for their workers; Greenbelt, for example, or Linda Vista, or Maplewood (see pages 232, 236, and 129). In such cases the planner is given a chance to co-ordinate the shopping center with the rest of the community. It has often been successfully combined with the social and civic center of such a newly created village.

In most communities of this sort the size of the population to be served, even its average income level, is clearly established in advance. The Trading Area is usually quite exactly delimited. Of the examples quoted immediately above, only Park Forest has a shopping center larger than community size intended to draw trade from beyond its boundaries.

The average, less privileged, promoter has a far more difficult job on his hands. He must try to distinguish the center of gravity created by a number of new residential groupings built and to be built. He must then be the first to erect a shopping center; and he must make a successful, well-informed guess at its requisite size. A shopping center which is not sufficiently comprehensive (and remember that success may depend upon its springing forth full-grown, rather than adding gradually to its size) can be just as unsuccessful as a center that is too large for the population served. It is only a mistake of this nature which will give the latecomer a chance.

Two examples may, perhaps usefully, be cited here. Shaker Square (see page 184), had it been on one side only of the main road, and had it been allowed sufficient space to expand, might well have grown into a very much larger store group. Northgate (see page 214) was but one of two large centers projected for the northern suburbs of Seattle. Northgate is already built, and operating most successfully; there is probably no longer opportunity left for any rival of equal scale, at least until the population density in that area has shown a large increase.

Increased use of automobiles and buses

Between 1925 and 1940 the number of automobiles in the U.S. increased from approximately 20 million to 32 million. Between 1925 and 1950 the number of passenger cars has more than doubled. The increase in their use has been even more striking: from approximately 200 billion passenger miles in 1925 to 500 billion in 1940. (The cutback in auto production during World War II has distorted the figures from 1940 to 1950.)

Automobile ownership and use is not evenly distributed geographically. The newly developed West and Southwest, with its more widely scattered communities and less complete public transportation system, naturally depends more upon the private automobile. In 1950 there were 8.7 persons per passenger car in New York City, only 2.9 in Los Angeles. Car registrations in Los Angeles are only 18% less than those of New York and Chicago combined. A car has become as essential there as a pair of shoes, with significant results upon business. In 1929 about 33% of the total retail business in Los Angeles was done in the downtown stores. In 1949 the percentage had dropped to only 12.5.

Obviously Los Angeles is an exaggerated example; but there are very good reasons to suppose that it may be a new species rather than a sport among U.S. cities. The automobile has become the preferred method of transportation. Drive-in movie theaters are now a commonplace feature of the landscape everywhere in the U.S. In Texas, as might be expected, this has been carried one stage further—a drive-in concert. In Hollywood (which of course is in the stage beyond Texas) there is a drive-in church. And in White Plains, a New York suburb, they are trying out mailboxes which may be used by motorists without dismounting.

In public transportation the trolley car steadily declined from its peak use in 1923 to a low point in 1940. The trolleys' costly tracks, which formed a rigid armature within the growing city, and generated important store groups at intersections, have been gradually torn up.

Bus routes, with their infinite flexibility, do not so readily spawn bordering strips of commercial development. Bus routes can be quickly bent or lengthened in order to serve new suburban communities. The traffic which the bus can bring may be of considerable importance even to those shopping centers which are laid out primarily for the automobile.

However, there is also a trend to the use of private cars rather than buses. St. Paul, Minn., is an interesting example. The population increased from 260,000 in 1920 to 336,000 in 1940, a gain of 29%. But the number of passengers carried by the city's trolley cars and buses dropped during this same period from 84,561,000 to 36,462,000, a loss of 57%. Automobile registrations in St. Paul, on the other hand, showed an increase of almost 400%—from 17,500 in 1920 to 86,000 in 1940—whereas over the nation as a whole the increase in registrations was less than 250% in this period. Meanwhile trade in downtown St. Paul was declining, due to the lack of parking space, which made it an unattractive shopping center for anyone coming into the center of town by automobile.

It is hard to see how this downtown congestion in our cities can become anything but worse, given the facts outlined above. The private car occupies about half as much space as a bus, but carries on the average less than a tenth of the number of passengers. Other pertinent factors, such as driving skill, space between vehicles in motion, etc., will only emphasize still further this disparity between private and public transportation. The congestion will to some extent carry its own palliatives. It has been found, for example, that in cities with a population of less than 100,000, 81.2% of those en-

(text continued on page 10)

BOOM TOWN STORE BLOCK ALREADY HAS CURB PARKING AND CONTINUOUS OVERHANG, GOOD FEATURES BOTH COMMONLY FOUND IN MODERN SHOPPING CENTERS

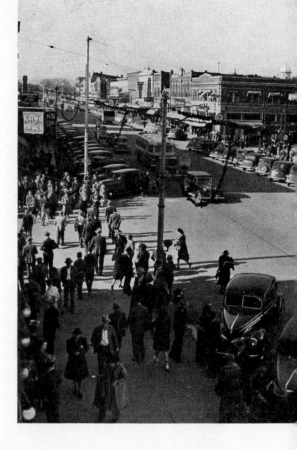

MAIN STREET, U.S.A. (IN THIS CASE GADSDEN, ALABAMA) WITH ANTIQUATED STORE BUILDINGS, AND INSUFFICIENT PARKING SPACE. BUT ITS COMPETITIVE PRICES, AND A WIDE SELECTION OF GOODS, WILL GIVE A STIFF FIGHT TO NEW, OUTLYING SHOPPING CENTERS

MODERN SHOPPING CENTER, MILES AWAY FROM DOWNTOWN CONGESTION, HAS COVERED WALKS FOR SHOPPERS, AMPLE HEAD-IN PARKING SPACE, UNIFIED DESIGN, SINGLE OWNERSHIP. (CAMERON VILLAGE, RALEIGH, N. C.)

MECHANIZED SELLING is not new. Cigarettes and candy have been sold through coin vending machines for many years. Now rising labor costs and increased adaptability of the machines have set almost all the large chain and department stores to experimenting with partial mechanization.

Coin vending machines are best fitted to handle fast-moving standard brands with low unit cost (up to $3.00 is the practical limit at this time). The newer ones are not restricted to standard-size packages, but at least one of the leading makes does set a maximum package size of 4 x 10 x 15 ins. Moreover no machine can yet be

relied upon to handle frozen foods — ideally suited to this mechanized selling.

One great advantage of the coin vending machine is its ability to serve as half a sales clerk, either helping out in a busy department, or taking over completely a department which is not large enough to justify the cost of a clerk. Of particular importance to the shopping center is a round-the-clock automatic branch store.

For supermarkets there have been various devices evolved for automatic collection from a central storage of items already ordered by the customer from samples on display. However, the housewife is by now accustomed and willing

MECHANIZED SELLING HELP IN DEPT. STORE

HOLES IN TAPE RECORD KEEDOOZLE ORDERS

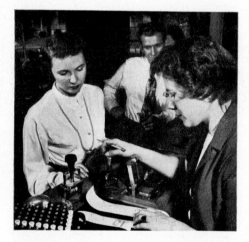

TAPE TOTALS COST, ORDERS UP GROCERIES

COIN VENDING MACHINES have already made a place for themselves as dispensers of soft drinks by the cup—choice of four flavors, mixed or plain, hot or cold, all from one machine. (Spacarb) Now mechanized selling is being tried in department stores, and in outlying branches of these stores set up in transportation terminals and shopping centers. Machines can be kept open 24 hours a day, 7 days a week. (Vendomatic)

MECHANIZED SUPERMARKETS may not be too far in the future. Each of the two systems illustrated here has been operating for at least a limited period.

Keedoozle (above) is Clarence Saunders' mechanized successor to Piggly Wiggly, one of the first self-service chains. Keedoozle was first brought out in 1935, soon closed because of mechanical difficulties. In 1948 a pilot store was opened again in Memphis. The sales room at this store

is small, lined with glass-fronted shelves holding one of each item available. Outstanding advantages of such a system are the saving of display space, and prevention of spoilage and theft. It can be used most effectively for branded goods in containers, where quality is known.

The operating mechanism of the whole ordering and accounting system is a roll of paper tape, housed in a "key". This key is inserted in sockets along the front

ASSUME MANY DIFFERENT FORMS

to do her own collecting, so probably such machinery will not be widely used. Meanwhile self-service is being improved by display racks like that shown at right. In a length of 84 ft. this can display more than 2,000 items. The shelves are kept filled by gravity. Restocking is done from behind, so the store aisles are never cluttered with stock carts.

By mechanized computing at the checkout gates, with code numbers replacing individual price tags (so that price changes are made by simply turning a screw on one machine instead of restamping hundreds of packages), the cashier's job can be made practically foolproof.

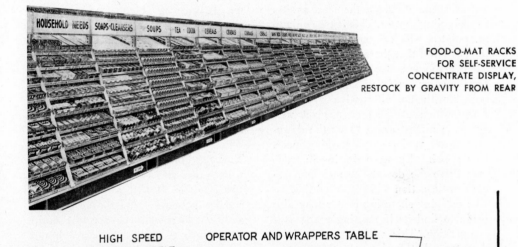

FOOD-O-MAT RACKS
FOR SELF-SERVICE
CONCENTRATE DISPLAY,
RESTOCK BY GRAVITY FROM REAR

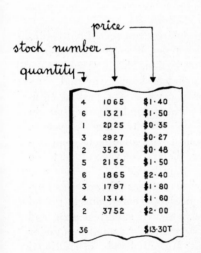

price

stock number

quantity

4	1065	$1·40
6	1321	$1·50
1	2025	$0·35
3	2927	$0·27
2	3526	$0·48
5	2152	$1·50
6	1865	$2·40
3	1797	$1·80
4	1314	$1·60
2	3752	$2·00
36		$13·30 T

SKILLMAN TAPE KEYED TO STOCK NUMBERS

of the display shelves. By pressing buttons a shopper pierces the tape with a series of coded holes which record her order. By putting this coded tape through a calculator the cashier automatically records the cost of each item, and the total order cost. The same tape actuates a series of feed chutes in the storage warehouse. These automatically tip the ordered goods on to a conveyor belt which **hustles them out to the waiting customer.**

HIGH SPEED
CONVEYER BELT

OPERATOR AND WRAPPERS TABLE

STREET FRONT

DISPLAY

SKILLMAN COLLECTING MACHINE

STORAGE SPACE
WITH COLLECTOR MACHINE
MAY BE DISTANT FROM SALES ROOM

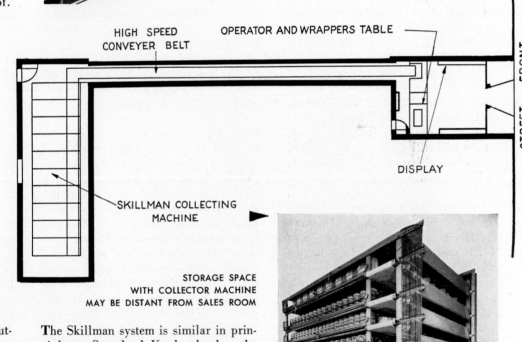

The Skillman system is similar in principle to Saunders' Keedoozle, has the special merit of using standard telephone exchange parts. A cashier records the quantity and stock number of all items ordered from the sample shelves. This automatically records the cost (above left), and signals the collector machine (right) to forward items on moving belts to the customer. This system could operate at night with a single employee.

9

(text continued from page 7)

tering the central business district came in their own cars. In cities with a population of more than 500,000, only 41.1% of those entering the central business district came in their own cars*. This also suggests that, in the larger metropolitan areas, public transportation terminals in the central city, and bus and railroad stopping places in the surrounding suburbs, become increasingly important as traffic generators, and therefore as sites for shopping centers. This is true only to the point at which decentralization is so far advanced that there is no more than a trickle of commuter traffic left.

On the other hand, if shoppers are presented with an alternative group of stores, which satisfies their needs as well (or even almost as well) as the downtown stores, yet has ample parking space, then a painfully steep decline in trade may drive the downtown merchants to the drastic action which is essential.

The outlying shopping center may also begin to find itself meeting really stiff competition. This will come not from downtown but from competing centers on the outskirts of the center's own Trading Area. Shoppers will have a choice of centers, and ample free parking will be a commonplace. The automobile shopper, having once mounted her car, would just as willingly drive five miles as two. But she will still want one-stop marketing, so she will probably be drawn to the biggest center within reasonable distance provided that its values are in line with those of its competitors.

The successful center must, of course, be easily accessible by road *(see page 21)*. It can usually be a little off the main highway, provided that its promotion is loud and skillful. It can usually be on cheap land (cheap at least by downtown standards), so that low rent may be held out as a bait to the downtown department store, and to the other, smaller tenants.

Gas stations were the first to realize the possibilities of running after their customers on the highway by setting up stations outside the towns. Then retail businesses which require large store areas— furniture stores, automobile salesrooms —began moving out of the center of town to less expensive sites along the highway.

Then the department stores saw cheap land in the suburbs as a possible way to satisfy their urge for expansion. Their downtown stores were hemmed in. The cost of expansion was too high, particularly for such a comparatively unproductive use as parking. In the suburbs they could acquire ample space (necessary for the volume of traffic upon which they depend), and yet still make tremendous savings in overhead.

Three types of shopping center

The shopping centers illustrated and discussed in this book will usually fall into one of three categories: neighborhood centers, community centers, regional centers. The distinction here is partly by size and partly by the variety of store types included in the project.

THE NEIGHBORHOOD SHOPPING CENTER will be designed to serve a *minimum* of 750 families. It will always contain a small supermarket and a drug store. In addition there will be several service stores such as a dry cleaner, a beauty parlor, shoe repair, laundry, barber; also possibly a variety store. If the supermarket has no satisfactory bakery department a separate bakery will be needed. There should also be a filling station.

THE COMMUNITY SHOPPING CENTER, designed to serve a larger number of families, will probably contain, in addition to the stores mentioned above, a service grocery with phone order and delivery service, florist, milliner, radio, children's shoes, gifts, candy, lingerie, liquor, women's apparel, restaurant, book store, children's wear and toys, haberdashery, athletic goods. In older centers of this size a theater would have been normal. Now the development of television will probably confine theaters to the larger centers.

A bank and post office should be included as a public service, if they are not available elsewhere in the neighborhood. They do not pay well, any more than service stores do, but often in a shopping center it is more important to have a balanced variety of stores, than a group of 100% pullers."†

In order to make this truly a community center it may also be advisable to include

offices for doctors and other professional men. However, it is generally considered among developers that office workers usurp a great deal of parking space all day without drawing sufficient trade to compensate for this. Offices are generally put on the second floor of one of the store buildings, or in a separate building which may be used as a buffer between the stores and the surrounding residences.

THE REGIONAL SHOPPING CENTER is much larger than either of the two types so far considered. It is a suburban equivalent of the existing downtown shopping center. It will contain, in addition to all the stores listed above, at least one department store (many planners are now advocating two or more, in order to gain the stimulating effect of competition), backed up by a wide selection of women's apparel stores. The larger the concentration of such stores, the more business each will do. In a center of limited size it may be advisable to increase the number of these stores at the expense of a more rounded selection such as would normally be advocated. The regional center will provide a wide choice of fashion shopping goods, also home furnishings and household equipment of all types. Women will find here an ample selection. They will spend time making a choice, shopping around, comparing prices, value. The parking turnover will therefore be lower than in either of the other two types of center. Many women will come from comparatively far, though not very often, to do their shopping here.

Such a large center as this, covering anything from 20 to 50 acres, must be placed in a thickly settled suburban area, and be easily accessible by a number of major highways. Huston Rawls of National Suburban Centers *(see page 199)* demands 300,000 to 900,000 people within 30 minutes driving time. Then, if only 15% of these shoppers spend upward of $500 each year at his center, its gross sales will total at least $22,500,000.

---

*Eno Foundation for Highway Traffic Control: "Investigation of 8 typical cities under 100,000 population, and 10 typical cities over 500,000 population."

†These recommendations are adapted from those in "The Community Builders Handbook", published by the Urban Land Institute.

There has in recent years been considerable research done by city planners and commercial developers in an attempt to discover the most desirable ratio between residences and stores. The recommendations of the several authorities vary widely.* Villanueva, for example, recommends ten times more net acreage per 1,000 people for Local Shopping than does Lillibridge. The number of stores recommended ranges from 0.8 per 1,000 people (Lillibridge) to 6.3 per 1,000 people (Stein & Bauer).

One interesting fact, brought out in data collected by Harrison, Ballard & Allen for a planned rezoning of New York City, is that the number of stores per 1,000 people is higher in the more densely populated areas; and that more space (measured in front feet of business per 1,000 people) is used for retail selling in low-rent areas.

For example, in the Sunset Park area of Brooklyn, where population density is 150 persons per acre and rents average $35 per month, there are approximately 353 ft. of commercial use (i.e. retail stores) per 1,000 people. In the South Greenfield section of Brooklyn, on the other hand, where population density is only 75 persons per acre and rents average $50 per month, there are only 143 front feet of commercial use per 1,000 people. These facts appear to run directly contrary to Lillibridge's assumptions. as discussed in the first paragraph above.

Any positive space allotment is further confused by considerations of profitable management which demand that every store be planned to do a maximum amount of business in a minimum amount of space. So the average in ideal, or subsidized, communities is almost inevitably higher than that found by experience to be desirable in store groups carefully run for profit.

Organization of a planned center

For a choosy shopper the modern planned shopping center has three outstanding advantages. First, the cumulative pull of a carefully selected group of stores. Second (a corollary of the first advantage), all of a day's average shopping can be done at one place; this is one-stop marketing. Third, there is always ample parking space.

In larger centers the shopper will not be content unless she is given the opportunity of comparison shopping. So many experts now feel that in a regional center it would be more profitable to have two department stores than one.

If the center is large enough to support more than a single supermarket, then usually the two rivals will prefer to be next door to one another. It is normal practice, likewise, to group all the other food stores—bakery, meat market, fish market, delicatessen, and so on—around the supermarkets. The smaller women's apparel stores and specialty shops are, in similar fashion, grouped around the flanks of the department store.

Obviously such a grouping of stores makes life easier for the shopper who wishes to compare values. It will also act to the advantage of the smaller stores, which are better able to take advantage of the traffic generated by the big pullers. And competition will almost inevitably add to the volume of all the stores.

But how should these minor groupings be disposed within the bigger group of the complete shopping center? Suppose that in a big regional center there are two department stores, should they be set one almost next door to the other (like Macy's and Gimbel's in New York), in order to stimulate shopping excitement by concentration? Or should they be set at opposite ends of the center, in order to spread their pulling power through a larger number of small apparel stores? Or again, might it not be more advantageous still to reduce the scale of a big center like this by breaking it into two sections, each centered on a department store of a different class?

These are questions to which there is no agreed, complete, or inevitable answer. The layout of the centers shown later in this book *(pages 78 to 279)* suggest some of the many possible alternatives.

In any center, large or small, the arrangement of stores is usually dictated by the pullers: supermarket, drug, variety, and department stores. In neighborhood centers the order has now become practically inevitable; supermarket at one end, drug store at the other, and variety store in the center of the store block. This gives to the two most essential tenants the corner sites which they still demand, and at the same stroke helps to distribute shopping traffic more evenly throughout the entire store group.

In some of the medium-size, or community-type centers, the store grouping is roughly by type of goods sold: convenience goods, shopping goods (whether style merchandise or service goods), and service stores. This tends, however, to a somewhat lopsided distribution of traffic, and overcrowding of the parking space which serves the convenience goods stores. The shopping goods area, in contrast, will often appear depressingly empty.

There are certainly many affinities between stores, most of them fairly obvious. For example a group of women's apparel stores could well be put alongside a gift shop, or a tea shop; but a liquor store might be a fish out of water in such company. It might better be grouped with a sporting goods store, which in turn would fit in comfortably alongside a hardware store or a hobby shop.

Consideration should also be given to possible grouping by class (i.e. price) of merchandise sold. While Sears Roebuck, for example, and a variety store might be a well-assorted pair, they should probably both be kept separated from the better apparel stores.

As a theater is busiest in the evening, it is often set apart in what may be termed a night section. Here beside the theater there will be a restaurant or drug store, a candy store, florist, perhaps a liquor store. In the near future there may also be automatic vending units to take the place of those stores in the other part of the center which are closed in the evening and on weekends. The vending units may come to be considered as branch stores open round the clock every day.

In a shopping center on a through highway, it will often pay to have a good restaurant on the highway edge of the center near the gas station. It will persuade passing motorists to stop off and perhaps do some impulse buying in the other stores which make up the group. Services such as banks and post offices, also miscellaneous service stores such as dry cleaner, laundry, barber, shoe re-

*Marcel Villanueva: "Planning Neighborhood Shopping Centers". Robert M. Lillibridge: "Shopping Centers in Urban Redevelopment". Clarence S. Stein & Catherine Bauer: "Store Buildings & Neighborhood Shopping Centers."

pair, beauty shop, etc. are so essential—and such low-rent tenants—that they may usually be set off to one side in a less busy location than the main pullers and their satellites. These services, however, do bring in a certain amount of trade to the other stores in the center; and they are certainly essential in composing a balanced group for one-stop shopping. They contribute an important share of the center's cumulative pull.

This is a typical instance of the four-way benefit that the planned shopping center may confer: on the shopper, the large store, the small store, and the promoter. The shopper we have already considered. The large store, in return for its prestige and pulling power, is given a low rent and a protected location. It acquires some control over its surroundings without actually owning them (though there are several cases in which a large store owns a whole center). The small store, in return for a somewhat higher rent than might be demanded elsewhere, can take advantage of the traffic generated by its larger neighbor. In most cases it is also guaranteed against direct competition within the center. By joining a group it is able to share facilities such as parking, landscaping, even public toilets and children's nurseries, which it could never afford were it on its own.

The modern planned shopping center may well cut down the appalling rate of failure now obtaining among retail stores. During the last half century, regularly every year more than a quarter of a million retail businesses have failed; and in most years an even larger number of new ones started. Most of these failures result from poor location.

Then let us not forget the promoter, the man who owns the group of stores. Naturally enough he benefits also from the success of his shopping center. If he has the normal percentage leases the more business the center does the more he benefits. And he almost certainly deserves to benefit, for upon him rests all the responsibility of decision.

He must decide what tenants he wants; and then make do with those he can get. Should he try for independents or for chains? The independents may pay a higher percentage rent, but the chains may draw more customers because of their wide reputation, spread through national advertising. But they will probably be more difficult to keep in line. They will consider themselves, more likely than not, strong enough to break the rules set by the promoter (and his architect) in his efforts to impose a certain uniformity, especially in the matter of signs. And when a chain wants to grow bigger it will probably set up another branch in a rival shopping center nearby, whereas the independent is more willing to grow with the center by taking more space. As a general principle it is only those centers which completely dominate their own Trading Area which can afford to take a chance with independents.

By varying the rates of percentage leases, the smaller tenants are forced to subsidize the larger *(see table page 20)*. The long-term percentage lease is almost universal for the larger tenants. In some centers the smaller merchants are still on short-term fixed-rent leases, so that they can be moved to another position if necessary. This is often the case with service stores, which the promoter may later wish to move to a less busy location.

Larry Smith, one of the most experienced analysts and management consultants in the West, offers the following pointers on how to obtain the most productive leases in a modern shopping center. "The most profitable lease with a major tenant will be based on a *low* minimum rental rather than on a high. The major tenants take the attitude that if they are required to *guarantee* a fair return on the total valuation of land and buildings, they should pay no percentage rent. If they do pay a percentage it will be more in the nature of an inflation clause, rather than a full percentage on sales. When the major tenants are located, there will be an assurance of pedestrian traffic which will allow you to obtain higher minimum rents and more generous percentage clauses with the smaller tenants than would otherwise be possible. . . . . The guaranteed rent for the major tenants should be limited to not more than 4% on the land valuation and 5¾% on the buildings, plus an allowance sufficient to take care of the taxes. If guaranteed rents are higher than this rate you will either lose the tenants or lose part of the possible percentage rents."

(text continued on page 16)

HOW A SMALL

REHABILITATION of existing town centers, though common in the bulky reports of planning experts, is usually forced into being only by the impulsion of some disaster or emergency. In Mount Kisco it was the elimination of a grade crossing. This entailed moving the New York Central tracks and station about 200 ft. northwest; East Main Street was then carried across the tracks by an overpass. To an outsider this would seem nothing more than a small and desirable improvement. To many of the merchants clustered along East Main Street it meant starting afresh in some new location. Many of these "D.P.s" decided that South Moger Avenue was the most promising spot for the new stores which they would build. Normally such a movement would have got under way haphazardly, one by one, with no overall pattern of development. Fortunately in Mount Kisco the Northern Westchester Joint Planning Program, led by the Village Planning Board, brought forward a plan for improving this whole section of the town. Beside a new shopping center for the displaced merchants, and a new parking space for the relocated railroad station, the plan included a general cleanup of the swampy area beside Branch Brook, which had recently been released from New York's watershed acreage. This gained useful parking space at the rear of the new store group. The complete program is now under way. The sketch at right and the descriptions below are taken from a broadsheet issued by the sponsors of this town remodeling during their campaign to gain public support. It may suggest both objectives and methods to other communities. The plan is divided into six stages:

1. The grade crossing on East Main St. will be eliminated in the near future. To make space for the overpass and new station, many stores will be demolished. In order to vacate when necessary, merchants must move into new buildings, which will go up as soon as the Village Fathers give the cue by endorsing this plan.

2. The new shopping center will be concentrated east of the station on both sides

TOWN SET ABOUT REMODELING ITS SHOPPING DISTRICT

of South Moger Avenue, and extending to Branch Brook. A new service street and adjacent parking area are therefore necessary. Charting out the street and parking area is an essential before the store buildings go up. You will note that the new service street links East Main St. with Lexington Avenue. It will ease the present traffic problem by taking trucks off the main thoroughfare. It will afford hasty shoppers a convenient parking space directly behind the stores, or allow leisurely shoppers access to the adjacent, tree-framed, parking lot.

3. Mount Kisco's new stores and new movie theater will be grouped in a center convenient to the surrounding 50,000 people. Linked by a shaded, landscaped walk, which will run from the Municipal Building to the station, stores will be accessible to pedestrians and motorists.

4. An extensive new parking area, accommodating more than 500 cars, is situated to the east of the new service street. Note its central location, and the fact that it will be attractively landscaped.

5. In order to provide space for the new parking lot adjacent to the shopping center, Branch Brook must be relocated. The swampy brook will become a tree-lined canal, one of many efforts which will be made to combine beauty with practicality in the future Mount Kisco.

6. The new boulevard, linking Lexington Avenue to Jeff Feigel Square, will be a four-lane, divided thoroughfare. From it the motorist will view a landscaped village green with its public buildings on the east, and on the west an attractive retail shopping center across the inviting, tree-dotted parking area.

7. Negotiations are now under way to acquire property for the village from the railroad, to be used for additional parking space when the new station is built. When this is accomplished, the present parking lot, now used by commuters, can be sold. Such sale might well add a quarter of a million dollars to the village's working capital, taxable property now exempt, and an even larger amount in new taxable construction.

MOUNT KISCO, N. Y., BEFORE RELOCATION OF RAILROAD TRACKS AND STATION. BRANCH BROOK TRAVERSES SWAMPY, UNDEVELOPED AREA IN FOREGROUND

PLAN OF REMODELING DESCRIBED IN TEXT, AND NOW UNDER WAY. CORRESPONDING VIEW TO THAT SHOWN IN PHOTOGRAPH ABOVE

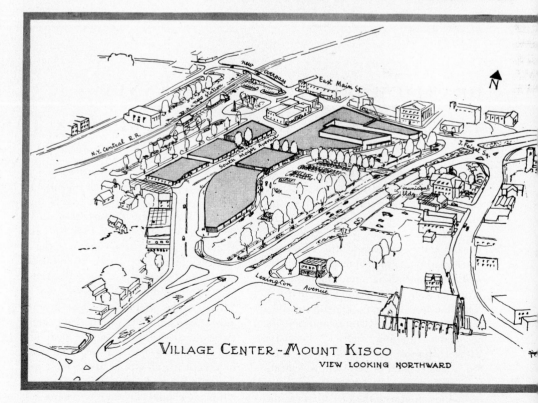

VILLAGE CENTER — MOUNT KISCO
VIEW LOOKING NORTHWARD

EXISTING BUSINESS BUILDINGS
EXISTING PUBLIC BUILDINGS

THESE CONDITIONS STARTED IT ALL

DRASTIC IMPROVEMENTS PLANNED

TO REJUVENATE HEART OF SUBURBAN TOWN

"**TRAFFIC CONDITIONS** at both ends of the shopping center are congested and confusing. Through traffic of private cars and trucks, as well as buses, makes the whole business length of Purchase Street unsafe and inconvenient for shoppers. Street parking is inadequate, obstructive, and time-consuming; and modern off-street parking is almost non-existent."

Thus the city of Rye, N. Y., with startling honesty, described existing conditions in its main shopping district (Purchase Street). Here was the urgent justification for a master plan of civic improvements prepared by the Planning Commission in co-operation with the City Council, the Community Chest, the Board of Educa-

tion, several advisory committees, and an impressive list of technical consultants. Rye happens to be a small suburban town in Westchester County, three-quarters of an hour from New York by train. More than half of its six square miles is taken up by private homes. Its residents have been described as "typically American". Its problems are equally typical.

"Even if the architecture and general appearance of Rye's business center miraculously could be made ideal, the job of reaching it by car, finding a place to park while shopping, still would present chronic and exasperating delays.

"It is no wonder then that too many dollars which rightfully should be dropping

into the tills of Rye shopkeepers now fatten the balances of stores in New York, White Plains, and smaller nearby communities. In 1944, according to Dr. Homer Hoyt, at least $3 million worth of trade — a third of the $9 million annual retail total spent by Rye people — went to stores outside of Rye.

"It has become a vicious circle: people can't shop conveniently in the Purchase Street district, so they buy out of town; this cuts down volume for Rye's merchants and discourages them from keeping adequate and varied stocks; then the people who do reach these stores fail to find what they want. Inconvenience of shopping, inadequacy of merchandise,

HOW THE TRADING AREA IS DELIMITED
HOW TO FIND THE NUMBER OF FAMILIES, AND THEIR INCOME
HOW MUCH DO THEY SPEND IN RETAIL STORES?
HOW MUCH WILL THEY SPEND AT THE NEW CENTER?

Bankers and prospective tenants are far more easily influenced by well-presented economic facts than by architectural renderings. So the market analysis of a proposed shopping center becomes of far greater value to the promoter than the architect's plans which, after all, will be constantly modified to suit the tenants' whims. Moreover the market analysis is of inestimable value to the promoter in the planning of his own program, by suggesting the most suitable tenants and forecasting anticipated rentals on a percentage basis.

Such an analysis will be most telling in its effect when prepared by some authoritative but neutral expert, such as a research institute or a professional economist. This becomes especially important if, as is normally the case, the market analysis is to be used for promotion.

The analysts' basic purpose is always to discover how many stores, of what type and of what size, can reasonably expect to operate profitably in the proposed shopping center. With rents based on percentage leases, the landlord is just as closely concerned as the tenant in avoiding unprofitable business.

The overall pattern of these market analyses is by now well-established. First the Trading Area is mapped, i.e. the limited district from which the new center may reasonably expect to attract trade. Second, calculation is made of the Buying Power within the Trading Area, i.e. the amount of retail purchases made by those living within the Trading Area. The simple, empirical method of allotting so many square feet of store area for each family is completely outmoded, even for preliminary calculation. When applied to a newly-created, isolated community, with a controlled population size and often, too, a controlled income level, economic surveys can easily be made to appear simple and inevitably correct in their conclusions. To cope, however, with the more normal realities of free competition, shifting population, and widely varying income levels, the successful economic analyst must be a person of considerable ingenuity and one with wide experience in the field.

Typical of his difficulties is the fact that almost all of the basic figures upon which his analysis must rest are inevitably out of date. The nation-wide U.S. Census remains his basic sourcebook; but a new edition is compiled only once every ten years. So the conscientious analyst is immediately forced into a whole set of assumptions, long before his ultimate forecast is even under way. It is small wonder that the most respected economic surveys are usually the work of analysts who appear to treat the available facts most conservatively.

An economic survey for a new shopping center will usually try to provide factual answers to the following five questions, in this order:

1. How large is the Trading Area?

The size of the Trading Area will depend to a large degree upon what the new shopping center has to offer when compared with what is available in other stores serving the same area.

What type of stores, how big, and in how great a variety, are to be found in this new center? The Trading Area of a small neighborhood center with a supermarket, drug store, and a few service stores will obviously be much more confined than the Trading Area of a 30-store center—assuming that each was to be placed on the same site.

Will the new center offer any advantage in the general price level of its merchandise? Will there be a predominance of well-known chain stores? Will there be directly competitive stores to spur comparison shopping? Will this new center offer better physical comforts than existing stores, air-conditioning for example, short walking distance between stores, at least a pleasant, relaxed atmosphere of comfort, with well-kept flower gardens and a safe place for the children to play while mother goes shopping?

Above all will this new center be more accessible than the existing stores? How long does it take to reach it, by automobile, or by public transportation? There can be no absolute standards of time-distance. The Trading Area will contract or expand according to the relative accessibility of competing store centers. Its geographical boundaries may in some cases be best defined by driving-time isochrons (see Clearview, Princeton, page 196), in other cases by neighborhoods which have, in their turn, been formed by natural features such as rivers, canals, railroads, or highways (cf. Northgate,

Seattle, page 219). Normally the Trading Area will not be accurately delimited by a circle. When measuring the pull of a large regional center, Reilly's Law may be applied just as aptly as it has been to downtown shopping centers: "Two cities attract retail trade from an intermediate city or town in the vicinity of the breaking point approximately in direct proportion to the populations of the two cities, and in inverse proportion to the square of the distances from these two cities to the intermediate town."

If the shopping center (as it normally does, once it passes the neighborhood size), includes a variety of stores with different ranges of attraction, the Trading Area will be subdivided into a number of roughly concentric areas of different size. Each will represent the magnetic range of one or a group of stores. Food stores, for example, will never exert such extensive attraction as a department store. People are willing to go quite a long distance to buy furniture, or an evening dress. These are comparatively expensive goods and seldom bought; they warrant comparison shopping, which may mean a trip downtown or to a regional center. Whereas for a bottle of aspirin almost no one considers going further than the corner drugstore.

Homer Hoyt would divide the Trading Area of a large shopping center into three separate zones:

Zone 1, immediately surrounding the center. Here the nearest food, drug, and service stores are in the new center.

Zone 2 already has neighborhood stores (food, drugs and service) nearer than the new center. But this zone lacks department and clothing stores of a quality equal to those in the new center.

Zone 3 is a fringe area. It has all the same types of store as the new center, and nearer. But these customers may be lured away by greater selection of goods, better values, more comfort and convenience — if the new center can offer such inducements.

2. How many families live in this Trading Area as now determined?

Population data is gathered decennially (1940, 1950, 1960, . . .) by the Bureau of the Census, a branch of the Dept. of Commerce. The figures are tabulated by

small census tracts, and to simplify calculations the Trading Area boundaries are often made to coincide with census tract boundaries.

During the years intervening between one census and the next, population figures must be brought up to date with whatever information happens to be available locally. Building permits filed, the number of new light and water meters installed by the local utility company, the number of new telephones — all these may be helpful in bringing the population figures up to date.

3. What is the income of these families?

The U.S. Dept. of Commerce and the U.S. Dept. of Labor both compile figures on family income. Again, however, it will be found that the available figures are almost invariably out of date. They can be adjusted in accordance with the changing level of national income. They can also be checked against state income tax returns, where these are available.

4. How much do these families spend in retail stores?

The Bureau of Labor Statistics in the U.S. Dept. of Labor made a nation-wide survey of family expenditures in 1944. Since 1945 they have made similar studies — analyzing spending patterns by income groups for families of two or more persons and single consumers — in three cities each year. In 1951 they will undertake another nation-wide survey to give both individual city and regional averages. As an example of the type of information which these tables provide, we reproduce one of those concerned with Houston, Texas, in 1948 (published Dec. 1949).

Another commonly used source is the "Survey of Buying Power" published annually by *Sales Management* magazine. This lists population estimates, and estimates of retail sales by counties and towns. The retail sales estimates are divided into four groups: food, general merchandise, drugs, home furnishings (including household goods, radio). These figures are more up to date but less detailed and specific than those of the Bureau of Labor Statistics.

5. How much of this retail spending will be done at the new center?

Here the economic analyst must use discretion as well as ingenuity. In a controlled community under single ownership, with a shopping center at the hub, prognostication is not difficult. A very accurate survey should be possible under these conditions because, with an exclusive franchise, such a center will have no competition.

Under more normal conditions, with many overlapping zones of attraction between competing store centers, with the influence of big cities such as New York and Chicago spreading out hundreds of miles beyond their physical boundaries, the analyst must apply percentage reductions. In setting their extent he must depend almost entirely upon his own experience and his acute judgment of local conditions. Some analysts, however, are now making use of questionnaires. The latter are employed as a means of increasing the analysts' understanding of local shopping habits and requirements. Distance from competing stores, the quality and extent of competition, relative accessibility, established habits — all these will be taken into account when deciding the percentage discounts which should be applied to the retail expenditures expected from various districts within the established Trading Area.

These percentage discounts will vary for each Zone of the Trading Area *(see under 1. How large is the Trading Area, above)* and for each type of store. In Zone 1, for example, which is that immediately surrounding the new center, 50% or more of the total expenditures for food may be expected to go to the new center. From Zone 2, on the other hand, the analyst may expect no more than 10%, and from Zone 3 none at all. However, in the case of apparel the new center may expect to draw almost as much trade from Zone 3 as from Zone 1. This is partly because there is less immediate competition, partly because women especially are used to spending some time on buying clothes, and always are willing to go further if they are able to find a better selection by so doing.

The analyst will now be in a position to compile an itemized list of potential sales at the new center in the many different

Houston, Tex.—White and Negro families of 2 or more persons: Average money income, expenditures, and savings, by net income class, 1948

Item	White families: Annual money income after personal taxes[1]										Negro families: Annual money income after personal taxes[1]					
	Under $1,000	$1,000 to $2,000	$2,000 to $3,000	$3,000 to $4,000	$4,000 to $5,000	$5,000 to $6,000	$6,000 to $7,500	$7,500 to $10,000	$10,000 and over	Under $10,000	Under $1,000	$1,000 to $2,000	$2,000 to $3,000	$3,000 to $4,000	$4,000 and over	Under $4,000
Percent of families in each class	2.4	10.4	13.4	27.5	19.5	9.1	7.3	6.7	3.7	96.3	2.3	18.2	47.7	18.2	13.6	86.4
Average family size[2]	2.5	2.9	3.4	3.2	3.6	3.5	3.1	3.1	4.3	3.3	(10)	3.5	2.4	3.6	3.5	2.9
Average number of earners	1.0	.9	1.4	1.4	1.5	1.6	1.7	2.0	1.5	1.4	(10)	1.6	1.5	1.8	1.8	1.5
Expenditures for current consumption	$2,073	$2,440	$2,725	$3,596	$4,521	$5,750	$5,864	$6,926	$10,161	$4,108	(10)	$1,804	$2,583	$2,898	$4,769	$2,441
Food[3]	640	884	1,008	1,186	1,362	1,448	1,608	1,663	2,656	1,241	(10)	850	772	1,026	1,130	831
Housing, fuel, light, and refrigeration[4]	330	341	416	447	601	663	787	767	1,782	528	(10)	200	401	270	344	325
Household operation	96	132	161	147	273	462	472	446	771	247	(10)	58	106	121	326	98
Furnishings and equipment	123	213	182	254	295	461	559	634	785	314	(10)	96	235	254	586	204
Clothing	134	315	262	492	536	861	777	1,221	1,485	548	(10)	239	513	479	1,184	436
Automobile	15	138	159	417	477	784	318	631	947	395	(10)	0	76	176	284	79
Other transportation	10	30	67	46	58	63	112	108	312	60	(10)	54	70	94	83	70
Medical care	362	172	215	201	414	280	278	219	245	262	(10)	49	102	104	290	93
Personal care	56	50	62	95	101	164	143	185	149	102	(10)	59	107	117	138	97
Recreation	15	37	70	146	171	231	433	652	517	191	(10)	105	83	77	186	85
Tobacco	14	75	77	68	82	64	62	88	145	72	(10)	60	58	91	87	64
Reading	24	28	23	31	47	54	52	57	58	38	(10)	11	21	17	44	18
Education	0	1	7	22	29	68	94	21	197	28	(10)	15	9	11	33	10
Other	254	24	16	44	75	147	169	234	112	82	(10)	8	30	61	54	31
Gifts and contributions	45	66	66	161	192	288	519	344	1,495	193	(10)	46	105	169	769	104
Insurance	43	84	77	118	202	260	393	310	596	172	(10)	44	85	98	211	78
Net surplus	0	0	0	0	0	0	0	936	1,306	0	(10)	0	0	230	0	0
Personal taxes[5]	13	26	90	226	352	613	591	1,061	2,249	328	(10)	19	113	198	219	108
Money income[1]	642	1,606	2,587	3,481	4,502	5,374	6,694	8,645	14,357	4,073	(10)	1,630	2,512	3,414	5,213	2,470
Other money receipts[6]	4	0	0	0	50	30	0	0	0	13	(10)	0	0	0	0	0
Net deficit	1,625	939	218	356	302	719	192	0	0	353	(10)	240	206	0	240	120
Balancing difference[7]	+106	−41	−63	−38	−61	−175	+110	+129	+799	−34	(10)	−24	−55	+19	−296	−33
Surplus:																
Percentage reporting	0	5.9	18.2	37.8	46.9	26.7	58.3	72.7	66.7	35.4	(10)	12.5	19.0	62.5	33.3	26.3
Average amount for those reporting	0	$90	$176	$382	$391	$542	$1,138	$1,757	$2,298	$667	(10)	$90	$326	$457	$100	$368
Deficit:																
Percentage reporting	75.0	82.3	54.5	60.0	53.1	73.3	41.7	27.3	33.3	58.2	(10)	50.0	61.9	12.5	66.7	50.0
Average amount for those reporting	$2,167	$1,146	$458	$834	$913	$1,178	$2,054	$1,256	$677	$1,012	(10)	$502	$433	$440	$410	$434
Percent of expenditure for current consumption	100.0	100.0	100.0	100.0	100.0	100.0	100.0	100.0	100.0	100.0	(10)	100.0	100.0	100.0	100.0	100.0
Food[3]	30.9	36.2	37.0	33.0	30.1	25.2	27.4	24.0	26.2	30.2	(10)	47.1	29.9	35.4	23.7	34.0
Housing, fuel, light, refrigeration[4]	15.9	14.0	15.3	12.4	13.3	11.5	13.4	11.0	17.5	12.9	(10)	11.1	15.5	9.3	7.2	13.3
Household operation	4.6	5.4	5.9	4.1	6.0	8.0	8.0	6.4	7.6	6.0	(10)	3.2	4.1	4.2	6.8	4.0
Furnishings and equipment	5.9	8.8	6.7	7.1	6.5	8.0	9.5	9.2	7.7	7.6	(10)	5.3	9.1	8.8	12.3	8.4
Clothing	6.5	13.0	9.6	13.7	11.9	15.0	13.3	17.6	14.6	13.3	(10)	13.3	19.9	16.5	24.8	17.9
Automobile	.7	5.7	5.8	11.6	10.6	13.6	5.4	9.1	9.3	9.6	(10)	0	2.9	6.1	6.0	3.2
Other transportation	.5	1.2	2.5	1.3	1.3	1.1	1.9	1.6	3.1	1.5	(10)	3.0	2.7	3.2	1.8	2.9
Medical care	17.5	7.0	7.9	5.6	9.2	4.9	4.8	3.2	2.4	6.4	(10)	2.7	4.0	3.6	6.1	3.8
Personal care	2.7	2.0	2.2	2.6	2.	2.9	2.4	2.7	1.5	2.5	(10)	3.3	4.1	4.0	2.9	4.0
Recreation	.7	1.5	2.6	4.0	3.8	4.0	7.4	9.4	5.1	4.6	(10)	5.8	3.2	2.7	3.9	3.5
Tobacco	.7	3.1	2.8	1.9	1.8	1.1	1.1	1.3	1.4	1.8	(10)	3.3	2.3	3.1	1.8	2.6
Reading	1.1	1.1	.8	.9	1.0	.9	.9	.8	.6	.9	(10)	.6	.8	.6	.9	.7
Education	0	0	.3	.6	.6	1.2	1.6	.3	1.9	.7	(10)	.8	.3	.4	.7	.4
Other	12.3	1.0	.6	1.2	1.7	2.6	2.9	3.4	1.1	2.0	(10)	.5	1.2	2.1	1.1	1.3

ANALYSIS OF CONSUMER EXPENDITURES TYPICAL OF THOSE ISSUED BY THE U.S. DEPT. OF LABOR, BUREAU OF LABOR STATISTICS

categories of merchandise available. The potential sales figures can then be translated into square feet of store space. Each type of store will do a different amount of business per sq. ft. (cf. the table prepared for Clearview, Princeton, page 198).

From these estimates of gross business to be expected, the developer can calculate his potential income from rents, which are based on a percentage of this gross. These percentage rents vary to some extent, but the table on page 20 is representative of the general relationship between rents for different types of stores at the time of writing.

The developer will next compare this prospective income from rents with the projected cost of the buildings and site required to produce this income. And then he will be forced into modifications of all kinds (many of them drastic) in order to suit the tenants whom he is able to sign up, and to satisfy the bankers or investors to whom he must run for working capital.

Yet in most of the centers so far built actual business done has far outstripped the predictions of the economic surveys. This may be in part due to wilfully conservative estimates, but more perhaps to inexperience, which makes it difficult as yet to estimate how much the cumulative pull of a shopping center exceeds the sum of the pulls exerted by the individual stores gathered there.

PERCENTAGE OF GROSS INCOME PAID FOR RENT*

TYPE OF STORE	McMICHAEL	BROWNLOW	BANGS	RUBLOFF	CAMPBELL
Art Shops	6–10	—	7–9	8–10	8–10
Auto Accessories	3–5	—	6–8	5–8	5–7
Auto Agencies	3–4	—	3–4	3–4	3–4
Bakeries	4–6	—	6–8	6–8	6–8
Barber Shops	8–12	—	10–12	15	15
Beauty Shops (Merchandise)	8–10	—	10–12	10–12	10–15
Beauty Shops (Service)	8–10	—	to 20	15	15
Beer Parlors	7–8	—	—	10	8
Books and Stationery	6–8	—	8–10	8–10	10–12
Books, Second Hand	8–10	—	10–12	12–15	10
Candy	5–8	10	7–9	8–10	8–10
Candy (with Luncheon)	5–8			8–10	8–10
Cigars, Luncheonette, Sundries	3–5	8	4–5	6–8	4–5
Cleaning and Dyeing	6–8		8–10	8	8
Cocktail Lounges	5–7		7–8	9	8–10
Credit Clothing	5–7	7	5–7	6–8	5–6
Department Stores	2–3	4–5	3–4	3–4	3–4
Drug Stores (Chain)	3–5	6–7	4–5	5–7	5–8
Drug Stores (Individual)	5–6	7	7–8	8–10	8–10
Electrical Goods	4–5		5–7	6–8	8–10
Florists	8–10		10–12	10–12	10–15
Fruit Stores	4–6		12	10	10
Fruits and Vegetables	3–5		8–10	6–8	10
Furs	6–10		7–9	8–10	8–10
Furniture	4–7		6–7	5–6	6–8
Furniture (Credit)	5–8	7	5–6	5–6	4–7
Garage (Storage)	30–40		30–35	50	40
Gas Stations (Cents per gal.)	1		1–1½	1–1½	1–1½
Grocery Stores (Ordinary)	3–4		4–5	5	3–5
Grocery Stores (Chain)	2–3	3	2–3	2–3	2–3
Hardware	5–7		6–8	6–8	6–8
Hosiery and Knit Goods	7–10	10	7–9	7–8	8–10
Jewelry	6–8	10	6–8	8–10	10–12
Jewelry (Cheap Costume)	8–10		7–10	10	12
Jewelry (Exclusive)	6–8		5–6	8–10	12–15
Linens	8–10		10	8–10	10–12
Liquor Stores	5–8		6–8	6–8	7–8
Meat Markets	4–5		4–5	4–5	5–7
Meat Markets (Chain)	2–4		4–5	4–5	4–6
Men's Clothing	5–7	7	5–7	5–6	5–7
Men's Furnishings	5–8	10	8–10	8–10	10
Men's Hats	7–8	10–12	7–9	8	8–10
Men's Shoes	5–7	7	6–8	8–10	7–8
Men's Shoes (Volume)	6–8	7	5–6	6–7	6–8
Men's Tailors	6–7		6–7	8	7–9
Millinery	8–10	10–12	10–12	12½–15	10–15
Motion Pictures	10–18		12–15	12½–15	15–20
Optical Stores	8–10		8–10	15–20	10–12
Paint, Wallpaper Supplies	5–6			6	8–10
Parking Lots	30–40		35–40	50	30–40
Pianos and Musical Instruments	5–7		6–8	6–8	10
Radios and Television	6–10		5–7	5–6	8
Radios and Electrical	4–6		6–8	—	8
Restaurants	6–8		7–9	6–8	8–9
Cafeterias	5–7		6–7	6–8	7–8
Luncheonettes	7–8		8–10	8–10	8–10
Tea Rooms	7–8		8–10	8–10	10
Specialty Stores (Non-Advertising)	6–7		6–7	8–10	8–10
Sporting Goods	6–7		6–7	6–8	7–9
Theatres (Combination Vaudeville and Motion Pictures)	8–15			12½–15	12–15
Trunks and Leather Goods	5–8		7–9	8–10	10
Women's Cloaks and Suits	5–8	8	6–7	6–8	6–8
Women's Cotton Wear	6–8	10		—	8
Women's Furnishings	6–8	10	7–8	—	8–10
Women's Shoes	7–8	8	7–9	8–10	7–8
Women's Shoes (Volume)	6–7	7	6–7	6–7	6–8
5-10c or 25c-$2 Stores	4–6	6	5–6	5–6	3–5

*The five realtors quoted are from (L. to R.) Santa Barbara, Calif., Knoxville, Tenn., Washington, D. C., Chicago, Ill., and New York, N. Y. Each expert is quoting average figures for his section of the country.

WHAT MAKES A GOOD SHOPPING CENTER SITE?

ACCESSIBILITY DEPENDS UPON MORE THAN DISTANCE
HIGHWAY CAPACITY MORE IMPORTANT THAN TRAFFIC COUNT
VISIBILITY FROM THE HIGHWAY. ZONING
HOW MUCH IS IT WORTH PAYING FOR A SITE?

The most important factors to consider when judging a prospective shopping center site are accessibility to shoppers with the required Buying Power, topography, cost and zoning; and usually in that order. The developer will already have decided, on the basis of local need and the amount of money available for the project, exactly what type of center he hopes to create.

Is this to be a neighborhood store group, with a supermarket, drug store and a few service stores, designed to serve a limited area immediately adjacent to the center? Or is it to be at the other extreme of size, a regional center, which will contain all the elements of a neighborhood center, and then in addition at least one department store, a number of apparel stores, specialty shops, home furnishing stores, a movie theater, restaurants, and perhaps a post office.

Or then again it may be a community center, in size about midway between a neighborhood and a regional center (see page 10). But this is often a dangerous size at which to aim, for it may not have a sufficient choice of goods, to compete with existing or future centers nearby.

Accessibility

The accessibility of a shopping center depends upon much more than distance. A store that is two miles away, but on the way to work, may be much more accessible than a store which is only a mile away, but in the opposite direction.

A regional center served by wide highways with little traffic, and planned with ample parking space, may be more ac-cessible to the automobile shopper than a congested downtown shopping area, even though the latter may be very much closer if the mileage alone is considered. This can be most dramatically illustrated by the use of a map marked off in isochrons. These are the contour lines of driving-time-distance, which is one of the controlling factors in accessibility for automobile shoppers. By this measure the center may prove more accessible to a shopper living 9 miles away than to one 2 miles nearer (cf. map on page 197).

It is still true, however, that in the case of a neighborhood center distance is likely to be the most important kind of accessibility. The most desirable site for such a group of stores has usually proved to be on a main highway corner, at the edge of some rather dense new development. It should be adjacent to the area where further densening of the population seems most probable, and on a highway thickly used by local traffic. It may be of advantage to be on the homegoing side of the street, if this can be established with any accuracy.

Nearness in itself is not enough, even in the case of a neighborhood center; and as the store group increases in size this quality becomes less and less important. Once the housewife has been forced to take the car out of its garage—and she must shop by car if she is to take full advantage of the supermarket's economy —then it is very little more trouble for her to drive three miles than to drive one.

The automobile is bound to no particular route or distance. The automobile shopper can easily and quickly change her shopping habits if some more distant market seems to offer better value in choice or price of goods, or in general comfort and convenience.

Market analysis (as described in the preceding section of this book) will of course be the dominant factor in site selection. It will discover how much and what type of Buying Power a new center in this neighborhood may hope to tap. With a neighborhood center it will be necessary to consider only the immediate surroundings. A larger center will hope to attract buyers from a wider area.

For this reason one of the most desirable sites for a regional center will often be where the city joins the suburbs. Being on the downtown edge of a growing suburban area, the center will intercept the natural flow of shoppers to the downtown stores.

It is necessary to consider conditions not just as they exist today, but in relation to the trend of development in the area as a whole. It will be found, for example, that most cities spread out further and faster on one side; suburban growth has a certain predictable lopsidedness.

A neighborhood of small homes will support a wider variety of stores than a group of apartment houses. New home developments will contain a majority of recently married couples with babies and young children. Both houses and children are insistent in their needs. On the other hand much of the young family's income will be subtracted by mortgage payments on their home.

In older developments, where the average age of the residents is higher, their needs change; and the variety of stores in the neighborhood center will also have to be modified. These shoppers will be more interested in stores offering luxury goods such as high-quality gift shops and specialized food stores.

In buying a site the shopping center promoter is actually making an investment in Buying Power, part actual, part potential. In the case of a neighborhood center this Buying Power should be concentrated, so that the stores may hope for a virtual monopoly. In the larger regional and semi-regional centers, which count on drawing trade from a much wider area, good highway access becomes the crucial requirement in selecting a site, once the general area has been chosen.

The continued prosperity of downtown shopping centers in big cities is largely attributable to their position at the hub of a rapid transit network. This makes it easy for shoppers to reach the center quickly and directly from all the surrounding region. It must be made even easier for the automobile shopper to reach the new regional center.

This implies a perceptive study of the amount and type of traffic on main highways bounding the center. Of first importance is a study of their capacity, a complicated subject which can often be judged almost as accurately by amateur observation and local experience as by professional charting.

Highway capacity

Important features affecting capacity are the number and width of lanes, the number of heavy trucks, length and steepness of grades, sight distances for overtaking, traffic signals, parked cars, street cars and buses.

Calculations which attempt to include all conditions are liable to be misleading. For example, the theoretical capacity of a multi-lane divided highway with 12 ft. lanes is 1,000 cars per hr. per lane at 45-50 m.p.h. At 35-40 m.p.h. the capacity is increased to 1,500 cars per hr. per lane. However, on a three-lane highway, at 45-50 m.p.h., the total cars per hr. *in all three lanes together* is only 1,500. Or consider a normal four-lane business street. At peak-hour capacity it should be able to carry about 700 vehicles per hr. in each lane. However, in the curb lanes, due to parked cars, trucks, bus stops, etc., the capacity is no more than

350 vehicles per hr. And then, because of the disturbance caused by vehicles moving in and out of this slow lane, the practical capacity of both lanes together is reduced to only 800 vehicles per hr.

The size and comparative slowness of trucks, particularly on grades, will have a drastic effect on road capacity. Congested areas and traffic lights will influence conditions for many miles.

A clear distinction must always be made between traffic volume (the number of cars per hr. passing a given point) and traffic density (the number of cars on a given stretch of roadway at one time). Traffic density will be high when the traffic is forced to travel at low speed. Roads with high traffic volume will have widely spaced traffic. Heavy density and high volume will not occur together.

In a downtown shopping center, or in one of the centers now being mooted around suburban rail and bus terminals, a certain congestion is encouraging. Here a count of pedestrian traffic, particularly if some attempt is made to sort these passers-by qualitatively, may be used to advantage in choosing a site. Such pedestrian counts could also be a useful guide in choosing a site for one store in relation to other stores *within* a center designed primarily for the motorist.

Any congestion which may face the automobile shopper who is trying to reach the center in her car must be avoided at all costs. High traffic density is most undesirable. Traffic volume is slightly more desirable, provided that the road capacity is sufficient to take the extra traffic caused by the proposed shopping center without becoming congested.

The fact of interest here is not the existing traffic volume, but the *gap* between that and the capacity volume of the highway. Is this gap more than sufficient to accommodate the shoppers which the new center hopes to attract? If not, its trade may well be strangled.

The traffic volume of course will vary from hour to hour, and traffic arriving at and departing from the center will also have its peaks and valleys. Often a road which is heavily traveled at night, or in the morning and evening, is comparatively empty during the daytime when the shoppers will want to use it. The point to emphasize is that "high traffic counts" are seldom to be considered as an essen-

tial advantage, and should indeed be looked at with suspicion as a potential hindrance to development of a shopping center on that site.

Sites to be seen

The passing motorist will seldom make a sudden decision to stop and shop, except at a gas station or a restaurant. But this is no reason for not installing deceleration lanes with plenty of "magazine space", wide center strips, and entrances from side roads as well as main highways, for not, in other words, making it as easy as possible to stop off.

For the same reason billboards and road signs should give plenty of advance notice along the highways leading to the center, and the center itself should be carefully arranged to draw the utmost attention to provide the greatest advertising value from its roadside position. Here the same rules apply as in the siting of billboards: at a curve where the traffic slows, or just beyond a traffic light, at an angle to the general direction of travel. Signs must be large enough to be read at 40 m.p.h., window displays also, if they are expected to stretch their appeal beyond shoppers who have already reached the stores and become pedestrians. Show windows themselves and the displays within them must take on the proportions and the broad, impressionistic appeal of a poster. Like a well-sited billboard, they should be set at an angle to the traffic flow.

As the store buildings should be of more interest than parked automobiles, it may be advisable to make use of changing levels on the site to put the buildings on a slope behind but above the parking; or to sink front parking so that the buildings can be clearly seen from the highway though both are on the same level. Landscaping can, of course, always be brought into play (with far greater effect than has been generally achieved so far), both for bright, poster effects, and for close-up charm around the stores. No longer should all but the flat, open site be rejected as impractical. With the present popularity of the two-level department store in suburban centers, developers have actually put their bulldozers to work creating two different entrance levels on a flat site.

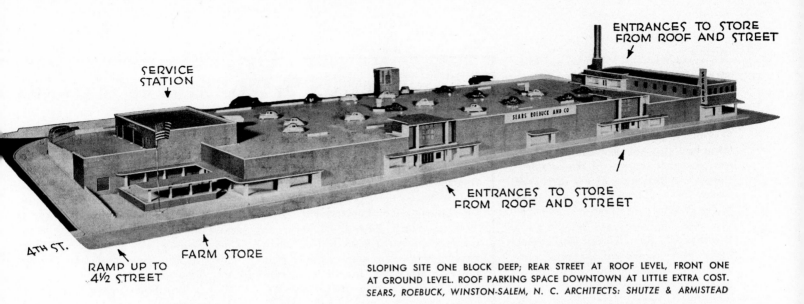

SERVICE STATION

ENTRANCES TO STORE FROM ROOF AND STREET

ENTRANCES TO STORE FROM ROOF AND STREET

4TH ST.

RAMP UP TO 4½ STREET

FARM STORE

SEARS ROEBUCK AND CO

SLOPING SITE ONE BLOCK DEEP; REAR STREET AT ROOF LEVEL, FRONT ONE AT GROUND LEVEL. ROOF PARKING SPACE DOWNTOWN AT LITTLE EXTRA COST. SEARS, ROEBUCK, WINSTON-SALEM, N. C. ARCHITECTS: SHUTZE & ARMISTEAD

Far more important to consider when judging topography are the sub-surface conditions. These may make development unreasonably expensive if special deep foundations are necessary. It will be at least as expensive if considerable rock blasting is required. Any physical feature which has to be mastered rather than turned to advantage should be regarded with suspicion.

Zoning

A similar observation could be made with regard to local zoning ordinances which affect the proposed site. For any but the smallest neighborhood center it will almost certainly be necessary to have some change made in the zoning. Seldom will there be a sufficiently large parcel of land available in a section already zoned for commercial development. And it is never advisable to assume that a center will not later need to expand (except of course in a planned community of predetermined size). Sufficient land should be bought before development gets under way.

If controlled by old-fashioned "strip" zoning, the 50 ft., or even 100 ft. width will not be sufficient to accommodate economically a well-designed modern center of regional or semi-regional type. Consequently it will be necessary to petition for a change from Residential to Commercial; and this will normally be unpopular with the neighboring residents. It may, therefore, become advisable for

the shopping center promoter to make concessions, perhaps dedicate a wide boundary strip as public park, *(see page 194)*, or call in leaders of local opinion as consultants upon the building design and landscaping.

It must be remembered that zoning, troublesome though it may appear to the harassed promoter, may actually be of advantage to him by denying sites to his prospective competitors. However, zoning can be changed; it is very open to political pressure. A better assurance of stability in the neighborhood pattern is a belt of recent home development and the lack of any large undeveloped sites. Contrarywise, provided the zoning can be changed, the most valuable site for a large shopping center is a big tract of open and undeveloped land left in the middle of an area otherwise fully built-up with private homes and apartments. This may be a former golf course, as in Broadway-Crenshaw, Los Angeles *(page 174)*, or Country Club Estates in Philadelphia *(page 208)*. Or it may be a large private estate, as was the case in Cameron Village, Raleigh *(page 147)*, and in Great Neck, Long Island *(page 124)*.

Where the zoning regulations include parking requirements, the promoter will find no difficulties; for even the most stringent of such regulations do not insist upon parking ratios as large as those already accepted as necessary by all forward-looking merchants.

A new type of zoning regulation which may well become increasingly popular is

one which allows for neighborhood shopping centers in high-income residential neighborhoods. Such centers would be very closely supervised both in plan and appearance, a modern and improved version of the old crossroads store.

They would satisfy the city planner's ideal of the community as a series of neighborhoods, each centered on a school and some stores. They might even appeal to the downtown merchant, as a means of alleviating congestion in the central store area, and as an opportunity for him to set up branch stores which would be more convenient to his customers for that small, day-to-day shopping which does not warrant the time and trouble of a trip downtown. Such neighborhood centers exist, even in speculative communities like Levittown *(see page 260)*.

How much to pay for the site

Eventually the question will come up: how much is it worth paying for this site? It is of course impossible to give a generally applicable answer in dollars and cents. But there are certain general principles which will affect the answer.

First, it is wise to remember that the cost of utilities must be added to the site cost, so that a site with mains and sewers already in place will be worth more than one to which these must be extended.

Second, the site will bring no returns until developed and built up with stores, so that any awkwardly placed rock or sub-surface conditions that require expensive foundations will actually make the site cost higher than it appears.

Third, it must always be kept in mind that no more than one quarter of the site will be yielding direct returns in the form of rent. The other three quarters will be taken up by parking space, landscaping, etc. So that if the cost of the complete site were, for example, $1 per sq. ft., the cost of the building site for the stores would be actually $4 per sq. ft. plus the cost of development.

It will be seen that high-cost land cannot therefore be considered for any center except one which would have a high concentration of pedestrian traffic, in addition to the anticipated automobile shoppers. This might be the case if a center were built up at some public transportation terminal.

The cost of the site itself is often quite a minor item in the total cost of a large regional center. As Homer Hoyt, one of the most experienced market analysts, has pointed out: "In a large regional center the total cost of the buildings, parking surfacing, etc., might be as much as $7,000,000. The 40 acres required for this center may be obtained for $2,000 an acre on the periphery and at $10,000 an acre for a vacant tract surrounded by development. By taking the better and closer-in location the total cost of the project is raised only from $7,080,000 to $7,400,000, an increase of but 5 per cent. The higher-priced location might well produce 50 per cent more sales and net income."* A large tract of open land in the middle of an already developed area may have for a shopping center promoter a value out of all proportion to the per acre cost of smaller, widely separated parcels in the same neighborhood. When assembling a large site there may be one or two lots breaking into the edge which it has not been possible to buy at what seems a reasonable price. As far as possible competition goes these are too small to matter; any stores put there will be troublesome only as their customers may "borrow" parking space. The danger here is lack of control over the type and quality of these stores; they may not enhance the high reputation built by the large, controlled center.

*"Market Analyses of Shopping Centers:" Technical Bulletin No. 12. Urban Land Institute.

COMBINATION OF COMMUTERS' RAILROAD

Mount Vernon, N. Y., a close-in suburb of New York City, is served by the New Haven railroad, with an efficient commuter service which has been in part responsible for the striking growth of the suburbs on the New England side of New York. Financially the railroad, like many others, has been less successful, and it has recently put up for sale all its station property along this line. The railroad would be given a station free of taxes and maintenance, the buyer would acquire what might turn out to be a valuable site. Plans have already been drawn for developing the station as a shopping center. This would have parking in the basement and on the roof (total: 400 cars). At ground level there would be 36 stores and a theater. Entrance to the station platforms would be through a store-lined arcade in the center of the building.

It still remains to be seen whether commuter traffic and shopping traffic can be profitably mixed, and how much the two may overlap. In parking, especially, there may be some conflict between all-day commuter parking, and local shopping traffic with its much faster turnover. However, in this particular instance the question is not clearly posed, the station is very near the business district.

Owner: Mt. Vernon Terminal Shopping Center Inc. *Architects:* Boak & Raad.

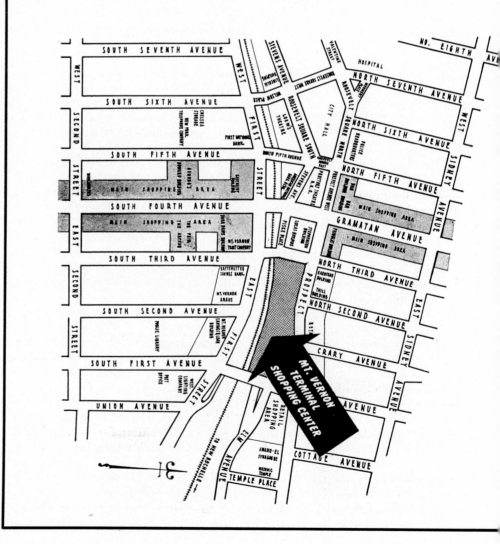

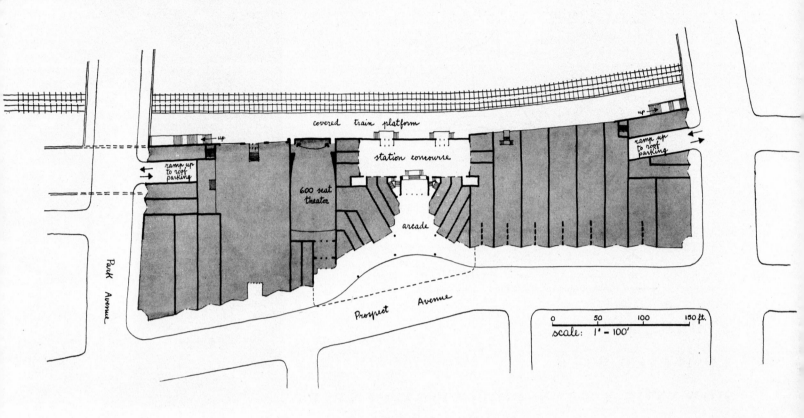

covered train platform

station concourse

ramp up to roof parking

600 seat theater

arcade

ramp up to roof parking

Park Avenue

Prospect Avenue

scale: 1' = 100'

0   50   100   150 ft.

BYRT SULLIVAN
1950

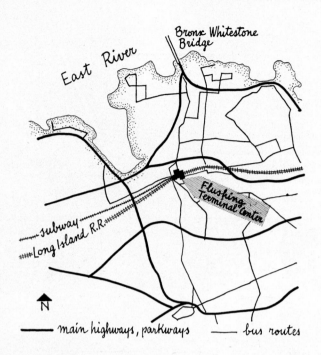

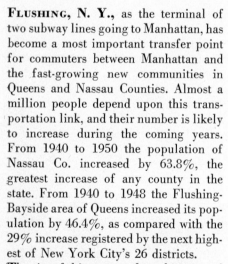

— main highways, parkways — bus routes

STORES AND PARKING

COMBINED WITH

DOWNTOWN TRANSPORTATION CENTER

FLUSHING, N. Y., as the terminal of two subway lines going to Manhattan, has become a most important transfer point for commuters between Manhattan and the fast-growing new communities in Queens and Nassau Counties. Almost a million people depend upon this transportation link, and their number is likely to increase during the coming years. From 1940 to 1950 the population of Nassau Co. increased by 63.8%, the greatest increase of any county in the state. From 1940 to 1948 the Flushing-Bayside area of Queens increased its population by 46.4%, as compared with the 29% increase registered by the next highest of New York City's 26 districts.

The site of this proposed combination of transportation terminal and shopping center is in the very heart of downtown Flushing. These streets and many of the present business buildings date from the time when Flushing still had some semblance of a quiet suburban town. They are entirely unfitted to accommodate the tremendously increased population which

has now become dependent upon them both for transportation and shopping. Twelve bus lines, with an average weekday load of 100,000 passengers, converge on Main Street and Roosevelt Avenue. The subway station and the Long Island Railroad station are within two blocks. Buses obstruct the curb and slow down all traffic. Because of the general congestion and confusion the local stores, which formerly thrived on their hub position, are beginning to lose customers to the many new, better-planned shopping centers recently built in the surrounding communities where the customers live. Public parking space is very limited. It could not be extended sufficiently to attract the large potential drive-in trade, without changes more drastic and expensive than the town and its merchants will at present consider.

The proposed development shown in model form on these two pages was designed by Lester C. Tichy, architect. It is being promoted by realtor William Zeckendorf, the dynamic head of Webb

& Knapp. Undoubtedly this plan will be modified in many details before it finally gets under way, but it does clarify the ideas behind this type of development. The transportation transfer point is in the block between Roosevelt and 41st Avenues, from Bowne Street to Union Street. Below street level here would be the Long Island Railroad station. This would be joined by escalators to the bus station at ground level, and the parking space on the roof. There would be an underground arcade connecting with the subway station one block west. All freight traffic would be ramped down to basement loading docks, all private automobile traffic would be ramped up to the extensive parking area on the roof. Shoppers, having parked their cars, can descend on escalators through the department store, or walk across a covered bridge to the theater and restaurant on the other side of 41st Avenue. Adjacent to the store buildings, the plan envisages three multi-story blocks: a hotel, a professional building, and an office building.

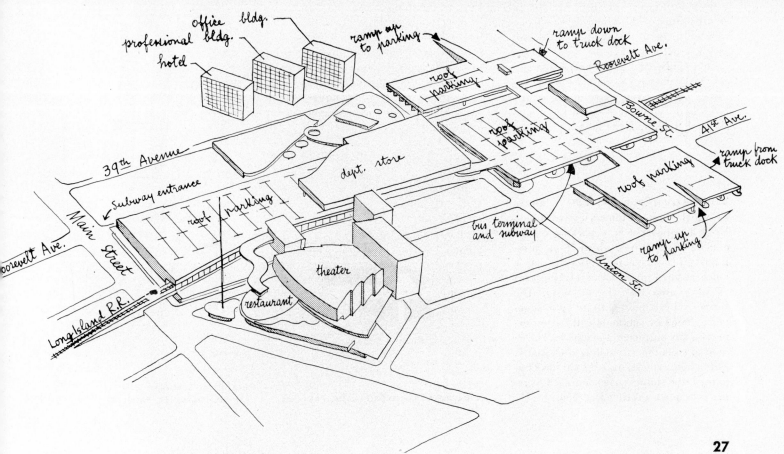

EVOLVING THE SITE PLAN BY CORRELATION

IS A SHOPPING CENTER PLAN SUGGESTED BY SITE?
SHOPPERS IN CARS, SHOPPERS ON FOOT, FREIGHT
EACH OF THESE ELEMENTS MUST HAVE FREE CIRCULATION
AUTO-SHOPPING AND PARCEL PICKUP IDEAS

More often than not it is the site which makes the site plan. The shape of the lot, its size, its topography, and the length of its highway frontage will almost immediately narrow the choice of site plan. For example, a long shallow strip of land along the highway will almost inevitably be best suited to a long strip of stores, while, on the other hand a deep site with small frontage will immediately suggest some type of shopping court or pedestrian mall scheme.

However, when planning a large center, the site itself is of such a size, and the store buildings occupy such a relatively small section of the whole (perhaps one quarter, or less), that the planner is usually without fetters. He is free to evolve a site plan based on what he considers to be best from the viewpoint of merchandising policy, irrespective of slight differences in physical shape between one site and another. These latter differences become of only modifying importance in the whole long and complex work of correlating requirements.

On these two pages we have collected the plans of ten centers. Each shows a different way of relating the stores to the highway and to the parking areas *(shown hatched)*. These plans range from a modernized version of the traditional crossroads store group, where the highway traffic is channeled between the store buildings, to some in which the stores turn their backs on the highway and retreat beyond a strip of parking space.

In some the shopper can drive up to the front entrance of the stores and park at the curb. In others the car must be shed before entering the shopping enclosure, just as Moslems relinquish their shoes at the door of a mosque.

On page 30 are three examples of site plans fitted to awkwardly shaped lots at highway junctions.

ALL DRAWINGS ON THIS AND THE FOLLOWING TWO PAGES ARE AT SCALE 1″ = 600′

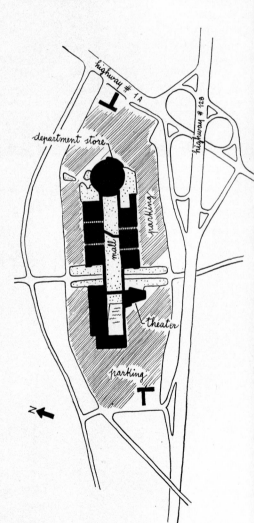

TURNING **THEIR BACK** to the highways by which their customers arrive, Linda Vista and Beverly have parking on the outside of the stores, which front on an interior pedestrian mall. Beverly has a much larger proportion of parking area to store area than Linda Vista. The former relies almost entirely upon shoppers coming by automobile, the latter expects many customers to come by bus or on foot from the surounding community. But in both centers, once the car has been parked, the shopper is encouraged to relax in a quiet, protected garden.

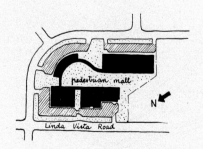

LINDA VISTA, SAN DIEGO, CALIF. PAGE 236

NATIONAL SUBURBAN CENTERS
BEVERLY, MASS. CF. PAGE 199

ON ONE SIDE of important highway intersections, Shirlington and Cameron Village furnish their own interior roadways, for circulation of shoppers in cars and on foot. The stores front on these roads. Shirlington reproduces the downtown shopping street, with abundant rear parking added. Cameron Village has much front curb parking, which is easier for the driver but, by causing the store blocks to be widely spaced, is more hindering to the pedestrian who wants to cross from one store to another.

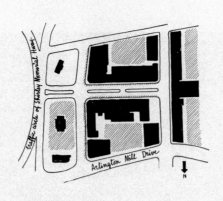

SHIRLINGTON, VA. PAGE 180

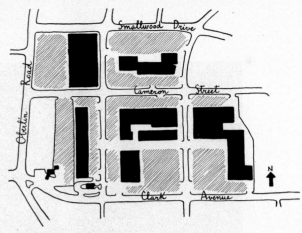

CAMERON VILLAGE,
RALEIGH, N. C. PAGE 147

ENCLOSING THE INTERSECTION of two busy highways, Hampton Village and Shaker Square are both cut into four pieces. This has the advantage of exposing the store fronts to a large volume of passing traffic, which is going by too fast to notice. The shoppers, on the other hand, are prevented by the hazards of crossing these highways from passing easily between one store block and another. The result is that such centers are liable to develop lopsidedly, with a great loss of cumulative pull. It is significant that the original plans for these two centers both date back 20 years.

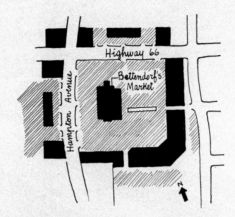

HAMPTON VILLAGE,
ST. LOUIS, MO. PAGE 188

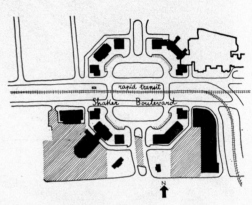

SHAKER SQUARE,
CLEVELAND, OHIO. PAGE 184

FRONTAGE WIDTH on the highway is less important than easy accessibility. Edmondson Village has the stores set in a long line parallel to the highway, but far behind the front parking where they are not easily seen by the passing motorist. Highland Park, on the contrary, with a comparatively narrow frontage, carries the line of stores back at right angles to the highway to form a small plaza. Once inside here, the shopper is surrounded by stores, whichever way he turns.

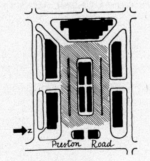

HIGHLAND PARK,
DALLAS, TEXAS, PAGE 90

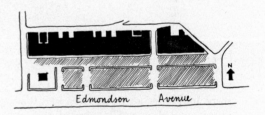

EDMONDSON VILLAGE,
BALTIMORE, MD. PAGE 138

PEDESTRIANS AND PARKING have usually been mixed in shopping centers so far built. Bellevue is typical of the plans in which the stores face on to streets used for both parking and traffic circulation. The motorist can park right in front of the store he wants to visit. In the typical Farmers Markets, automobiles are barred from the alleys between the shops, which stand like an island in the center of the parking area.

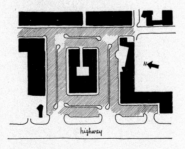

BELLEVUE,
NEAR SEATTLE, WASH. PAGE 222

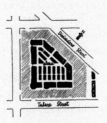

FARMERS MARKET,
FRESNO, CALIF. PAGE 96

29

CIRCLE ON A TRIANGLE. MAYBROOK CENTER, MAYWOOD, N. J. KELLY & GRUZEN, ARCHS.

HIGHWAY JUNCTIONS often create odd-shaped but valuable sites. When store values were estimated by the front foot, store buildings, even on sites like that above, would normally have followed the sidewalk along the highway edge. Now, even on a comparatively rectangular crossroads site *(right)*, the store blocks are set back to allow for some front parking space. In a neighborhood center in Washington, D. C., *(far right)*, the store block is even further withdrawn from the road junction, and set at an angle to traffic.

In the scheme for Maywood *(above)*, the narrow tip is abandoned to parking, next is a theater and restaurant, then the circle of stores—approachable from all sides —which faces into a quiet sheltered court for pedestrians only.

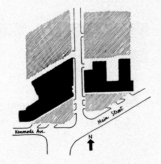

AMHERST, N. Y. GUELICH & BOEBEL

MICHIGAN AVENUE, WASHINGTON, D. C. PAGE

CIRCULATION OF SHOPPERS AND FREIGHT

THE MOST IMPORTANT INFLUENCE on the site plan of any shopping center is circulation—of shoppers in cars, shoppers on foot, and freight loading and unloading at the stores.

The most practical solution, in our age of open planning and romantic merging of space, still remains the old-fashioned one of customers' entrance and display windows on one side (the front), service entrance and loading docks on the opposite side (the rear).

Unfortunately this neat division between customers and freight does not work quite as smoothly as the plans (and the planners) may suggest. Truckmen may prefer to go to the front entrance, ignoring the site planner's intentions. To prevent this, policing is probably necessary but certainly uneconomic. A better method of prevention is to provide a more clearly marked and accessible service road.

Though many stores continue to have the traditional front and rear, the fronts may not face the highway. They may be turned round to face upon a quiet interior court, pleasantly landscaped and free of auto traffic. In the planners' language this is known as a pedestrian mall. The service entrances will, in this scheme, open on to a parking belt between shopping center and highway.

Because there is so much more of the site allotted to parking than to buildings (except in a center fitted on to a costly downtown site), the parking area becomes the dominating feature of the site plan. In the pattern of circulation it is an intermediate stage between the high-speed traffic on the highway and the pedestrian traffic within the center.

The parking area may be in front of the stores—even though this front does not face on the highway; we shall refer to this as *front parking*. Or the parking area may be at the rear of the stores—even though it then adjoins the highway; we shall refer to this as *rear parking*. A compromise plan, quite commonly found, is to have part of the parking in front, part behind the stores; we shall refer to this as *split parking*.

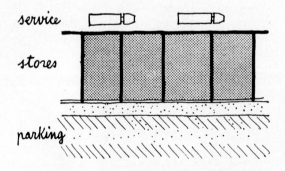

FRONT PARKING keeps the customers in front, the service traffic in the rear, thus separating these two circulations. This type of parking is especially well suited to the fast in-and-out shoppers, and is therefore found most frequently in small neighborhood centers. Many drug store chains consider front parking almost as essential as a corner site.

Front parking is actually the curb parking typical of Main Street. If much increased in depth it becomes inefficient. But its advocates claim—and there are very many experienced store owners among them—that the customer wants to have at least the opportunity of finding a parking space directly in front of the store that he intends to visit.

If the front parking space is between the store building and the highway, its rigid size may cause difficulties. If made big enough to handle peak loads (according to the Urban Land Institute, peak periods represent 15-20% of the total number of store hours each week), it will be so large that the store fronts are set too far back from the road for normal convenience and display. The passerby on the highway is separated from them by a concealing mass of parked cars, or by a bleak expanse of empty pavement.

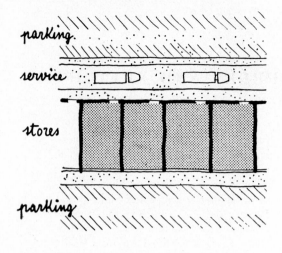

parking.

service

stores

parking

Split parking evades many of the difficulties of front parking *(see page 31)*, by adding a limited amount of parking at the rear or the side of the store block. The area in front of the stores is useful for quick in-and-out shopping (e.g. drug store and service stores), that at the rear

for longer visits and for overflow parking in peak shopping hours. Sometimes the customers are allowed to use the rear entrances of the stores, sometimes they are forced to detour through arcades in the store block to reach the front entrances *(see below)*.

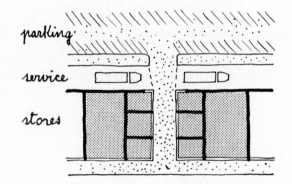

parking

service

stores

Rear parking is most often used when the shopping center is fitted into an already established shopping street, or when the stores turn their backs to the highway and face inward on to a pedestrian mall. Coming from a rear parking area the shopper will usually try to enter the stores by a back door, which is also the service entrance, and consequently cluttered with supplies and empty crates. Window shopping is not encouraged; customers may never see the store front displays, if they walk directly in and out of the rear entrance of a single store.

In many recently designed centers these objections have been partially overcome by making the rear entrance as attractive as the front. With truck deliveries limited to off-peak hours and strict supervision by the management, the traditional difficulties of using the same entrance for both freight and shoppers may be largely overcome. The ideal cure, of course, is a freight tunnel *(see page 51)*, but its high cost often prevents it from going beyond the architect's blueprints. And even so, two fronts complicate layout and supervision in most stores *(see page 55)*.

parking

service

stores

Rear parking, with arcades cut through the store block at frequent intervals, does overcome many of the objections raised by shoppers and freight sharing the rear entrance. Moreover the funneling of traffic through these arcades makes them extremely valuable for the display and sale of impulse goods. If these arcades do not occur frequently enough, shoppers will tend to resent the

detours to which they are subjected, and will use the rear service entrances for greater convenience in going to and from the parking area.

This rear parking with arcades is most suitable for leisurely shopping (e.g. women's fashion goods). It is often used in combination with interior pedestrian malls, where the rear entrances of the stores face the highway.

Distances between parking and stores can be substantially reduced, and also be made less apparent, by interlocking parking pockets with the stores. Arcades join these parking areas directly to the heart of the interior shopping court. In Los Alamos *(right)* the total parking area is broken down into a number of dispersed units, so that the shopper can park near the group of stores which she wants to visit. In Norgate *(far right)* parking and stores are interlocked for a combination of convenience and display value. Sidewalk shoppers are drawn into the plaza along the store fronts.

NORGATE, MONTREAL, CANADA
A DESIGN BY THE AUTHORS

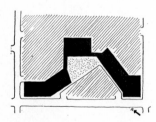

LOS ALAMOS. PAGE 242

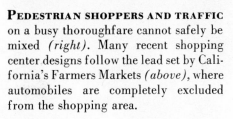

PEDESTRIAN SHOPPERS AND TRAFFIC on a busy thoroughfare cannot safely be mixed *(right)*. Many recent shopping center designs follow the lead set by California's Farmers Markets *(above)*, where automobiles are completely excluded from the shopping area.

THE REAR ENTRANCE. What's it for? Customers? Or freight and garbage? In most centers with rear parking it is supposed to serve both, with the result that neither is served as well as it should be. That customer emerging from the supermarket *(right)* is one of those who can keep a store in business or put it in the bankruptcy court. A little more thought should be given to her convenience. And those pathetic little rear entrances *(below)* are not going to attract and stop customers as a window display might. The larger stores *(above)* have an advantage here; they can invite the rear parkers to use the store as they would an arcade, as a short cut to the main front. An alert display manager will use all his wiles to stimulate their impulse buying.

33

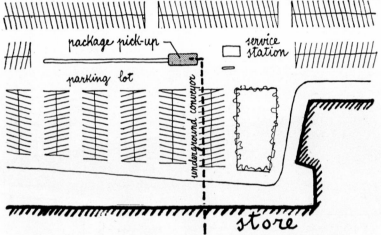

ABOVE: PICKUP STATION IN PARKING AREA. CONNECTED WITH STORE
By UNDERGROUND CONVEYOR. *RAYMOND LOEWY ASSOCIATES, DESIGNERS*

BELOW: PICKUP STATION WITH AMPLE MAGAZINE SPACE, TO SERVE
WHOLE SHOPPING CENTER. *HOWARD T. FISHER & ASSOCIATES, ARCHITECTS.*

AUTO-SHOPPING AND

THE MISSING LINK in almost every shopping center is between the stores and the automobile which the customer is using as a delivery van. Even in the best planned and most modern centers a distance of 300 ft. or more from the stores to the limits of the parking area is not infrequent. As a result the shopper will demand home delivery for packages which she would gladly take with her, if she didn't first have to carry them to her car. The supermarket alone has considered it economic to provide help *(above, left)*; but it is an expense which the supermarket would like to eliminate as much as the department store would like to cut down on home delivery. Other stores are also affected, indirectly. For a shopper encumbered with packages will be discouraged from window shopping. The answer may be some form of pickup station, where the shopper can have all her purchases sent for loading in her car when she drives off at the end of a shopping spree. This is already being attempted by some supermarket chains. The customer hands over her package after going through the check-out gates, and receives a numbered check. Later she

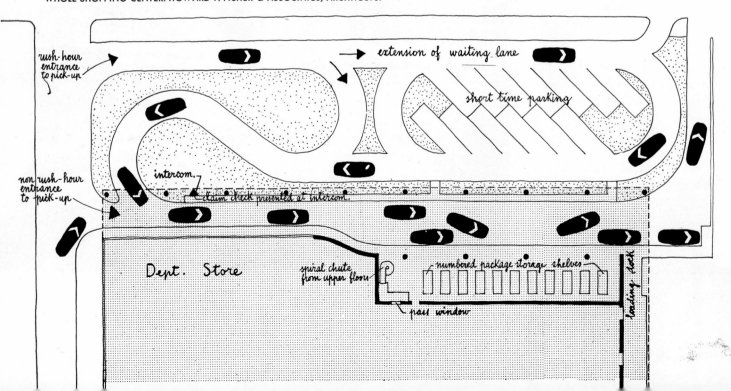

PARCEL PICKUP IDEAS

fetches her car from the parking lot, draws up at the curb, shows her check, and an attendant loads the packages. The two plans on the opposite page show more elaborate pickup ideas. To avoid the traffic jams which might plague a pickup station in the parking area, that shown at the bottom of the page has a great deal of magazine space for waiting cars. A clerk at the intercom phone relays claim check numbers from these waiting motorists to a clerk at the storage bins, so that the right package is ready immediately each car reaches the pickup point. Auto-shopping, where the shopper never leaves her car, is another possibility. It has already proved popular and successful in many banks *(below)*, where it has the additional appeal of greater safety for those carrying large sums of money. However, auto-shopping may appeal to the jaded customer more than to the budgetwise promoter. A shopper on foot occupies less than one hundredth of the space required by an automobile. And the pedestrian is infinitely more maneuverable. No fenders either. Auto-shopping is probably best suited to service stores, where customers spend little time in selection of goods, and where it is often necessary to handle large bundles (e.g. laundries and dry cleaners). As auto-shopping layouts are often wasteful of space if designed for peak loads, it will be advisable to provide ample bypass lanes and alternative parking.

ONE OF THE TWO TELLERS' WINDOWS
ST. PETERSBURG, FLA.

THE DRIVE-IN SECTION IS A NEW ANNEX
W. B. HARVARD, ARCH. J. B. DODD, ASSOC.

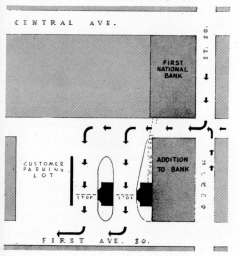

PARKING FOR SHOPPING CENTERS

HOW MUCH PARKING? SELF-PARKING OR ATTENDANT-PARKING?

MULTI-STORY PARKING SPACE. THE COST OF PARKING

EFFECT OF BUILDING SHAPE ON PARKING RATIO

DIMENSION TABLES AND LAYOUT OF PARKING AREAS

Everyone agrees that a modern shopping center should have "ample" parking. But how much is ample? The answer must be stated in economic terms.

Economic analysis of the prospects for a certain store group will establish certain anticipated sales figures. These will in turn have been based upon a certain number of customers each spending a certain amount of money at these stores. Obviously the parking space provided should be at least big enough to accommodate this number of customers. Unfortunately the flow of customers is not regular. It will vary from one day to another during each week, and from one season to another during the year. So if the parking space is truly to satisfy the customer, it must even be large enough to handle the crowds of the last Saturday before Christmas.

Unit Sales Method

This system for calculating the amount of parking space required relates the number of parking stalls to sales volume. Wurdeman & Becket, applying this system to the projected Hillsdale shopping center, near San Francisco, concluded that at least one parking space would be required in that center for every $15,000 of expected annual sales volume.

Their conclusions were based upon the following sequence of reasoning:

a. Average Unit Sale $5.40
c. Customers per car 1.4
m. Minimum car turnover per
space 3.3
Customers arriving by car . . . 50%

Minimum sales per day per parking stall (only for those customers arriving by car) were calculated as $a \times c \times m = \$25$. But as it had been estimated that only 50% of the shoppers would arrive by car, the minimum sales per day per parking stall should actually be $50.

Assuming 300 selling days per annum, the minimum annual sales for each parking stall will be $15,000. As Hillsdale's annual gross sales were estimated at $35,000,000, the required number of parking stalls would be $35,000,000 \div 15,000 = 2,333$.

Being based on the *minimum* turnover per parking stall, this calculation should successfully take account of seasonal peaks when not only turnover and income per stall will be higher but average sales per car will be higher.

There is, of course, no generally applicable formula for calculations of this type. Each of the figures must be changed to fit local conditions. The annual gross sales per parking stall, for example, may vary from $15,000 to $60,000 according to the type of store. Those handling lower-price goods, because their success must depend upon volume—a large number of individual sales—will need the largest amount of parking space. For this reason the Unit Sales method of calculating the required parking area may be a good deal more sensitive than the Area Ratio method described below.

Area Ratio Method

The ratio between the gross area of the parking space and the gross floor area of the stores has established itself during the past few years as the magic formula which can solve all parking calculations with a pair of figures and a colon. Its greatest merit, and the most understandable reason for its popularity, is that it is easy to apply. It is therefore especially useful for preliminary site planning.

As a rule of thumb the Urban Land Institute recommends a 2:1 ratio for "average conditions" (where do they exist?). Waverly Taylor, with wide and lengthy experience in the developing and management of shopping centers in Washington, D. C., has come to the conclusion that a ratio of 2:1 is the essential minimum, even when 60% of the customers arrive on foot.

In the projected Hillsdale center (where 50% of the customers are expected to come on foot) the gross floor area of the stores is 640,000 sq. ft. The parking space, arrived at by the Unit Sales Method as described above, totals 700,000 sq. ft. (allowing 300 sq. ft. per stall). In other words, at Hillsdale the Area Ratio would be only a fraction over 1:1.

In centers which rely almost exclusively on automobile shoppers an Area Ratio of 3:1, or even more, is generally advocated. An important consideration here is the type of shopping expected at the center. Is it to be the leisurely selection which we anticipate with women's fashion goods, or will there be more of those quick in-and-out errands associated with drug stores, service stores, banks?

In the past matters have often been still further confused by the failure to reckon with multi-story buildings. Obviously the

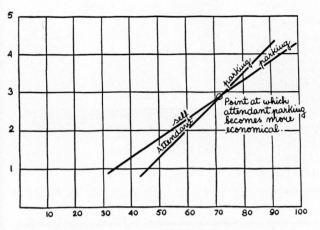

PARKING COSTS. SELF VS. ATTENDANT PARKING

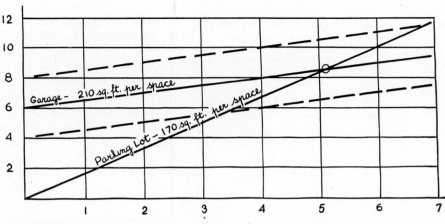

WHEN IS MULTI-LEVEL PARKING CHEAPER?

figure that counts here is gross floor area, not ground coverage only. The same considerations apply to basements, if these are used for selling.

For theaters a separate ratio is generally used: the number of seats compared with the number of parking stalls. Such a figure is often found now in zoning regulations. It will vary according to local conditions. In some Fairfield County, Connecticut, towns it has recently been set at one parking stall to every 6 seats. Guelich & Boebel, for a string of shopping centers in upper New York state, consider one parking stall for every 3 seats an adequate ratio.

Parking space limited

The gross area of parking space per car (including access roads) will vary with the layout of the parking area (see page 41). It will also depend upon whether the motorist parks his own car (self-parking), or whether he leaves it in the hands of a skilled attendant who does the actual parking (attendant-parking). The great majority of present and proposed shopping centers have self-parking at ground level. This is costly in space.

Most planners have come to accept 300 sq. ft. per car as an adequate allowance Our figures show that 350 sq. ft. is the minimum that can be considered satisfactory (see diagrams, page 43).

In some cases it will not be practical to extend ground-level self-parking space as far as the calculated number of parking stalls may demand. There may be insufficient land, or the land may be too expensive to justify this extravagant use.

Due to the shape of the lot, the parking area may stretch too far away from the stores to be used for anything but employee parking.

For these or similar reasons a shopping center may decide to install attendant parking or multi-deck parking. The pros and cons of these are outlined below.

Self-parking vs. attendant-parking

Cost is not the only factor to consider when making a decision between self- and attendant-parking. Self-parking usually runs more smoothly. The customer never has to wait for his car to be delivered. Self-parking is practically essential where there is high turnover.

It is comparatively simple to determine at what point the added cost of attendant parking becomes justified. The graph shown above was prepared by the American Automobile Association. It is shown as an example of the method to be used in setting up a similar graph for use in any specific case under consideration. The data used here were as follows:
Basic Expenses
(same for self- and attendant-parking)
Taxes: 25 mills.
  Maintenance & Miscellaneous: $14 per space per year.
  Interest on Investment: 6%
Added Expense in Self-Parking
  Additional space required: 70 sq. ft. per car.
Added Expense in Attendant-Parking
  Attendants' wages: $17 per space per year.
From the graph based on these figures it can be seen that the critical land price,

above which self-parking becomes more expensive than attendant parking, is $2.85 per sq. ft.

Multi-level parking

Changing from self-parking to attendant-parking can give only a limited saving in land area (about 30%). When land is so expensive or so impossible to acquire that an even greater number of cars per acre must be accommodated, then it is necessary to expand in a vertical direction by providing a multi-story structure with upper levels being reached by ramps or some type of elevatoring.

This may be operated with either self-parking or attendant-parking; but that must be decided in advance, for it affects the design of the structure. Self-parking will require more spacious parking stalls, wider and less steep ramps (probably not more than 10%). Attendant-parking will require sufficient magazine space where customers hand over their cars to the attendants. (cf. pages 85 and 50)

The point at which multi-story garages become economical can be computed by a comparative graph of land construction costs, as shown above. Costs will of course vary in each case. This table is based on a construction cost of $600 per stall (gross area 210 sq. ft.); this includes ramps. The broken lines are for costs of $400 and $800 per stall. Contrasted with these is a gross area of 170 sq. ft. per stall in the parking lot.

The graph shows that, when the land cost exceeds $5.10 per sq. ft., multi-decking at $600 per stall becomes more economical than ground-level parking.

BUILDING SHAPE
LIMITS PARKING RATIO

IN SUBURBAN SHOPPING CENTERS, although land is plentiful and cheap, there is one other factor which may affect the amount of parking space provided: the influence of building shape upon the ratio between building and parking areas.

The further the parking space stretches away from the stores, the less desirable it becomes. It is now generally agreed that in a suburban center, the maximum distance between the far edge of the parking area and the stores should not exceed 500 ft., and preferably should be less than 300 ft. This fading of usefulness might be checked by shuttle buses or moving sidewalks between the stores and the outlying parking areas, which could be operated only at peak hours.

Having established a certain maximum desirable distance between the far edge of the parking area and the store buildings, then it will be found that there is a definite relationship between the shape of the store block and the ratio between store area and parking area.

THE BLOCK DIAGRAMS on these two pages are simplified for the sake of quick and easy comparison. The buildings are assumed to be 100 ft. deep, the parking areas (diagonally shaded) 100, 200 and 300 ft. deep. In actual practice these exact measurements will probably not be found the most suitable. They are used here to simplify the demonstration of basic principles. No allowance has been made for walks, service yards, or landscaping; these may in reality cover as much as 20% of the site.

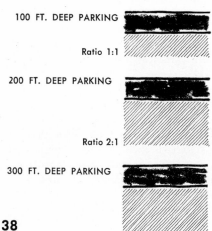

100 FT. DEEP PARKING

Ratio 1:1

200 FT. DEEP PARKING

Ratio 2:1

300 FT. DEEP PARKING

Ratio 3:1

THE L SHAPE has always been the favorite among small neighborhood centers. The more the difference in length between the long and the short leg is increased, the more the area ratio improves. But it never reaches the same high ratios as the straight row. An L-shape center is usually turned with the parking area between the highway and the stores. And 300 ft. deep front parking would not satisfy most merchants; they would want their stores nearer the highway traffic.

PARKING
100 FT. DEEP

Ratio 0.5:1

Ratio 0.8:1

THE U SHAPE, with parking confined to the court formed by the two arms, will always have less good parking ratios than the L shape. It is not until the U opens its jaws a considerable distance that the parking ratio begins to rise. Even then it always trails behind the ratios obtainable in L plans with the same frontage. Perhaps it is mainly for this reason that many U-shape centers have split parking, the additional rear parking being reserved mostly for overflow needs.

PARKING
100 FT. DEEP

Ratio 0.3:1

Ratio 0.7:1

THE RECTANGLE, with parking on the outside edge of the stores, is capable of achieving the highest area ratios. Because of the four corner areas (shown with opposite diagonal lines) this type of plan can give better ratios than even the straight line of stores. By using the inner court for parking, the ratio can be increased still further. Alternatively, if inner court parking is added, the same ratios can be achieved with a narrower band of parking on the outside, which would reduce the distance between the stores and the far edge of the parking area. More parking stalls would then be closer to the stores. In most centers of this type the store fronts are not visible from the highway. They face inward toward the central court.

PARKING
100 FT. DEEP

Ratio 1.7:1

Ratio 1

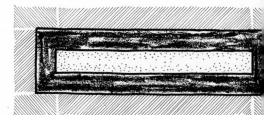

PARKING
200 FT. DEEP

Ratio 0.8:1

PARKING
300 FT. DEEP

Ratio 1:1

Ratio 1.5:1

Ratio 2:1

PARKING
200 FT. DEEP

Ratio 0.5:1

PARKING
300 FT. DEEP

Ratio 0.6:1

Ratio 1.1:1

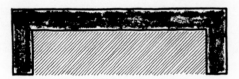

Ratio 1.5:1

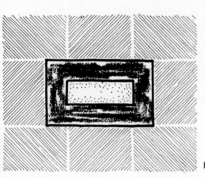
PARKING
200 FT. DEEP

Ratio 4:1

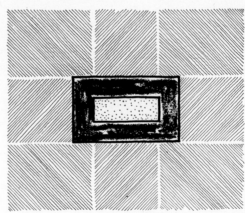
PARKING
300 FT. DEEP

Ratio 7:1

Ratio 5:1

Ratio 3:1

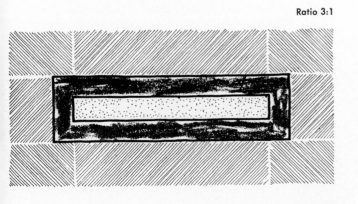
PARKING
200 FT. DEEP

0°
(PARALLEL)

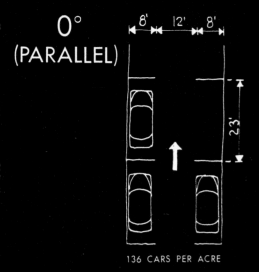

8' | 12' | 8'

23'

136 CARS PER ACRE

45°

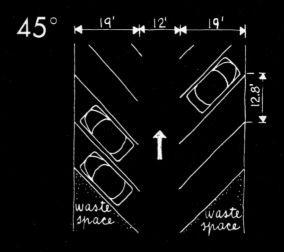

19' | 12' | 19'

12.8'

waste space   waste space

136 CARS PER ACRE (WASTE SPACE NOT COMPUTED)

60°

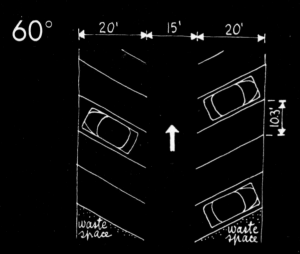

20' | 15' | 20'

10.3'

waste space   waste space

154 CARS PER ACRE (WASTE SPACE NOT COMPUTED)

90°

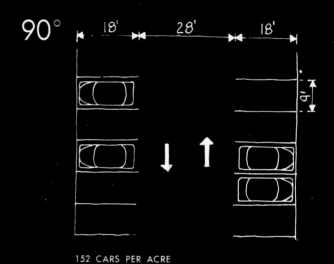

18' | 28' | 18'

9'

152 CARS PER ACRE

45° OVERLAPPED

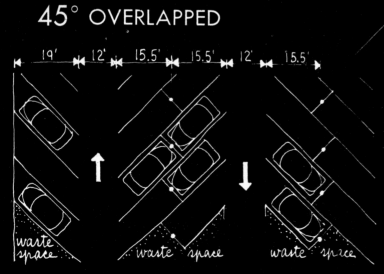

19' | 12' | 15.5' | 15.5' | 12' | 15.5'

waste space   waste space   waste space

158 CARS PER ACRE (WASTE SPACE NOT COMPUTED)

45° HERRINGBONE

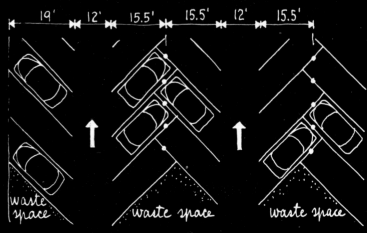

19' | 12' | 15.5' | 15.5' | 12' | 15.5'

waste space   waste space   waste space

158 CARS PER ACRE (WASTE SPACE NOT COMPUTED)

STANDARD DIMENSIONS for parking space — whether self-parking or attendant-parking—are normally for maximum use of the available space. This is satisfactory for the planning of downtown parking lots, where shoppers are so thankful to find any space at all that they are not too fussy about overcrowding. For the increasingly competitive field of suburban shopping centers, ease of parking, of entrance and exit, cannot be so lightly disregarded. Moreover it is most essential to provide sufficient space around the car so that large bundles may be loaded through the side doors and into the trunk with ease and safety. If the stalls are made too small, or too awkward to drive into, shoppers will disregard the painted demarcation lines and lap over into the next stall. This haphazard parking will waste far more space than provision of slightly larger stalls. Accordingly we have been brought to the conclusion that a stall measuring 9 x 18 ft. is desirable for self-parking in the typical outlying center where the land is available. Even so there will still be a few cars more than 18 ft. long which will stick out into the aisle. In very large parking areas it may be advisable to reduce the size of those stalls on the outer fringes of the area which are only in use at the busiest shopping periods.

Varying the angle of parking, as the diagrams and table show, will vary
(a) the length of curb per car,
(b) the width of the parking unit,
(c) the area per car,
(d) circulation within the parking area.
Varying the angle of the stall may also vary the ease with which one can enter it. A diagonal stall, for example, is considered easier to enter than a perpendicular or a parallel one.

For all angles up to 75° the width of the aisle required to turn into the stall is not sufficient to serve also for two-way circulation. The minimum desirable aisle width for two-way traffic is 24 ft.

For parking angles from 80° up, the width of aisle required to enter and leave the stall is also sufficient for two-way circulation. This is a definite advantage, for two-way circulation is much less irritating for the driver who is searching for an empty stall. Also one-way circulation requires a large number of directional signs; and at peak periods, if it is to work

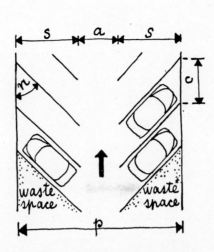
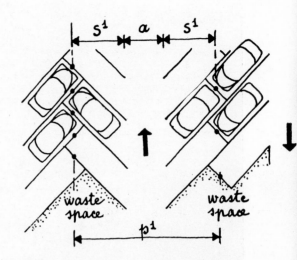

n parking angle degrees	p width of parking section in ft.	s depth of stall in ft.	a width of aisle in ft.	c curb length per car in ft.	A* area per car sq. ft.	p¹ width of parking section in ft.	s¹ depth of stall in ft.	A¹* area per car sq. ft.
0	28	8	12	23	320	28	8	320
30	46	17	12	18	415	38	13	342
35	48	18	12	15.8	380	41	14.5	325
40	49	18.5	12	14	343	42	15	295
45	50	19	12	12.8	320	43	15.5	275
50	51	19.5	12	11.8	302	45	16.5	266
55	53	20	13	11.1	294	48	17.5	266
60	55	20	15	10.3	282	50	17.5	258
65	57	20	17	9.9	282	53	18	262
70	59	20	19	9.6	283	56	18.5	269
75	61	20	21	9.3	283	59	19	274
80	63	19.5	24‡	9.2	290	62	19	285
85	64	19	26‡	9.1	291	63	18.5	286
90	64	18	28‡	9	288	64	18	288

*Waste space at end of row and access roads are not included.
‡Width of aisle required for turning permits two-way circulation.

COMPARATIVE DIMENSIONS FOR DIFFERENT PARKING ANGLES.
8 x 18 FT. STALLS

effectively, it has to be supervised by a number of attendants.

Deciding upon the best parking angle depends mainly upon the size and shape of the parking area. It may sometimes be advisable to use different parking angles in the same parking lot, in order to use the available space to greatest advantage. Another method of space-saving, as shown by the last three columns of the table above, is by the use of overlapping and interlocking patterns of parking.

AT FRESH MEADOWS (*SEE PAGE 248*) THE MOST IMPORTANT STORES ARE AT LEFT CENTER, SO PARKING AISLES LEAD IN THAT DIRECTION

ROAD SHARED BY PEDESTRIANS, CARS......

BECAUSE RAISED PATHWAY IS TOO NARROW

PEDESTRIAN CIRCULATION may share the roadways with cruising automobiles *(left)*, or be encouraged to use raised pathways between the rows of parked cars *(right)*. Unlike the example shown, there should be at least 7 ft. clear between bumpers, to allow two people carrying bundles to walk abreast. The parking lines should be set at right angles to the most-used line of stores, so that pedestrians do not have to make blind crossings and worm between cars.

LAYOUT OF THE PARKING AREA

THREE IMPORTANT CONSIDERATIONS will influence decisions on the layout of parking areas: (i) circulation of pedestrians between cars and stores; (ii) circulation of cars in and out of the parking area, and looking for a place to park; (iii) space saving.

There should be as few obstacles as possible to the movement of motorists on foot back and forth between the stores and their parked cars. Therefore the parking aisles should be set at right angles to the stores, parallel to the main flow of shoppers using the center *(cf. picture opposite)*. If the aisles are set parallel to the stores, shoppers have to squeeze between cars, and make a blind crossing at each aisle.

Such a layout is justified only in shallow parking areas not more than two aisles in depth, where the aisles double as access roads *(see diagram right)*. Any other parking pattern would waste an undue percentage of the space on a separate access road.

Wide aisles—economical only with 90° parking — are preferable when pedestrians and automobiles share the same roadways; pedestrians are thus given a better chance to see and to be seen.

The more quickly a driver can be directed to an empty stall near the store she wants to visit the happier she will be. The faster each automobile shopper can be accommodated the less she will contribute to traffic congestion within the center caused by shoppers cruising around on the lookout for a place to park.

In smaller centers this difficulty will not arise, for the arriving motorist can usually appraise the whole parking area at a glance. But in the large centers, especially during peak shopping periods, it has been found necessary to install some means of guiding automobile shoppers to empty stalls. The usual method is by means of a spotter high up on the store building who communicates his findings to arriving motorists by means of traffic lights *(see page 44)*; or using loudspeaker or intercom, he may direct attendants in the parking area.

In the case of parking aisles at right angles to the stores, there will have to be

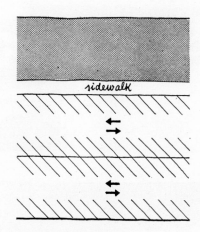

45° Shallow (above)

Number of cars per 1,000 sq. ft.
of store area 3.1
Sq. ft. per car 396
Area Ratio (parking to stores) . 1.2:1

90° Deep (right)

Number of cars per 1,000 sq. ft.
of store area 9.4
Sq. ft. per car (including feeder
roads shown on plan) . . . 339
Area Ratio (parking to stores) . 3.18:1

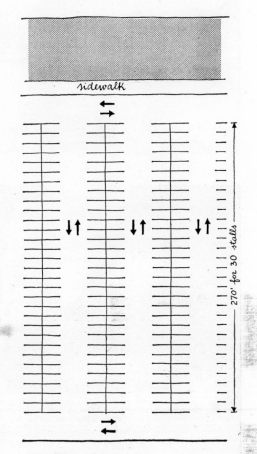

at least a two-lane access road running along the front of the stores. Two-way circulation here will be easier on the drivers; but one-way traffic will give a smoother flow to the parking aisles.

This roadway is also useful for unloading and picking up passengers. It should be kept free of any longer parking, so that there will be no stoppage in the free flow of traffic to the parking aisles.

A roadway at the store end of the aisles is essential. Exit to a public street, or to another access road at the far end of the aisles is desirable but not essential. It will prevent departing shoppers returning to congest the access road in front. Circulation within the parking aisles may be two-way, or one-way in only one direction, or one-way with the direction alternating from one aisle to the next.

As shown in the drawing at right, two-way circulation is best suited to a 90° parking pattern, because the aisle width

required for parking is in itself large enough to allow this.

The combination of diagonal parking with two-way circulation requires a much larger amount of space for roadways, and is therefore seldom used except for shallow front parking where the aisles double as access roads. This is particularly effective in small neighborhood centers with a great deal of quick in-and-out shopping.

In all other cases diagonal parking will normally be combined with one-way aisles. This is popular in larger centers, although it requires clear marking and careful policing if it is to work effectively. Most commonly found are one-way aisles with the direction alternating from one aisle to the next *(see pages 46 and 174)*. One-way aisles all running in the same direction are less common, but can be effective if under centralized control, as shown on the following page.

AISLES OF 60° PARKING STALLS RUN
AT RIGHT ANGLES TO MAIN STORE BLOCK

PARKING DIRECTED BY TRAFFIC LIGHTS
CONTROLLED FROM LOOKOUT IN STORE TOWER

SEARS, ROEBUCK & CO., at their Wayside store in Houston, Texas, station a controller high up on the store to oversee the whole parking area. When one-way aisles (with 60° stalls) are as long as this, it becomes exceedingly difficult for the arriving motorist to see from one end if and where there is an empty stall. So at the entrance of each aisle is a traffic light managed by the controller. As long as there is a single empty stall in an aisle the light at its end will show a green arrow. When the aisle is full the controller will switch that light to red. Were it not for this control it would scarcely be feasible to economize in space by emptying the aisles directly on to a public street, instead of having a service road within the site. *Architect:* Kenneth Franzheim.

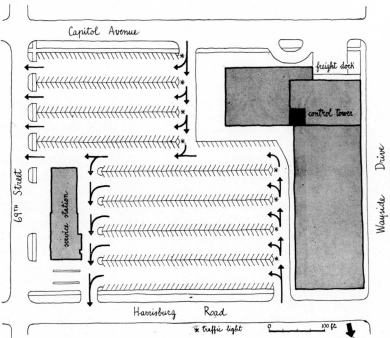

Capitol Avenue

69TH Street

service station

Harrisburg Road

freight dock

control tower

Wayside Drive

* *traffic light*   0   100 ft

A ROOFED SHELTER KEEPS OFF SUN AND RAIN. *LAMAR CENTER, RIVER OAKS, HOUSTON, TEXAS*

SOME OTHER VARIETIES OF PARKING

MORE COMPLEX PARKING structures are usually the result of the topography of the site or the scarcity (and high cost) of land. Even extremes of climate may cause elaboration *(above)* of the common open parking area at ground level. In the project sketched below the store is built right over part of the parking area. Connection between store and parking here is by escalator, as at Milliron's, Los Angeles *(page 48)*, where parking space is above the store, on the roof.

The most reasonable and economical use of the roof for parking is usually on a sloping site where there is no need for expensive ramps (expensive both in construction and waste of space). In the Sears, Roebuck store at Winston-Salem, for example *(page 23)*, the roof is at street level in the rear. At Bullock's-Pasa-

dena *(page 46)*, the parking area is split into two levels. The upper level, to the north of the store, spreads over part of the roof of the lower floor. The latter opens on to the lower level parking area to the south.

The parking space which surrounds Wanamaker's store, at Cross County Center, Yonkers, N. Y. *(see page 172)*, is divided into three levels, so that each level of the store has a ground floor entrance. This is a more elaborate example of the split-level pattern which has become so popular for suburban department stores *(cf. pages 163-173)*.

One other possibility remains: a multi-story garage. The economics of these are discussed on page 37. One designed for self-parking is shown on page 85, one for attendant parking on page 50.

BENEATH A STORE RAISED ON STILTS, SHOPPERS GO TO AND FROM THEIR CARS UNDER SHELTER. *KETCHUM, GINA & SHARP, ARCHITECTS*

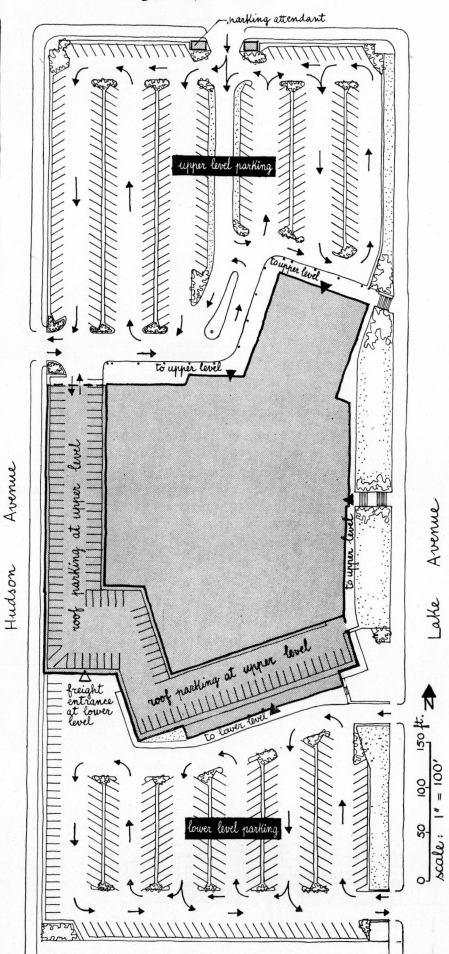

Del Mar Street

parking attendant

upper level parking

to upper level

to upper level

Hudson Avenue

roof parking at upper level

Lake Avenue

to upper level

roof parking at upper level

freight entrance at lower level

to lower level

lower level parking

N

scale: 1" = 100'

0   50   100 150 ft.

PARKING AREA ON TWO LEVELS.
ALTERNATING ONE-WAY AISLES,
WITH ONE-WAY ACCESS ROAD AT EACH END.
SPOTTER ON ROOF CONTROLS PARKING,
THROUGH ATTENDANT AT GATE

roof parking

freight entrance

roof parking

ENTRANCE TO ROOF PARKING IS CLEARLY MARKED, INVITING

ROOF PARKING, without benefit of a sloping site, is clearly demonstrated at Milliron's store in Westchester shopping center, Los Angeles *(see also page 168).* The two one-way ramps, a concrete scissors along the rear of the store, are 20 ft. wide and have a grade of only 11%, probably the maximum for self-parking. With access and exit points fixed by the ramps, alternating one-way aisles parallel to the ramps are practical and economical. Clearly marked pathways cross the aisles, through the lines of cars, to store entrance escalators in the middle.

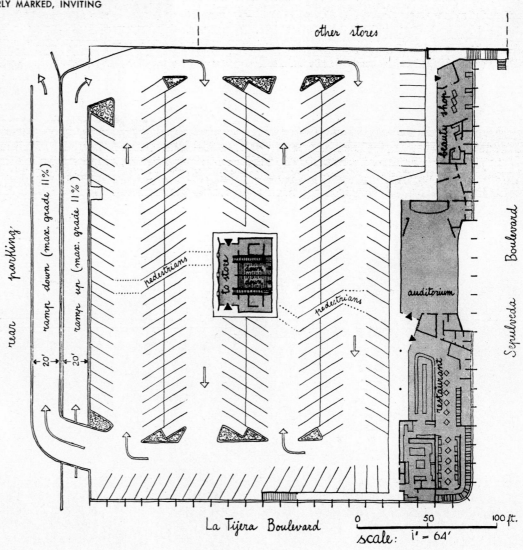

other stores

rear parking

ramp down (max. grade 11%)

ramp up (max. grade 11%)

20' 20'

pedestrians

to store

pedestrians

beauty shop

auditorium

restaurant

Sepulveda Boulevard

La Tijera Boulevard

scale: 1' = 64'

0 50 100 ft.

RAMPS TO AND FROM ROOF PARKING MAKE A STRIKING DECORATION FOR THE REAR WALL OF MILLIRON'S STORE, LOS ANGELES

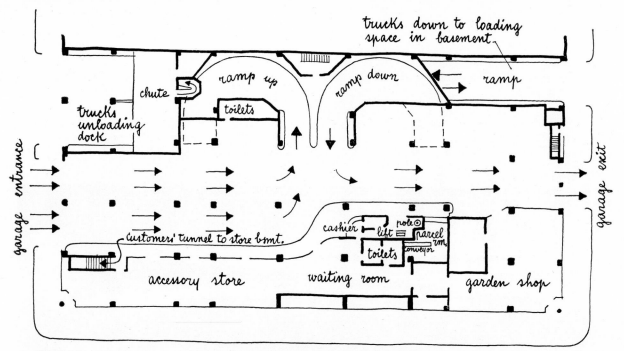

GRADUATED PARKING RATES DISCOURAGE LONG-TERM PARKING. ATTENDANTS USE MOVING LADDERS GOING UP, SLIDE POLES COMING DOWN. AS A RESULT, MAXIMUM DELIVERY TIME: 2 MINUTES

MULTI-STORY PARKING garages are usually operated by attendants, so that connecting ramps between floors can be narrower, steeper, and more sharply curved, thus reducing this unprofitable space to a minimum. Foley's five open-sided floors in Houston, Texas, can house almost 600 cars. An underground pedestrian passage connects with Foley's windowless department store, which occupies all the adjoining block. There is a four lane entrance and magazine space on one side of the garage, a two-lane exit on the other. The basement connected to the store by underground conveyor belts, is used for all the store's freight handling. Customers' purchases can be delivered from any part of the store to a pick-up desk near the garage exit. *Architect:* Kenneth Franzheim. *Retail Planners:* Raymond Loewy Associates.

THIN CONCRETE EYEBROWS PROTECT OPEN-SIDED PARKING FLOORS FROM WEATHER

STEEP NARROW RAMPS CUT DOWN WASTE SPACE

SEPARATING FREIGHT AND CUSTOMER TRAFFIC
HOW TO INCLUDE SERVICE COURTS IN NEW STORE GROUPS
DIMENSION DATA FOR FREIGHT DOCKS
SUPERMARKET FREIGHT HANDLING. GARBAGE COLLECTION

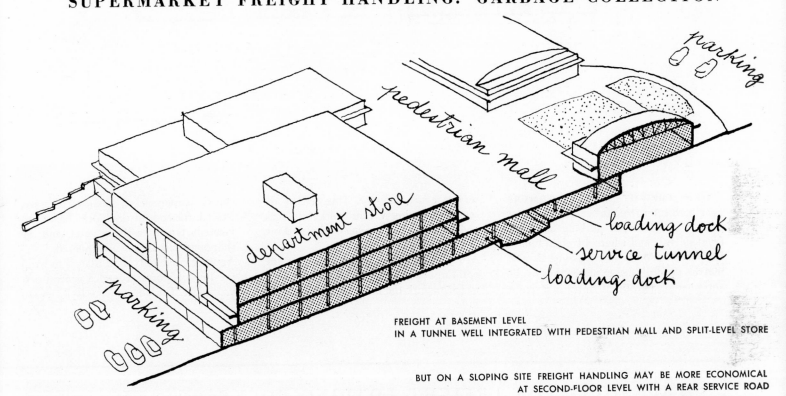

FREIGHT AT BASEMENT LEVEL
IN A TUNNEL WELL INTEGRATED WITH PEDESTRIAN MALL AND SPLIT-LEVEL STORE

BUT ON A SLOPING SITE FREIGHT HANDLING MAY BE MORE ECONOMICAL
AT SECOND-FLOOR LEVEL WITH A REAR SERVICE ROAD

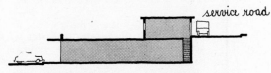

WITH FIRST-FLOOR-LEVEL FOR CUSTOMERS

Far too many of the shopping centers illustrated in this book fail to some extent in their handling of freight traffic. In some the loading and unloading facilities provided are not in themselves efficient. In others freight traffic is not adequately segregated from customer traffic. In the first case greater efficiency depends upon improvement in the design of service courts and loading docks; on the two following pages we have gathered examples and data which outline the problems involved and suggest ways of solving them.

But attention to such details is not in itself sufficient. More important (as already outlined on pages 31 and 32) is the circulation as dictated by the site plan. Many shopping center designers and operators still think wishfully that freight and customer traffic can be separated in time rather than space. So they attempt to limit freight and garbage handling to hours when the stores are closed. This almost never works well. Undoubtedly the idea which appeals most strongly to the designer (and the one which puts the greatest strain on the promoter's budget) is a freight tunnel. Then all freight handling is completely separated from customer traffic, and decently hidden in the basement. Moreover the basement floor can be set at dock level in relation to the tunnel roadway. Broadway-Crenshaw (page 174) led the way. Northgate improved upon the idea (above); the tunnel serves stores on both sides, and is effectively integrated with the building structure.

When a center has two-front stores, with the official display front on one side, but an equally important and heavily used front on the opposite side, then a freight tunnel is probably the only good answer. On a sloping site (above), as at the Naylor Road center in Washington, D. C., where it is simple to put a service road at second floor level, it may be a sound idea to switch from basement storage to second floor or mezzanine storage space.

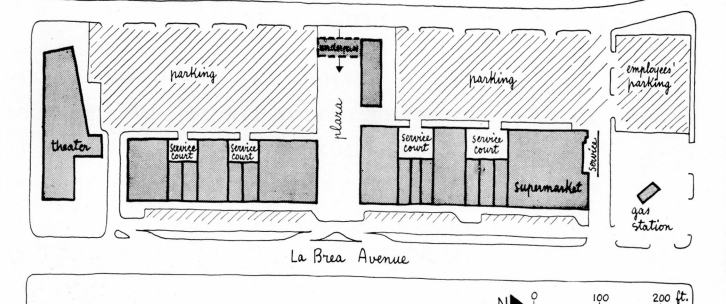

Baldwin Hills residential area

parking · plaza · parking · employees' parking

theater · service court · service court · service court · service court · supermarket · service · gas station

La Brea Avenue

N▶   0   100   200 ft.

SPLIT PARKING AND RECESSED SERVICE COURTS
AT BALDWIN HILLS SHOPPING CENTER, LOS ANGELES, CALIF. ROBERT E. ALEXANDER, ARCHITECT

WHEN FREIGHT AND CUSTOMERS must both enter from the same side of the store (e.g. with split parking and two-front stores), and where a freight tunnel for some reason is not feasible, then it may be a useful idea to merge the freight entrances of a group of stores in a single service court *(above)*. This can be recessed, allowing variation in store size, and shielded from the customers' parking area by a wall or fence.

A worthwhile trick, when arranging the buildings on the site, is to put those stores which require the most extensive service courts (supermarket, department store, etc.) at the ends of the block. There service courts can easily be inset, and the shoppers' circulation unhindered.

Another commonly used plan is to wrap the line of stores around a central service court. The stores themselves serve to

DIMENSIONS FOR FREIGHT LOADING DOCKS

RECOMMENDED OVERHEAD CLEARANCE: 14 FT.
RECOMMENDED MINIMUM ROAD WIDTH: 12 FT.
MORE NEEDED ON TURNS AS SHOWN BELOW

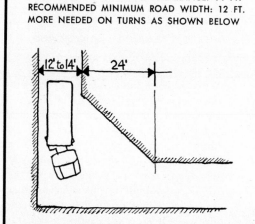

12' to 14' · 24'

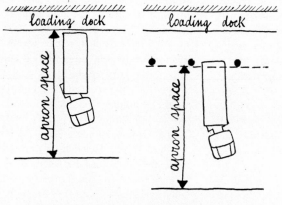

loading dock · apron space
loading dock · apron space

MOST COMMON *HEIGHT* FOR DOCKS IS 44 TO 50 INS.
BUT LIGHT TRUCKS HAVE A LOWER BED LEVEL

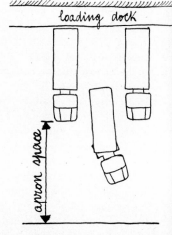

loading dock · apron space

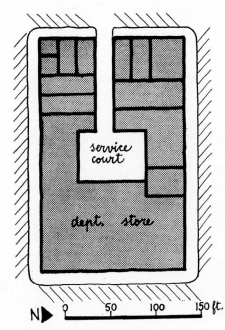

AT BELLEVUE (PAGE 222)
STORES SURROUND SERVICE COURT

WALLED SERVICE COURT ON STREET SIDE OF STORES AT HIGHLAND PARK (PAGE 90)

shield the court. If it is slightly larger than that shown above, this space can be used for extending certain stores at the rear as tenants may require (cf. plan on page 57). Such an arrangement is typical of the more conservative shopping centers, where stores are grouped in blocks surrounded by streets.

The ingenious arrangement of staggered stores at Aero Acres (below) not only provides a series of individual recessed docks on the rear service road, but also gives a most desirable variety in store depths, from 84 ft. to 48 ft.

A more elaborate (and expensive) version of the walled service court is that shown above. The outside—the street side —of the wall at left is, in addition, thickly planted. Such elaborate camouflage of the service court is required because there are residences across the street.

STAGGERED ARRANGEMENT OF STORES AT AERO ACRES (PAGE 128)
FORMS FREIGHT DOCKS ON REAR SERVICE ROAD

length of tractor-trailer in feet	width of opening in feet	apron space required in feet
	10	46
35	12	43
	14	39
	10	48
40	12	44
	14	42
	10	57
45	12	49
	14	48

ALL FIGURES ARE MINIMUM FOR BACKING INTO A DOCK IN A SINGLE MANEUVER

Courtesy Fruehauf Trailer Co.

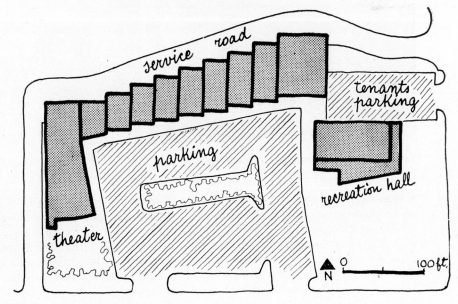

STANDARD BINS LOADED DIRECTLY ON TRUCK

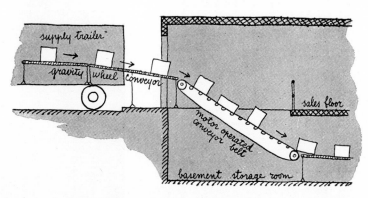

ROLLER CONVEYORS COMBINED WITH BELT CONVEYORS

FREIGHT HANDLING in a shopping center is at its most insistent and urgent in the supermarket. Two examples typify the improved methods now being evolved. To cut handling costs, Lucky Markets use large standard bins, each holding about 60 cases of merchandise. Two such bins form a truckload. They are loaded and unloaded with a fork lift, moved about the store on hydraulic lifts. (Raymond Loewy Assoc.) Most large supermarkets depend upon stock clerks working at night to fill the shelves.

To transfer freight from truck to store without need of a loading dock, use has been made of gravity roller conveyors. They are also used for moving goods within the store. Combined with a motor-operated conveyor belt between floors, they make the basement accessible storage space. (First National Stores)

LARGE METAL CONTAINER FOR GARBAGE AND TRASH ....

COLLECTED ON A SPECIAL HOIST TRUCK, REPLACED BY A CLEAN EMPTY

GARBAGE COLLECTION in a shopping center, like freight handling discussed above, will be of primary concern to the supermarket, of secondary importance to all other tenants except the restaurant. The crates and boxes which make up most of the supermarket's garbage are bulky; collection more than once a day is seldom feasible. Therefore the first essential is to provide a closed storage space, so that the garbage is kept out of sight and will not be blown around. However, there still remains the process of loading it on to the truck which will take it away; and this will inevitably be unsightly and dirty.

The system pictured above, now coming into increasingly wide use, avoids any transfer from one container to another. For a special hoist truck backs up to this container, attaches lifting chains, and carries the complete unit away to the garbage disposal unit, whether that be a dump or an incinerator. The same unit may be returned after emptying, or the full container may be exchanged for an empty. (Dempster-Dumpster)

WHAT IS THE BEST SIZE FOR A STORE BUILDING?
HOW TO ALLOW FOR FUTURE CHANGES IN SIZE
HOW TO AVOID SHOW WINDOW REFLECTIONS
AWNINGS, OVERHANGS, SIGNS, LANDSCAPING

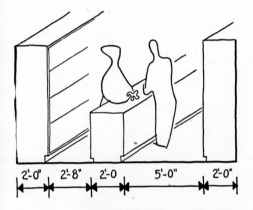

2'-0"   2'-8"   2'-0   5'-0"   2'-0"

THE ELEMENTS which must influence the size of store buildings are people and fixtures. A typical section of average people and average fixtures will give a minimum usable width of about 12-14 ft. with a display case at the side of the aisle. Double racks for garment storage will be 3 ft. 6 in. wide, rather than the 2 ft. common in most other storage fixtures; but then there won't be room for a counter case. Naturally all these dimensions, except the customer aisle width, mean very little if the store is divided crossways into two sections by a counter parallel to the store front. This arrangement is commonly found in service stores.

What size stores? This becomes of importance when planning the buildings to house smaller tenants. Those short-lease stores account for much of the center's revenue, but they also change occupancy more frequently than the larger stores. In the past, when store values were measured by the front foot, width was the most important dimension. Now, with the increased cost of building and the advent of two-front stores where the depth is frozen, store depth, and flexibility of construction to allow future changes, have become the two most important considerations.

The simplest way to achieve variety of depth is to build shallow blocks for the small stores, deeper ones for the big stores. But this tends to segregate stores by size rather than affinity.

If the stores are built around a central service court of good size, each store can expand in depth according to its own needs (see plan, page 57). To minimize the cost of such expansion the rear walls are kept free of ducts and piping. If one of these stores needs to expand still further, it may take over a section of the

neighboring store, thus expanding its own plan into an L, or even a T shape. This sort of arangement was a prime favorite of that vastly experienced Kansas City realtor, J. C. Nichols.

When the line of stores has but one entrance front, the smaller stores, even in a uniform rectangular block, can at least be kept to a desirable interior depth by partitioning off the rear section as storage, or allotting it to the next-door store for expansion. This may not be the most economical way to arrive at flexibility in store depth; but it works.

It is when the store block has two entrance fronts that the small stores become difficult to arrange. If the block depth is fixed to satisfy the needs of the big stores, then the small stores become narrow corridors. One way of avoiding this is to reverse the accepted practice by allowing the smaller stores to have the corner location usually reserved for a big puller. This allows a variety of width and depth (see plan at left), and reserves the two-front stores for bigger tenants, who are the only ones capable of benefiting from them. Any two-front store will operate much more smoothly if freight traffic is segregated in a tunnel, with loading docks and storage in the basement.

While store depth is affected by the general plan of a shopping center, store width is controlled more by the structural system of the buildings. Having decided on the best width for the smaller stores (and this may vary from 10 ft. which is probably too cramped, to 16 ft. which is probably wasteful, being neither big enough nor small enough) the structure should be such that two or more of

VARIETY OF SIZE AND SHAPE IN SMALL STORES AT END OF
TWO-FRONT STORE BLOCK. HUDSON'S, DETROIT: PAGE 200.

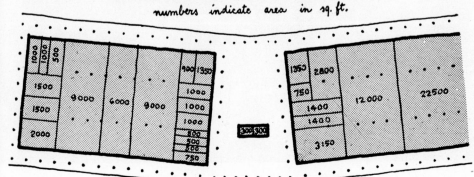

numbers indicate area in sq. ft.

the small units may be combined, when necessary, into a larger store without substantial alteration. In Fairlawn *(right)*, for example, the bearing walls—shown solid on the plan — are spaced 30 ft. apart. This 30 ft. unit can, when necessary, be divided with non-bearing partitions into smaller stores. Some of the bearing walls here double as fire walls; local building regulations require that in a non-fireproof building of this type the floor area shall be divided by fire walls into sections of not more nor less than 6,000 sq. ft.

At Ridgeway *(opposite page)*, instead of bearing walls there are steel beams supported by slender lally columns every 14 ft., which becomes the basic store width. The columns along the store fronts are for the most part encased in stone. When two units are merged, the center lally column, left bare, is quite inconspicuous behind the door jamb.

Basements are almost always worth their cost, even if they are not actually required at the time of construction. The cost of an unfinished basement is normally low, especially in those sections of the country where footings must be carried down 3-4 ft. below grade. Moreover, it is certainly a great asset to have a basement for storage, and also for later expansion of the selling area. The clear ceiling height should be not less than 9 ft., after allowance is made for air-conditioning ducts, which here become essential equipment.

To make a selling basement more inviting (and so more profitable) it should be opened to the first floor with a wide shallow stairway *(right)*.

Second-story offices for doctors, dentists and professional men are found in many centers, but there is considerable doubt as to whether they pay their way.

Second-story and basement store space gives a great increase of flexibility. By overlapping spaces, tenants can expand in many different ways *(right)*.

Store designers are now trying hard to abolish the old static conception of separate floors. By ramps *(page 199)*, split level plans *(pages 161-173)*, and shallow stairways which invite the customers to move up and down from one level to the next *(opposite page)*, the modern store may do without costly elevators, relying instead upon stairs and escalators.

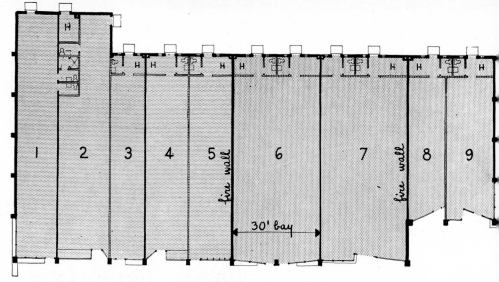

A VARIETY OF STORE DEPTHS, AND SOME NON-BEARING PARTITIONS FOR FLEXIBILITY IN WIDTH. *FAIRLAWN, STAMFORD: PAGE 104*

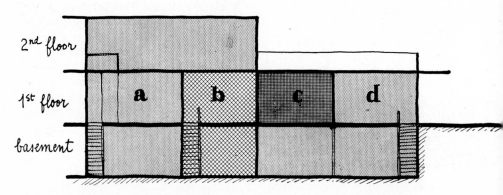

USING BASEMENT AND SECOND-STORY SPACE, STORES CAN EXPAND BY OVERLAPPING

SHOPPERS MORE WILLINGLY USE STAIRS THAT ARE WIDE, SHALLOW, PROMINENT
LORD & TAYLOR, EASTCHESTER, N. Y. STARRETT & VAN VLECK, ARCHS. RAYMOND LOEWY ASSOC.

VARIETY IN STORE DEPTH.
EACH STORE PROJECTS
AS FAR AS THE TENANT DESIRES
INTO A CENTRAL SERVICE COURT.
J. C. NICHOLS CO., PAGE 79

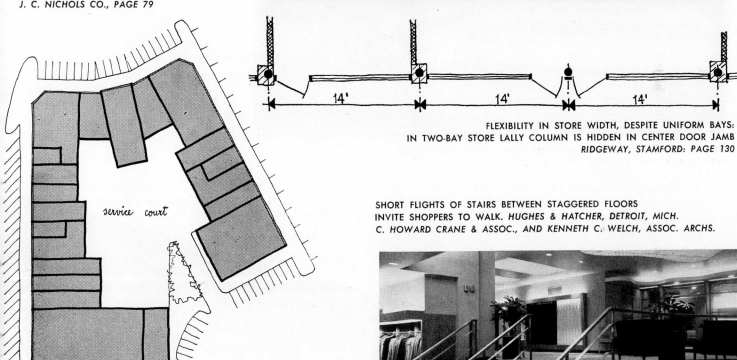

service court

0   50   100   150 ft.

FLEXIBILITY IN STORE WIDTH, DESPITE UNIFORM BAYS:
IN TWO-BAY STORE LALLY COLUMN IS HIDDEN IN CENTER DOOR JAMB
RIDGEWAY, STAMFORD: PAGE 130

SHORT FLIGHTS OF STAIRS BETWEEN STAGGERED FLOORS
INVITE SHOPPERS TO WALK. HUGHES & HATCHER, DETROIT, MICH.
C. HOWARD CRANE & ASSOC., AND KENNETH C. WELCH, ASSOC. ARCHS.

SECTION TO SHOW STAGGERED FLOOR ARRANGEMENT OF STORE

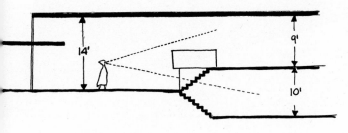

SMALL PANES GIVE COLONIAL CHARACTER IN NEIGHBORHOOD CENTER
SPRINGWELLS PARK, DEARBORN: PAGE 272

SHOW WINDOWS

A **CHARACTERISTIC** seen in almost all the shopping centers illustrated in this book is a certain uniformity of appearance along the store front. But within this uniform frame there is immense variety in the display fronts of the various stores. For the most part these follow precedents already set by downtown, street-front stores. Though there are many big glazed facades like that shown at far right, very few are so cleanly designed as this.

To harmonize with the residential neighborhood in which they are set, some shop-

ISOLATED DISPLAY CASES ATTACHED TO OVERHANG SUPPORTS AT EYE LEVEL
FARMERS MARKET, LOS ANGELES: PAGE 94

IDEAS FOR SHOPPING CENTER USE

OPEN FRONT UTILIZES WHOLE INTERIOR AS DISPLAY. *RIDGEWAY, STAMFORD: PAGE 130*

ping centers have reduced the scale of these open fronts by dividing them up into small panes *(left)*, a fairly successful attempt to impose a Colonial air.

Some large stores have come to the realization that, for them, the traditional show window has little value. The supermarket *(bottom right)* can make more effective use of a solid exterior wall, which is used for self-service display space on the interior. A strip of glass block high up still lets in natural light.

In cases where there are not likely to be any casual pedestrian window shoppers

(e.g. a suburban store back from the highway beyond an extensive area of landscaped parking), then the windows can be enlarged and used primarily for introducing daylight *(below left)*.

Whereas free-standing showcases would normally not be permitted on a city pavement, in a shopping center, where the environment is under private control, they may be used to extremely good effect, particularly when incorporated in the canopy supports *(opposite page, below)*. These isolated displays at eye level use daylight to excellent effect.

TALL WINDOWS AS IN A FORMAL MANSION. *LORD & TAYLOR, MANHASSET, N. Y. STARRETT & VAN VLECK, ARCHS. RAYMOND LOEWY ASSOC., DESIGNER*

INSTEAD OF SHOW WINDOWS A SOLID WALL FOR INTERIOR DISPLAYS. *BROADMOOR, SHREVEPORT: PAGE 142*

HOW TO DESIGN SHOW WINDOWS TRANSPARENT

THE GLASS OF A SHOW WINDOW is both transparent and reflective. Even clean plate glass has a reflection factor of 8%. If the glass is dusty, or if one's line of vision is not at right angles to the surface, the factor is much higher. In the window shown *(left above)*, one sees simultaneously the window display and the reflection of objects outside. If the brightness of the reflection is not as in-

tense as that of the display, then the latter will remain visible through the glass. But when the reflected images have the greater intensity, then the display will be obscured by a veiling glare.

A well-illuminated show window, with a light-colored background, in the shade, aided by natural light from the sky, will seldom have a brightness of more than 400 foot lamberts. Consequently it can-

not hope to compete with the reflections of white clouds, sunlit buildings, etc. *(see right)*. The window shopper will glimpse displays surrealistically mingled with fragments of street scene.

Satisfactory anti-reflective coatings for large sheets of glass are not yet available. So reflections must be stopped before they occur. They can be prevented by control of the environment. In this

WITH THE SUN IN FRONT an awning will not reduce the brightness of the pavement, which is reflected in the lower part *(a)* of the window. Dull surfacing on the pavement, and shadows cast by trees and bushes will help.

WITH THE SUN BEHIND the store building, an awning will shade the pavement in front. Beyond this band of shadow, dull surfacing and planting can be used to reduce the pavement brightness.

REFLECTION-FREE

respect the shopping center—a group of stores under a single ownership—has a great advantage over the single store in a street downtown.

To clarify discussion the reflection of the pavement *(a)*, cars and buildings *(b)*, and sky *(c)*, have been treated separately, in the drawings below. In reality, of course, their reflections are simultaneous, the remedies overlapping.

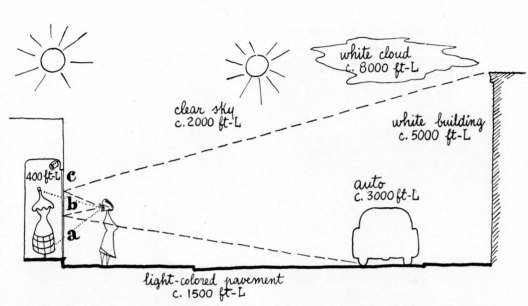

white cloud
c. 8000 ft-L

clear sky
c. 2000 ft-L

white building
c. 5000 ft-L

400 ft-L

auto
c. 3000 ft-L

light-colored pavement
c. 1500 ft-L

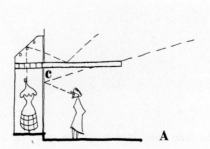

A

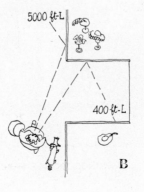

5000 ft-L

400 ft-L

B

REFLECTIONS AT EYE LEVEL, from cars and buildings across the street *(b)*, are the most difficult to prevent. They can be intercepted only by awnings hung from the edge of the canopy *(see page 62)*, or by high trees. Then the brightness of the buildings across the street can be reduced by painting them in dark, dull colors with a low reflective value.

A. OVERHANGS can eliminate sky reflections entirely, so that the area *(c)* remains unblurred. The upper surface of the overhang may be used to reflect daylight into the show window (through a transom), to boost artificial lighting.

B. VESTIBULES, and all types of slanted window, sidestep many reflection problems, for they reflect other show windows of equally low brightness. They avoid the bright reflections from opposite which plague the street-front windows.

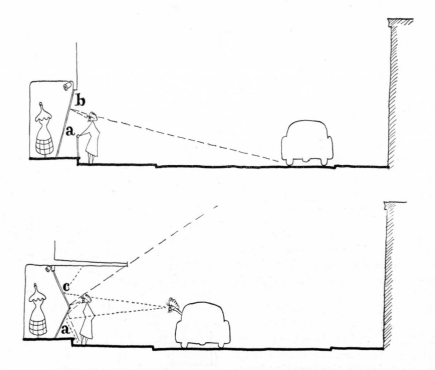

CURVED AND TILTED WINDOWS are the most effective in preventing unwanted reflections. One fitted with curved glass *(above)*, and patented by U.S. Invisible Glass Co., reflects only the black surfaces of its own parapet and soffit. No matter what there may be outside the window, veiling reflections will never be visible. The forward-tilted glass *(top right)*, if facing north, will reflect only the dark pavement in shadow, except in the small section *(b)* at top. The double-tilted window *(right)* must be combined with an overhang, to avoid interference by sky reflections.

AWNINGS can still substitute for a fixed canopy, to protect window shoppers from sun and rain, and to shade the display windows so that their brightness may better compete with that of the sunlight outdoors. Awnings have the great virtue of flexibility. Unfortunately too often the individual stores in a center create a hodge-podge like that above *(at Glen Oaks: page 264)*. But awnings of uniform size and pattern can be effective.

VERTICAL AWNINGS PROTECT STORES FROM LOW WESTERN SUN. *RIVER OAKS, HOUSTON, TEXAS*

GAILY STRIPED AWNINGS, OF UNIFORM SIZE AND PATTERN, DISPLAY STORE NAMES ON FRONT EDGE.
COLONIAL SHOPS, EVANSTON: PAGE 105

OVERHANG CO-ORDINATED WITH SIGNS AND LIGHTING. *SEE SECTION, PAGE 66*

OVERHANGS PROTEC

To encourage window shoppers, most shopping centers have some sort of continuous overhang along the front of the stores. Like the arcaded market square of a medieval town, these not only shelter the pedestrian from rain and sun but also reflect the benevolent despotism of a whole store group under single ownership. This is, of course, in contradistinction to the typical Main St. pattern, where there is not unity either of architectural style or of ownership.

The design of a shopping center overhang should be co-ordinated with the re-

HIGH, LIGHT-STUDDED OVERHANG HAS RIPPLING EDGE LINE.
RIDGEWAY, STAMFORD: PAGE 130

VINDOW SHOPPERS FROM WEATHER

quirements of signs, lighting, and general appearance. At River Oaks, Houston *(top left)*, a single continuous light source, at the root of this curving overhang, causes the store name letters to stand out in silhouette, and by reflection from the white stucco soffit provides overall lighting for the sidewalk. This overhang does very little, however, to prevent reflections veiling the store windows thereby decreasing their display value. For weather protection an overhang should be low and wide, like that at Bellevue *(lower right)* in the state of Washington, where rainfall is frequent. Many overhangs *(below, and bottom left)* accent the height of the ceiling within (of which they are an extension), but this height makes them inefficient as shelter if there happens to be a driving rain. In both these overhangs a row of down lights on the underside serves to light the pavement.

In the case of Oakland Gardens *(right)* the overhang is so high and narrow that its only remaining function is to carry a row of spots for lighting the sign strip over the stores.

OVERHANG LIGHTS ILLUMINATE SIGN STRIP
OAKLAND GARDENS, L. I.: PAGE 106

STORE ENTRANCE RECESSED UNDER CONTINUOUS HIGH OVERHANG
BULLOCK'S-PASADENA: PAGE 164

STEPPED OVERHANG FOLLOWS SLOPE OF SITE.
BELLEVUE: PAGE 222

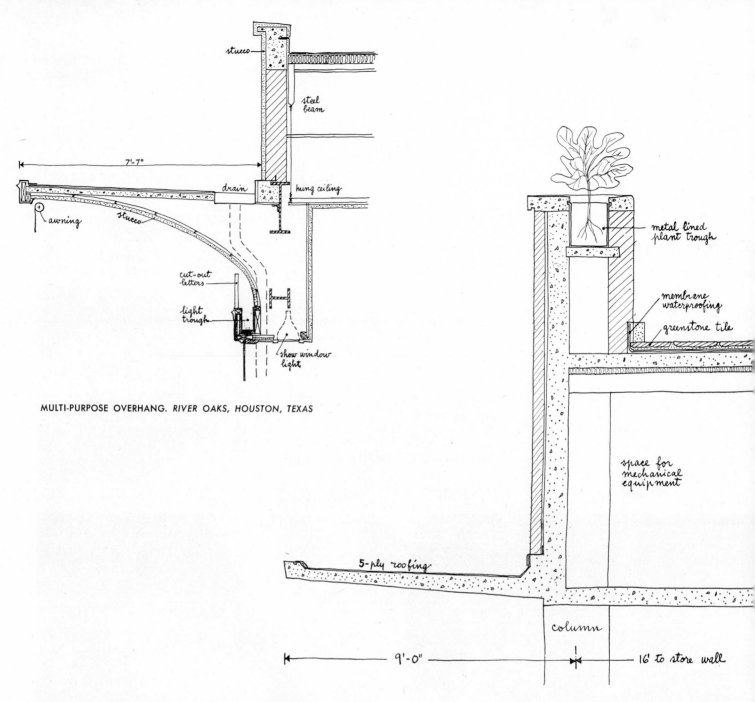

MULTI-PURPOSE OVERHANG. *RIVER OAKS, HOUSTON, TEXAS*

stucco

steel beam

drain

hung ceiling

7'-7"

awning

stucco

cut-out letters

light trough

show window light

metal lined plant trough

membrane waterproofing

greenstone tile

space for mechanical equipment

5-ply roofing

column

9'-0"

16' to store wall

DELICATE REINFORCED CONCRETE. *BULLOCK'S-PASADENA: PAGE 164*

A CONTINUOUS OVERHANG along the store fronts has now become practically standard in any new shopping center. Gathered on these two pages are construction details of five different types. That at River Oaks *(top left)* is among the most ingenious for the way in which the lighting, the store sign, the awning, and the sheltering roof are all coordi-nated. The detail shown is from the west side of the store group, where awnings are fitted to guard against the low after-noon sun *(cf. picture, page 62)*.

Structure and appearance in an overhang are obviously interdependent. A canti-levered overhang is usually more expen-sive than one supported on columns. Cantilevering may be in reinforced con-

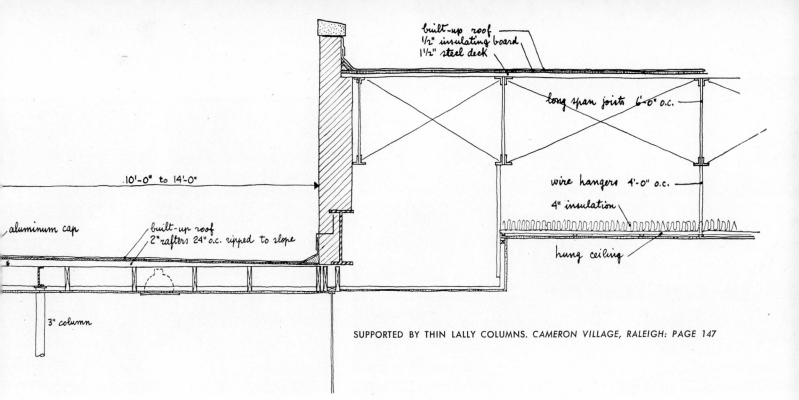

built-up roof
1/2" insulating board
1 1/2" steel deck

long span joists 6'-0" o.c.

10'-0" to 14'-0"

wire hangers 4'-0" o.c.

4" insulation

aluminum cap

built-up roof
2" rafters 24" o.c. ripped to slope

hung ceiling

3" column

SUPPORTED BY THIN LALLY COLUMNS. CAMERON VILLAGE, RALEIGH: PAGE 147

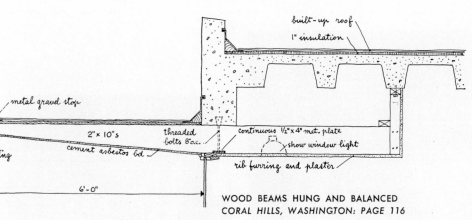

built-up roof
1" insulation

metal gravel stop

2" x 10"s

threaded bolts 8" o.c.

continuous 1/2" x 4" met. plate

show window light

um. olding

cement asbestos bd.

rib furring and plaster

6'-0"

WOOD BEAMS HUNG AND BALANCED
CORAL HILLS, WASHINGTON: PAGE 116

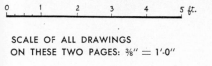

0 1 2 3 4 5 ft.

SCALE OF ALL DRAWINGS
ON THESE TWO PAGES: 3/8" = 1'-0"

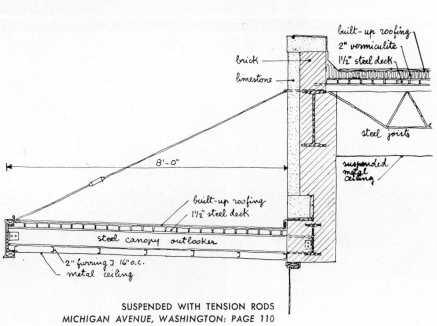

built-up roofing
2" vermiculite
1 1/2" steel deck

brick

limestone

steel joists

8'-0"

suspended metal ceiling

built-up roofing
1 1/2" steel deck

steel canopy outlooker

2" furring ⌶ 16" o.c.
metal ceiling

SUSPENDED WITH TENSION RODS
MICHIGAN AVENUE, WASHINGTON: PAGE 110

crete *(left center)* or in wood *(right center)*. The latter is most ingeniously balanced at the midpoint where 2 x 10s are bolted to the concrete roof structure. Where economy is of prime importance, and in cases where a wider than usual overhang is demanded, it may be supported by slim lally columns *(top right)*, or partly hung by tension rods *(right)*.

RESTAURANT BEHIND A GARDEN. CAMERON VILLAGE, RALEIGH: PAGE 147

SUPERMARKET PORTE-COCHERE FOR PICKUPS. LUCKY MARKETS
DESIGNED BY RAYMOND LOEWY ASSOC.

STORES LIT BY TRANSOM ABOVE OVERHANG. MAPLEWOOD: PAGE 129

OVERHANG BECOMES COLONNADE. GREENHILLS,
OHIO, U.S. RESETTLMENT ADMINISTRATION

OFFICE BUILDING HAS PATIO INSTEAD OF LOBBY
RIVER OAKS, HOUSTON, TEXAS

SHORTCUT LINED WITH SHOW WINDOWS
PARKCHESTER, NEW YORK: PAGE 246

AMENITIES CAN HELP TO CREATE ATMOSPHERE

MUCH OF THE ATMOSPHERE which the public finds so appealing in a modern shopping center is due to such formerly unexpected amenities as covered walks, arcades, patios, and lavish landscaping *(cf. page 74)*. These are what create that feeling of relaxation and make shopping at one of the best new centers a very different experience to shopping downtown. This creation of a special, different, atmosphere becomes of the greatest im-

portance in department stores which specialize in women's fashions. Their clientele is extremely conscious of gay touches like the bright-colored canvas lashed to a pipe frame, which has now become a recognizable characteristic of Lord & Taylor's suburban branches. Like Bullock's slatted sunshade it will appeal to women with a sense of fashion.

The Spanish fountain at River Oaks *(opposite, bottom left)*, in a courtyard be-

tween the residential area (through the arcade in the background) and the store fronts, has a somewhat dated air, but the idea behind its placing here is sound.

More functional, and certainly more modern in style, is the supermarket porte-cochere *(opposite, top left)*. It is placed a few steps away from the main entrance, to avoid congestion there, but connected with it by a covered walkway, for shoppers and their bundles.

BRIGHT CANVAS. LORD & TAYLOR, MANHASSET: PAGE 74

FOR TERRACE FURNITURE. BULLOCK'S-PASADENA: PAGE 164

STAIR TOWER AS SIGN FOR CENTER. *RIVER OAKS, HOUSTON, TEXAS*

SIGNS MUST BE

IF SIZED TO THEIR AUDIENCE, as they should be, shopping center signs can be divided into three categories. First, a tall sign on the roadway, to identify the center. Second, store signs to be read by the motorist on the highway or in the parking area. Third, store signs for the shopper walking from store to store.

If there is a continuous canopy along the front of the stores, the signs on the facade

THE CENTER'S OWN SIGN is increasingly important. The level of competition is shifting; rather than one store competing with another, one shopping center will compete with another. It is the cumulative pull of a store group which can lure the shopper on wheels. One-stop shopping is what attracts. It becomes essential, therefore, to promote the center as an entity in itself. For this a distinctive trademark sign, used in all advertising, on all direction signs, even on packages, would be of value.

The sign at the center must be tall and prominently placed. At the Lamar center *(above)* it is on the stair tower which serves the second-story offices. At Northgate *(right)* it is a tall pillar on the road at the freight tunnel exit.

PILLAR AND BILLBOARD AT FREIGHT TUNNEL EXIT. *NORTHGATE, SEATTLE: PAGE 214*

BOTH DESIGNED AND PLACED FOR SEEING

above, while they may be visible to the motorist at a distance, will be of no help to pedestrians window-shopping beneath the overhang. For them it will be necessary to hang small signs below the canopy, at right angles to the store fronts *(below right)*. This idea is not new *(right)*, just forgotten.

To accentuate the unified design of a shopping center, many owners attempt to control the store signs which their tenants erect. In some centers the owners have successfully insisted upon uniform lettering for all store signs. But this is not usually feasible except in the case of small independents. Chain stores particularly are very loath to give up their long-established trademark signs. A reasonable compromise may be to limit signs to a band of limited width *(bottom)*.

SIGNS FOR PEDESTRIANS AND MOTORISTS. EL RANCHO, SANTA ANITA: PAGE 140

SIGNS FOR PEDESTRIANS. LINDA VISTA: PAGE 236

ALL KINDS OF SIGNS, BUT CONFINED TO A STRIP
GLEN OAKS, LONG ISLAND: PAGE 264

71

BACK AGAIN. AND STILL NO NEW PRINCIPLES

TO BE SEEN FROM THE HIGHWAY by passing motorists, signs must be large, and turned at right angles to the flow of traffic. The two supermarkets shown below have carried their shouting to great heights. Even the bank, not wishing to be outshouted, has abandoned its traditional quiet conservatism. It is of course necessary with these low buildings to raise the sign on some sort of tower or scaffold, in order for it to be seen from a distance down the road. In the case of the Big Chain supermarket *(opposite page, top)*, reliance has been placed upon very thick letters atop the raised entrance marquee. These should stand out successfully against the sky.

Department stores, meanwhile, have become exceedingly restrained. Halle Bros. *(right)* has no sign at all along the street front, only a most restrained name plate on each side wall, dark against pale stone. Bloomingdale's has no more than a single trademark B on a gray marble panel at the entrance.

PRESTIGE MAY COME WHISPERING. BLOOMINGDALE'S, FRESH MEADOWS: PAGE 248

AT RIGHT ANGLES TO TRAFFIC: NAME TO BE SEEN. *HALLE BROS., CLEVELAND: PAGE 184*

SUPERMARKETS TAKE NO CHANCES. BROADWAY-CRENSHAW, LOS ANGELES: P. 174

LUCKY MARKET, SAN LEANDRO, CALIF. DESIGNER: RAYMOND LOEWY ASS

SUPERMARKET. *LAKE SHORE DRIVE, SHREVEPORT:* PAGE 144

STORE FACADE BILLBOARD. *BROADWAY-CRENSHAW, LOS ANGELES:* PAGE 174

THEATER. *BROADMOOR, SHREVEPORT:* PAGE 142

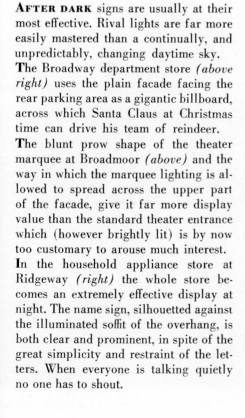

AFTER DARK signs are usually at their most effective. Rival lights are far more easily mastered than a continually, and unpredictably, changing daytime sky.

The Broadway department store *(above right)* uses the plain facade facing the rear parking area as a gigantic billboard, across which Santa Claus at Christmas time can drive his team of reindeer.

The blunt prow shape of the theater marquee at Broadmoor *(above)* and the way in which the marquee lighting is allowed to spread across the upper part of the facade, give it far more display value than the standard theater entrance which (however brightly lit) is by now too customary to arouse much interest.

In the household appliance store at Ridgeway *(right)* the whole store becomes an extremely effective display at night. The name sign, silhouetted against the illuminated soffit of the overhang, is both clear and prominent, in spite of the great simplicity and restraint of the letters. When everyone is talking quietly no one has to shout.

WHOLE STORE AS LIGHTED DISPLAY. *RIDGEWAY, STAMFORD:* PAGE 130

73

LAWNS, FRUIT TREES AND FLOWER BEDS, JUST LIKE THE NEARBY HOUSES
LORD & TAYLOR, MANHASSET, N. Y. STARRETT & VAN VLECK, ARCHS.
RAYMOND LOEWY ASSOC. DESIGNERS

LANDSCAPING CAN BE

LAWNS AND FLOWERING SHRUBS can give far greater delight to most women shoppers than even the most elaborate architecture. Landscaping can cover up many blunders of layout and appearance. It can endow the simplest buildings with charm and graciousness. It can also be remarkably expensive in maintenance if not planned from the start with economy in mind. Flowering trees and shrubs, for example, require very much less maintenance than flowering annuals. On the other hand these will give a longer and more variegated season of bloom, if carefully managed and frequently changed. And while a well-kept lawn is undoubtedly beautiful, its beauty is not achieved without considerable labor and expense. Cobblestones, bricks, flagstones —perhaps with rock plants or grass in the joints—can be just as attractive and considerably more economical on up-

MADE TO SERVE A SHOPPING CENTER'S PURPOSE

keep. Native plants are not to be spurned, particularly in regions where other plants require considerable irrigation *(below)*. For suburban stores in a residential neighborhood, some effort may be made to match the landscaping of the store with the surrounding home gardens *(opposite page, top)*. This is mostly a matter of scale. Planting may also be used to ease the change of level between upper and lower floors in these suburban stores where there is plenty of open space around the building. By turning and breaking the line of steps *(opposite page, bottom)*, they are made to seem less formidable. The walk *(right)*—between a rear parking area and other stores in the shopping center—along one side of a department store, is paved for heavy use, but also opened out into a sunken courtyard with a place to sit, which makes this an attractive place to linger.

TOWN & COUNTRY, SACRAMENTO: PAGE 98

RESTING PLACE FOR SHOPPERS BY STORE ENTRANCE. HALLE BROS., CLEVELAND: PAGE 184

PEDESTRIANS ONLY. FARMERS MARKET, LOS ANGELES: PAGE 94

SHOPPERS GOSSIP IN THE SHADE. LEVITTOWN: PAGE 258

PLANTING CAN RANGE all the way from a few shade trees in the jam-packed alleys of Los Angeles' Farmers Market *(left above)*, to the elaborate flower displays and fountains of Rockefeller Center's Channel Gardens in New York *(below)*. Both help to instill that mood of relaxation at which more recent shopping center designs are now aiming with the closed pedestrian mall ringed by stores. Trees and benches on a wide sidewalk *(left)* approach the same end more economically. Parking areas *(opposite page)* need not be vast and barren expanses of hot black asphalt. Shaded by trees and punctuated by flower beds (in strange but functional shapes), the parking area may be made less forbidding. If the site is not entirely flat, the total parking area may be divided into a number of smaller areas at different levels, the dividing banks covered with flowering plants and low shrubs.

ROCKEFELLER CENTER, NEW YORK. REINHARD & HOFMEISTER; CORBETT, HARRISON & MACMURRAY; HOOD & FOUILHOUX, ARCHS.

LANDSCAPING
FOR PEDESTRIANS AND CARS ALSO

FUNCTIONAL SHAPE IN PARKING AREA. MILLIRON S, LOS ANGELES: PAGE 168

B. ALTMAN & CO., MANHASSET, N. Y. HOPKINS & ASSOC., ARCHS.

PLANTING AND LIGHTING COMBINED. BULLOCK'S-PASADENA: PAGE 164

INTRODUCING AN ASSORTMENT OF 63 SHOPPING CENTERS, LARGE AND SMALL

On the following 200 pages is shown a wide variety of shopping centers. Each has some pertinent new ideas shown in plans, pictures and text. These store groups vary in size from a little ten-store neighborhood center, anchored on a supermarket and a drug store, up to regional centers planned to cover more than 100 acres and do a gross business of $100 million. Each center varies also according to local conditions: the climate, income levels, shopping habits.

Between conception and completion each center will have suffered many changes. Desirable tenants will always have power to modify the architect's original plans. A small promoter, as his capital runs out, will always try to cut costs, often at the expene of good design. Nevertheless, more and more, shopping centers as actually built are handsome, efficient and interesting examples of a building type very little restricted so far by established principles.

On the following pages the shopping centers have been arranged more or less according to plan-shape and size, starting from the short, straight line of stores, through L and U plans, to big store groups around a central mall. However, any rigid classification by types is not possible. Sub-groupings include planned communities, suburban department stores, historic forerunners, and many more. There is a complete index at the end of the book.

SYMBOLIC PICTURE OF SHOPPING CENTER HISTORY

TRIPLE-DECK PARKING GARAGE IN THE COUNTRY CLUB PLAZA, KANSAS CITY, MO.

SUMMED UP IN THIS PICTURE is the brief history of the shopping center, its aspirations, its misjudgments, and its possibilities. The Country Club Plaza *(left)*, was constructed in the late Twenties, so it happens to boast an elm-shaded Spanish wellhead as its symbol of refinement. Today neither the architect's taste nor the owner's pocketbook would permit such a piece of sheer decoration. But the value of shade trees and flowers is realized, even stressed, in more recent shopping centers.

The triple-decked garage, with its Mexican tile facing, *(described in more detail on page 84)* is the symbol of misjudgment. For the parking areas that seemed so ample, and such an idealistic waste of space in the Twenties, are now, in the Fifties, insufficient even when triple-decked. After some hard-headed calculation of future growth, even such expensive vertical expansion as this is now considered justifiable by practical real estate men trying to satisfy more and more automobile shoppers. Parking space still appeals most effectively.

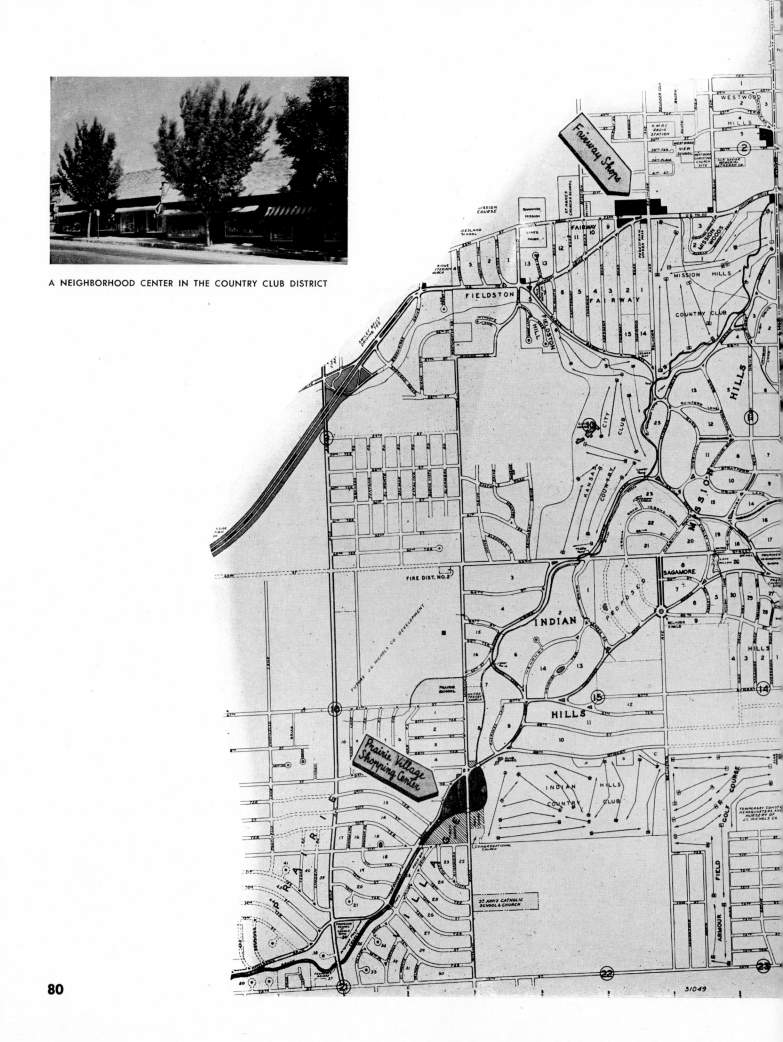

A NEIGHBORHOOD CENTER IN THE COUNTRY CLUB DISTRICT

KANSAS CITY DEVELOPER
PIONEERS INTEGRATION
OF HOUSES AND STORES

THE COUNTRY CLUB DISTRICT, Kansas City, Mo., was started by the late J. C. Nichols, and his associate J. C. Taylor, in 1908. It was then a 10-acre tract of swamp land, five miles south of the city and in a direction completely opposite to prevailing suburban growth. Today it spreads over 5,000 acres.

Inspired by a bicycle trip through Europe, Nichols determined to reproduce, in Kansas, a town as practical and beautiful as one of those ideal Garden Cities he had seen in England. Now the population of 50,000 is satisfied spiritually by 17 churches, educationally by 15 schools, and recreationally by 4 golf courses. For esthetic nourishment there is "The World's Greatest Outdoor Art Gallery", a million dollars worth of imported statuary, fountains, columns, and wellheads, scattered through the public parks and along the roadways.

Nichols realized very early that he would have to provide good shopping facilities. On the Kansas City edge of the District is a large downtown-type shopping area, the Country Club Plaza. Ten smaller neighborhood centers are distributed through the various subdivisions.

In creating the Country Club Plaza, Nichols intended to build a more profitable, more beautiful, and more convenient type of downtown shopping center. Nichols saw that if this was to substitute for downtown, it must contain a well-balanced group of stores giving complete and slightly competitive shopping. Apartment houses ring the store area. They act as a buffer strip between one-family houses and stores. They also produce more condensed buying power, with a profitable walk-in trade.

There had to be, of course, ample parking space. Nichols believed the most popular parking spot to be at the curb, directly in front of the store where the customer wanted to shop. Intermediate blocks reserved for parking fields he considered necessary but less desirable.

(text continued on page 84)

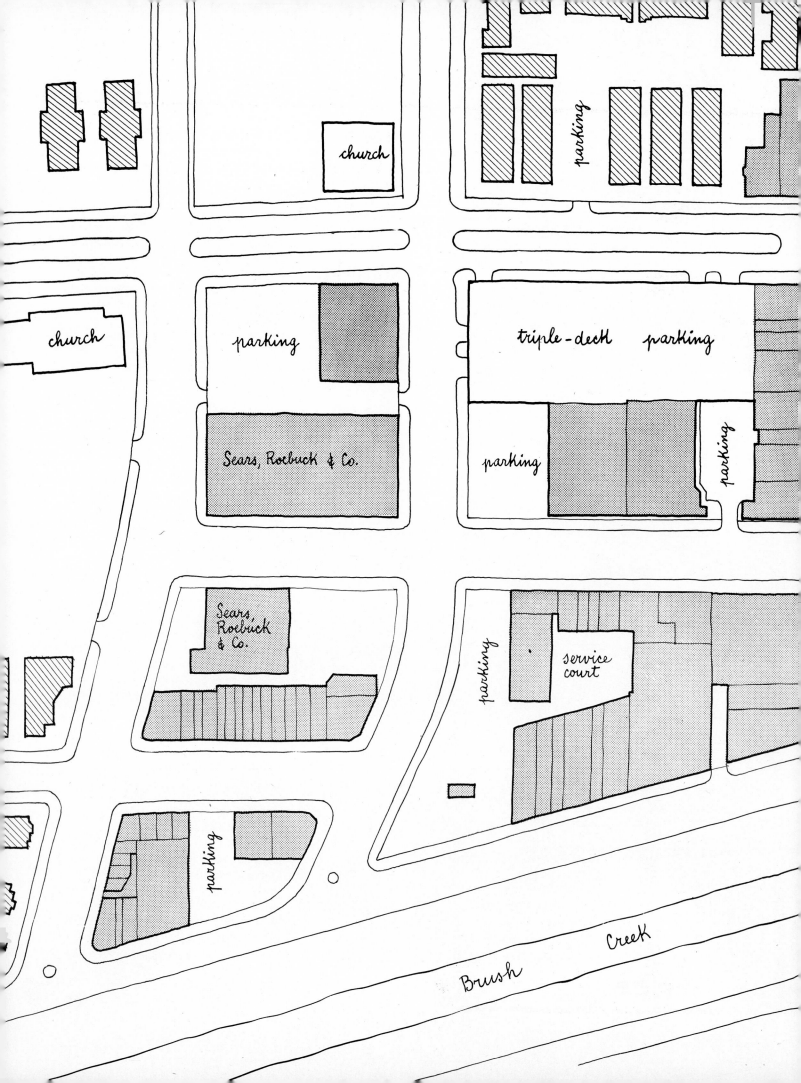

parking

to Kansas City ►

theater

sunken parking

sunken parking

parking

Parkway

Ward

N

0   100   200   300 ft.

stores and
offices

apartments

COUNTRY CLUB PLAZA SHOPPING CENTER

foot bridge

(text continued from page 81)

The importance of the late J. C. Nichols in the history of shopping center development is primarily his long experience in the actual operation of a planned neighborhood, as a real estate developer and as operator of both downtown-type and neighborhood-type centers.

To create more of what he considered 100% locations, Nichols preferred small store blocks, each with a hollow center used as a service court, *(see plan on preceding page)*. This also allows the stores to be extended at the rear, to fit each tenant's specific needs.

He justified development in small blocks by advocating a large ratio of street area to building area. In the Country Club Plaza it is approximately 46%. He claimed that this theory of design helps to solve the parking problem. This is accomplished by reducing the land available for building.

He also believed that small blocks allow more harmonious store-grouping, and enable merchants to pull trade from one side of a block to the other. To pull the trade all around a long block would be far more difficult.

He believed, further, that blocks radiating from a central core are more advantageous than any string type of arrangement along a single street. It was easier, he felt, to draw trade from a few blocks away than from half a mile down the street. Moreover, string development would extend what might be unsightly rear store entrances far into the residential area. This is of course a particularly important consideration for developers who own both the shopping center and the surrounding home sites.

Nichols was very much against high office buildings. He felt that their bulk would cut off air and light. But his prime concern was again with parking: all-day parking by office workers would sterilize too much of the available parking space. Investigation showed that the average shopper in the Country Club Plaza parks 20 minutes. Assuming that an office worker parks his car all day, he would preempt space that might otherwise be used by 24 shoppers. Office workers could never, Nichols believed, pay their way in a shopping center. The assertion was mathematically provable.

TRIPLE-DECKING MULTIPLIES PARKING

IN THE COUNTRY CLUB PLAZA, as in all other early shopping centers, the original parking space is now insufficient. It was in itself well-planned, especially one sunken area (shown below). Shoppers can see across and above the cars to the stores on the opposite side.

To gain more space, an area (162 ft. x 376 ft.) has been triple-decked, to accommodate 571 cars *(see opposite page)*. One end of the site is about 12 ft. higher than the other, giving the two-way access ramps (for self-parking), a grade of 10% or less, with wide-radius curves.

Yet experience shows that 8% grades would be even better.

The top deck is open, and pedestrians can go directly from here and from the middle level to the adjacent buildings. The middle level has a minimum clearance of 7½ ft. The basement has 13½ ft. headroom, so that it can be used for trucks. Parking stalls are at an angle of 68½°, with a width of 7 ft. 9 in., except on the roof level where it is 7 ft. 5 in.

Architects: Edward W. Tanner & Assoc.
Owner & Developer: J. C. Nichols Co.

COUNTRY CLUB PLAZA SUNKEN PARKING AREA—WELL-PLANNED BUT NOW INSUFFICIENT

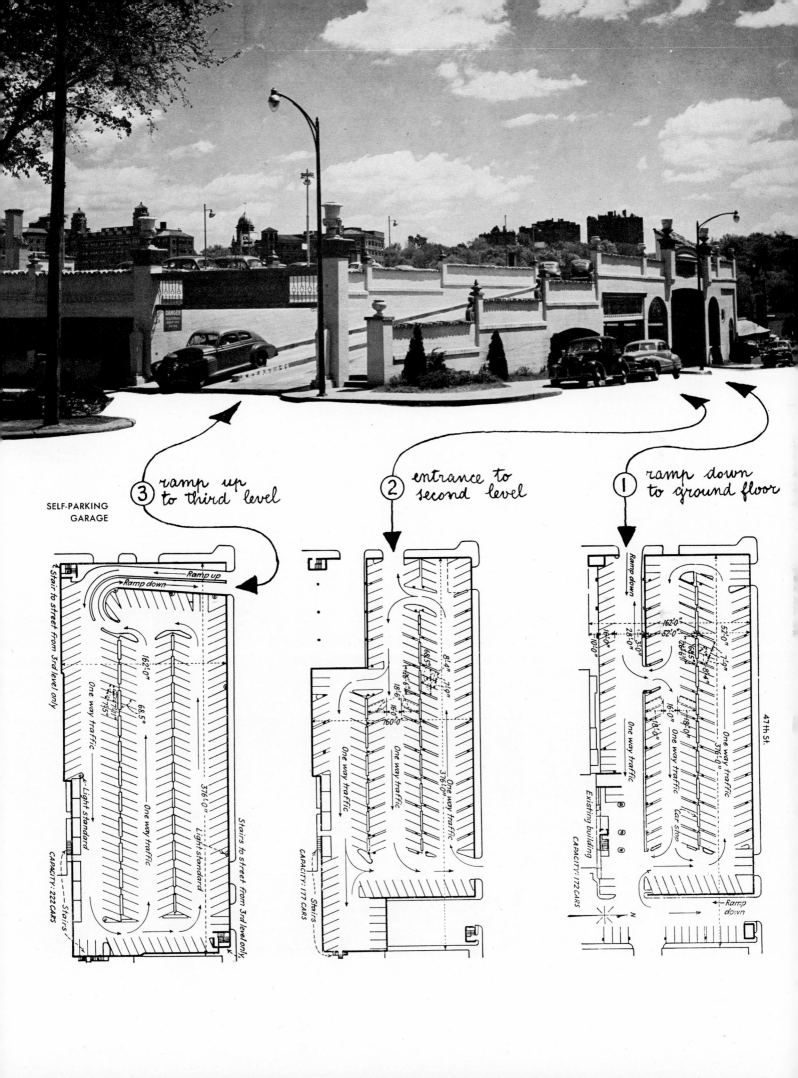

SELF-PARKING
GARAGE

③ ramp up
to third level

② entrance to
second level

① ramp down
to ground floor

Third level

Ramp up
Ramp down
162'-0"
68.5°
376'-0"
One way traffic
One way traffic
Light standard
Light standard
Stairs to street from 3rd level only
Stair to street from 3rd level only
CAPACITY: 222 CARS
Stairs

Second level

84'-0"
71'-9"
68.5°
18'-6" 16'-0"
160'-0"
376'-0"
One way traffic
One way traffic
One way traffic
CAPACITY: 177 CARS
Stairs

Ground floor

Ramp down
162'-0"
52'-0"
28'-0"
3'-0"
16'-0"
10'-0"
168.5°
71'-9"
48'-0"
16'-0"
18'-0"
376'-0"
One way traffic
One way traffic
One way traffic
Car shop
Existing building
CAPACITY: 172 CARS
N
47th St.
Ramp down

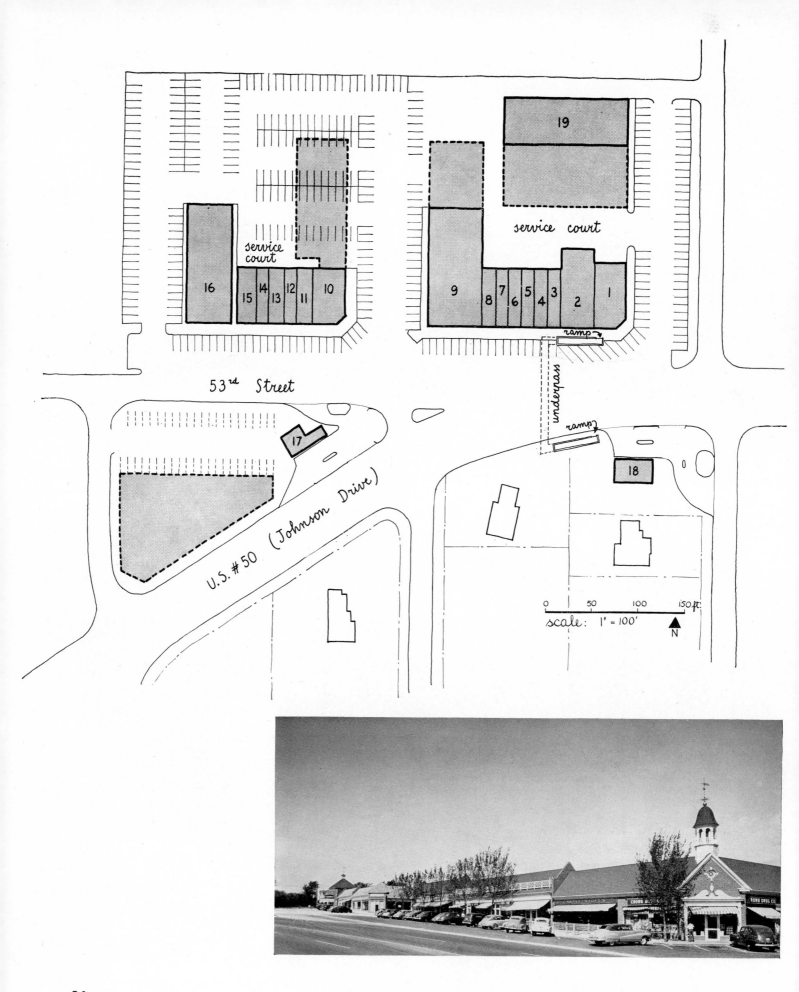

53rd Street

service court

service court

ramp

underpass

ramp

U.S. #50 (Johnson Drive)

scale: 1' = 100'

0   50   100   150 ft.

N

TYPE OF STORE	WIDTH, DEPTH	SQ. FT. AREA
1 Drugs	35 x 70	2,450
2 Variety	37 x 84	3,108
3 Grocery	14 x 62	868
4 Barber & Shoe Repair	14 x 62	868
5 Cleaners	14 x 62	868
6 Women's Wear	14 x 62	868
7 Beauty Shop	14 x 62	868
8 Bakery	14 x 62	868
9 Supermarket	60 x 125	7,500
10 Restaurant	35 x 60	2,100
11 Paints	17 x 60	1,020

TYPE OF STORE	WIDTH, DEPTH	SQ. FT. AREA
12 Children's Wear	13 x 60	780
13 Candy	17 x 60	1,020
14 Electric Appliances	13 x 60	780
15 Household Appliances	20 x 60	1,200
16 Theater	50 x 125	6,250
17 Filling Station		
18 Filling Station		
19 Frozen Food Lockers	50 x 135	6,750
Doctors' offices above Store 19		
TOTAL STORE AREA		38,166

UNDERPASS FOR SAFETY OF PEDESTRIAN SHOPPERS

FAIRWAY, one of ten neighborhood centers scattered through the Country Club District outside Kansas City, Mo., *(see map, page 80)* is at the junction of a main highway (U.S. 50, Johnson Drive) and three local streets.

Since most of the customers will come from homes south of the center, a pedestrian underpass has been built so that these customers (and their children) may cross this busy highway in safety.

Split parking, with curb parking along the street in front, and a large parking area behind, is typical of recent J. C. Nichols Co. centers. The arrangement of stores is more or less traditional: at the heart of the center is a big supermarket; the drug store is on a busy corner near the variety store.

A large building at the rear for frozen food storage lockers, with offices on the second floor, is an unusual addition to the list of neighborhood center tenants. It may well be a help in attracting new customers to this store group.

Typical of the Nichols centers are basements and individual heating plants for each store. In the few cases where a central heating plant is used, tenants are charged for heat on a square foot basis. Tenants who wish air-conditioning must install their own individual units.

Most of the percentage leases do not run for more than three or five years. Many of the smaller stores have fixed rental leases on a year-to-year basis.

Owner & Developer: The J. C. Nichols Co. *Architects:* Tanner & Mitchell.

N.B. In this and all of the store lists that follow, figures given in the column labeled **SQ. FT. AREA** represent the gross ground areas of the stores and do not necessarily correspond with the figures in the **WIDTH, DEPTH** column.

	TYPE OF STORE	WIDTH, DEPTH	SQ. FT. AREA
1	Filling Station		
2	Bank	34 x 84	2,856
3	Medical Center	20 x 65	2,100
4	Jewelry	15 x 50	750
5	Barber	12 x 50	600
6	Drugs	48 x 60	2,880
7	Beauty Shop	17 x 48	816
8	Books & Gifts	12 x 48	576
9	Bakery	15 x 48	720
10	Real Estate	15 x 48	720
11	Variety	35 x 82	2,870
12	Cleaners	12 x 48	576
13	Men's & Children's Shoes	20 x 48	960
14	Children's Wear	12 x 48	576
15	Women's Wear	17 x 48	816
16	Bedding	14 x 48	672
17	Self-Service Laundry	15 x 48	720
18	Cameras & Records	12 x 60	720
19	Hardware	17 x 60	1,020
20	Florist, Candy	15 x 60	900
21	Wallpapers, Paint	14 x 60	840
22	Men's & Boy's Wear	16 x 80	1,280
23	Furniture	38 x 80	3,040
24	Supermarket	58 x 125	7,250
25	Jewelry	40 x 22	450
26	Hobby Shop	14 x 30	420
27	Cleaners	14 x 30	420
28	Ice Cream	22 x 30	660
29	Shoe Repair	12 x 30	360
30	Law Office	12 x 30	360
31	Fabrics	40 x 15	440
32		35 x 40	1,450
33	Beauty Shop	16 x 53	848
34	Post Office	32 x 60	1,920
	TOTAL STORE AREA		41,586

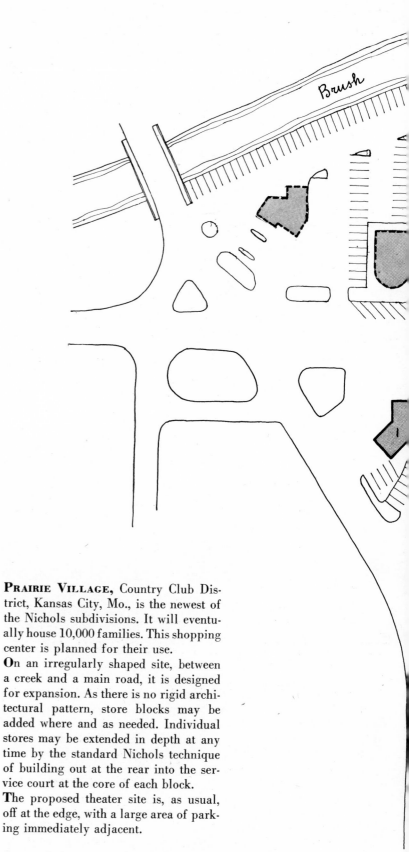

PRAIRIE VILLAGE, Country Club District, Kansas City, Mo., is the newest of the Nichols subdivisions. It will eventually house 10,000 families. This shopping center is planned for their use.

On an irregularly shaped site, between a creek and a main road, it is designed for expansion. As there is no rigid architectural pattern, store blocks may be added where and as needed. Individual stores may be extended in depth at any time by the standard Nichols technique of building out at the rear into the service court at the core of each block.

The proposed theater site is, as usual, off at the edge, with a large area of parking immediately adjacent.

Owner & Developer: The J. C. Nichols Co. *Architects:* Tanner & Mitchell.

Creek

theater

dept. store

Shawnee Mission Road

2

3

4
5

7 8 9 10

11

12

13 14

15 16 17 18 19 20 21 22 23 24

service court

ramp

34

33

32

31
30
29

28

27
26

25

Tomahawk Road

alternate theater

0   50   100   150 ft.

scale : 1" = 100'

golf course

filling station

Road

Preston

entrance to service yards

school

Theater

ARCHED WINDOWS IN THE CENTRAL BLOCK

START OF AN IDEA:
STORES TURN THEIR BACKS
TO THE HIGHWAY

HIGHLAND PARK, Dallas, Texas. It was under the influence of "J. C." Nichols *(see preceding pages)* that Hugh Prather, a fellow realtor, in 1916, set aside for this shopping center a ten-acre corner of his 1300-acre development outside Dallas. Not until 1913 was construction actually started on this super-block; and it is still not complete.

The layout, which has been widely copied, (notably at Bellevue, Seattle, Wash.; *see page 222)* was derived by Prather from the typical central plaza of a Texas county seat. The perimeter stores turn their backs to the street, face inward on to the plaza.

The buildings themselves (under the influence of "J. C." again) are Spanish in style. In fact Prather conscientiously took one of his architects to Spain, to obtain inspiration direct from the fountainhead. Largely because of this stylistic rigidity, the buildings do not have as much flexibility for changing needs and tenants as modern practice demands.

Looking back now from a distance of 20

A SPANISH PLAZA DESIGNED FOR CARS INSTEAD OF BURROS

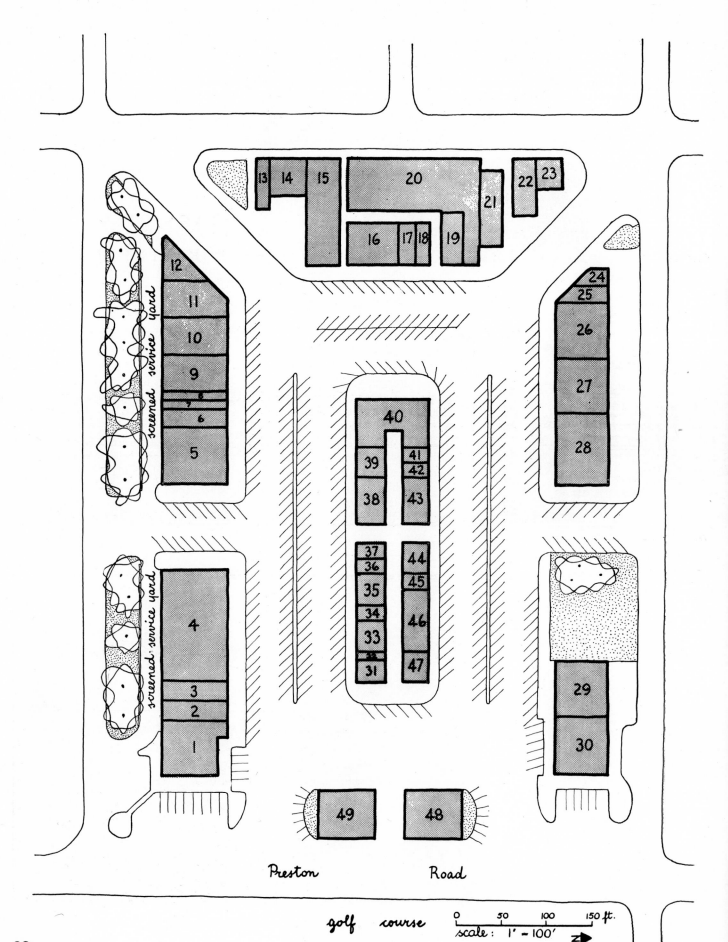

screened service yard

screened service yard

golf course

Preston   Road

scale: 1' = 100'

	TYPE OF STORE	WIDTH, DEPTH	SQ. FT. AREA
1	Drugs	60 x 60	3,600
2	Bakery	20 x 70	1,400
3	Women's Exchange	20 x 70	1,400
4	Supermarket	115 x 70	8,050
5	Grocery	60 x 70	4,200
6	Garden Supplies	20 x 70	1,400
7	Jeweler	10 x 70	700
8	Optometrist	10 x 70	700
9	Variety	40 x 70	2,800
10		40 x 70	2,800
11	Beauty Shop	40 x 60	2,400
12	Jewelry & Silverware	25 x 35	875
13	Administration	15 x 50	750
14	Lingerie	40 x 35	1,400
15	Tea Room	40 x 110	4,400
16	Electrical Appliances	55 x 45	2,475
17	Books	18 x 45	810
18	Gifts	15 x 45	675
19	Candy	25 x 55	1,375
20	Theater	50 x 140	7,000
21	Dance Studio	25 x 85	2,125
22	Dentist's Office	25 x 60	1,500
23	Dentist's Office	30 x 40	1,200
24	Ice & Dairy	15 x 20	300
25	Dance Studio	18 x 45	810
26	Offices	60 x 60	3,600

	TYPE OF STORE	WIDTH, DEPTH	SQ. FT. AREA
27	Post Office Basement Parking under stores 24 through 27	55 x 60	3,300
28	Department Store	75 x 60	4,500
29	Department Store	60 x 60	3,600
30	Bank	60 x 60	3,600
31	Florist	25 x 35	875
32	Jeweler	10 x 35	350
33	Beauty Shop	30 x 35	1,050
34	Electrical Appliances	15 x 35	525
35	Photographer	30 x 35	1,050
36	Millinery	15 x 35	525
37	Office	15 x 35	525
38	Women's Wear	50 x 35	1,750
39	Barber	30 x 35	1,050
40	Restaurant	80 x 50	4,000
41	Carpets & Drapery	15 x 30	450
42	Shoes	15 x 30	450
43	Sporting Goods	50 x 30	1,500
44	Camera Shop	35 x 30	1,050
45	Dressmaking	15 x 30	450
46	Shoes	65 x 30	1,950
47	Men's Wear	35 x 30	1,050
48	Gas Station		
49	Gas Station		
TOTAL STORE AREA			92,345

years, it is of course easy to see the faults in this pioneer development. Prather admits that he should have allotted 30 acres rather than 10 to this shopping center. And although the space allowed for parking was commonly thought to be excessive at the time it was planned, Prather now considers that he should have been less short-sighted.

Like many another developer he believes that customers prefer curb parking, directly in front of a specific shop. Parking space in the plaza itself is now supplemented by a basement garage and by a large vacant lot across the street to the north. A vacant lot within the center— a gap in the line of stores—is also used now for parking; but this, of course, is only a temporary relief. Due to cus-tomers moving cars in and out of the curb parking stalls, traffic within the plaza is quite slow, and presents no obstacle to pedestrians crossing from one store to another.

One of the most forward-looking ideas, and one which could be copied to advantage by many more modern centers, is a big walled service court behind the stores on the south side of the Plaza. This is particularly important where, as here, the service entrances of the stores abut on a residential street. The central store block has a service court down the middle. This is inevitably less well hidden, and unfortunately serves the restaurant.

Owner & Developer: Flippen-Prather Stores, Inc. *Architects:* Fooshee & Cheek.

HIGH WALL SHIELDS SERVICE YARD

COUNTRY-TOWN MARKETS

FOR SMART CITY SHOPPERS

THE FARMERS MARKETS which have been so successful in the West, are the modern equivalent of an old-time market square with parking added. They have usually settled on the outskirts of a town, where they could utilize what was originally cheap land, yet be accessible both to customers and producer-tenants.

The close-packed stalls are rented, usually by the month, mainly to small, independent suppliers of fresh farm produce and food specialties. These small producers would never survive if they set up shop on their own, particularly in a scattered community such as Los Angeles. Individuality (in direct contrast to the supermarket's standard brands) and direct-from-the-country freshness are the two qualities which account for the Farmers Markets' success.

In the plan of these markets we find the granddaddy of all the vast, currently popular pedestrian malls; but reduced to a calculated congestion and an intimate scale more reminiscent of the soukhs in a near-eastern bazaar.

The most famous, the "original", and the most successfully ballyhooed of all the Farmers Markets, is that in Los Angeles (designed by James Deleena and Edward Barber). Tucked in between Beverly Hills and Hollywood, this is where the "farmer meets the movie star".

Started by Roger Dahlhjelm during the Depression, it was pushed into prominence largely through the promotion of Fred Beck. His daily newspaper ads, a mixture of honesty and corn, are read even more avidly than Hedda Hopper.

HONEYS DIRECT FROM BEEHIVE TO YOU, CHOCOLATES MADE WHILE YOU WAIT

RELAXATION THAT SELLS FOOD AND DRINK

SHOPPERS SHED THEIR CARS BEFORE ENTERING THIS CALIFORNIAN SOUKH. FARMERS MARKET, LOS ANGELES

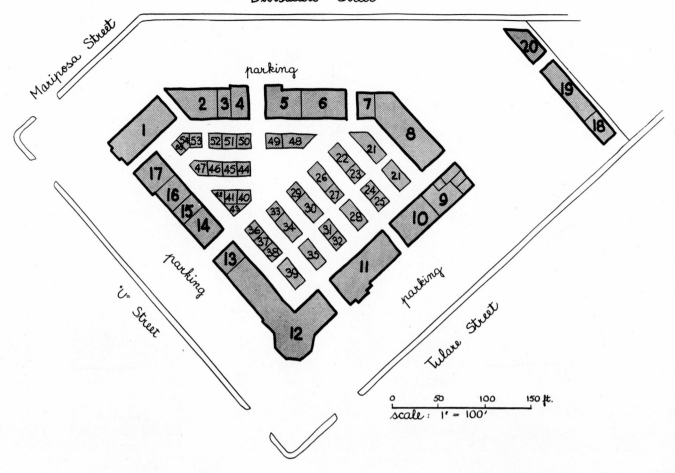

There is a peculiarly Californian slant in such items as "today I would like to discuss oranges. . . . There are two basic kinds . . . good oranges and Florida oranges." He may even advise against buying something being sold in his own market. "Peas", he may say, "are offish and overpriced this week because of the rain." Customers like such honesty.

One universal characteristic of these markets is the tremendous variety of services and goods for sale. The boast has always been that here you could buy anything from a truffle to a tripod, from an orchid to an ocarina. In Farmers Market, Los Angeles, there are 5 specialty meat shops, 3 poultry stalls, a sea-food shop, and also specialty kitchens where one may find "good-to-eat" things from all-over. If Mrs. Sawtell's Old London

Fish-and-Chip Shop doesn't tempt you, there is the alternative of a Chinese Kitchen, or a Farm Kitchen. Or you can continue on to Jim Boris' Cider Mill, where the apple juice is pressed while you wait.

Then of course, there are row after row of fresh fruit stands. Here owner Dahlhjelm particularly insists upon fine quality. If a farmer is caught selling boxes of fruit that are good only on the top layer, he is immediately expelled. This patriarchal gesture Dahlhjelm can make only because his tenants lease their stalls by the month, and the terms of the lease include a strict clause on "deceit and misrepresentation."

By chance perhaps, rather than by intention, the typical Farmers Market, such as that at Fresno (shown above and

opposite) has arrived at an extremely efficient plan. Perimeter parking is capable of giving the highest ratio of parking space to store area of any basic shape *(see page 38)*. Within this parking belt are the narrow pedestrian shopping streets, of a type which is now, 15 years later, being advocated by many advanced shopping center designers.

However, it should be remembered that the appealing characteristic of this plan is its intimate scale, the congestion, the close-packed stalls. If it is enlarged and spread over 50 acres, as suggested for some of the larger new centers, much of the shopping "excitement" that prevails here may well be lost.

Owner: The Farmers Market of Fresno.
Architect: Paul Emory.

FRESNO, CALIFORNIA
FARMERS MARKET

	TYPE OF STORE	WIDTH, DEPTH	SQ. FT. AREA
1	Electrical Appliances & Radios	80 x 32	2,560
2	Children's Wear	32 x 32	1,540
3	Jewelry	15 x 32	480
4	Gifts	20 x 35	700
5	Restaurant	40 x 35	1,350
6	Meat	50 x 32	1,600
7	Post Office	26 x 20	520
8	Grocery	72 x 32	2,560
9	Bakery	50 x 32	1,600
10	Drugs	50 x 32	1,600
11	Variety	80 x 40	2,800

	TYPE OF STORE	WIDTH, DEPTH	SQ. FT. AREA
12	Restaurant & Bar	100 x 60	5,000
13	Liquor	20 x 32	640
14	Men's Wear	32 x 32	1,020
15	Books	16 x 32	510
16	Lingerie	25 x 32	800
17	Women's Wear	32 x 35	1,110
18	Shoe Repair	30 x 20	600
19	Storage	70 x 20	
20	Incinerator	40 x 20	
21	Fruit & Vegetables	75 x 16	1,160
22	Fish & Poultry	30 x 16	480
23	Frozen Foods	15 x 16	240
24	Meat Pies	15 x 16	240
25	Fruit	15 x 16	240
26	Cheese & Sausage	30 x 16	480
27	Armenian Foods	15 x 16	240
28	Fruit & Vegetables	30 x 16	480
29	Spanish Foods	15 x 16	240
30	4 Farmers' Stalls	30 x 16	480
31	Plants	15 x 16	240
32	Nuts	15 x 16	240
33	Hot Dogs	15 x 16	240
34	4 Farmers' Stalls	30 x 16	480
35	Florist	30 x 16	480
36	Chili	15 x 16	240
37	Hobby Shop	15 x 16	240
38	Sporting Goods	15 x 16	240
39	Candy	30 x 16	480
40	Coffee Bar	15 x 16	230
41	Ceramics	15 x 16	240
42	Newsstand	15 x 8	120
43	Candy	15 x 8	120
44	Ice Cream	15 x 16	240
45	Gifts	15 x 16	240
46	Chinese Bazaar	15 x 16	240
47	Barber	15 x 16	250
48	Delicatessen	30 x 16	480
49	Coffee Shop	15 x 16	240
50	Luncheonette	15 x 16	240
51	Gifts	15 x 16	240
52	Dry Cleaner	15 x 16	240
53	Mexican Novelties	14 x 16	225
54	Keys	15 x 16	240
55	Photo Supplies	8 x 16	120
56	Outdoor Dining		
	TOTAL STORE AREA		27,850

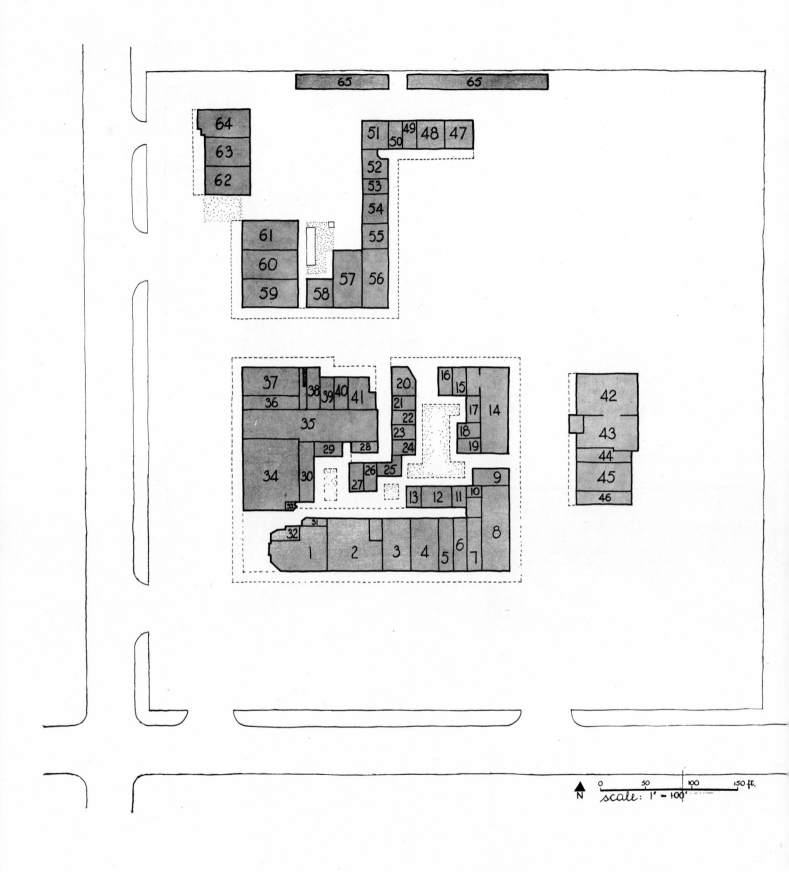

TOWN & COUNTRY VILLAGE SHOPS, SACRAMENTO, CALIF.

	TYPE OF STORE	WIDTH, DEPTH	SQ. FT. AREA
1	Drugs	60 x 45	2,250
2	Appliances	60 x 55	3,300
3	Children's Wear	30 x 55	1,650
4	Gifts	30 x 55	1,650
5	Photo Supplies	15 x 55	825
6	Boys' Wear	15 x 55	825
7	Girls' Wear	15 x 55	825
8	Bank	30 x 90	2,700
9	Paints	15 x 40	600
10	Art Supplies	15 x 10	180
11	Leather Goods	15 x 22	330
12	Pottery	30 x 22	660
13	Knit Goods	15 x 22	330
14	Grocery	40 x 90	3,150
15	Shoe Repair	15 x 30	450
16	Candy	15 x 30	450
17		15 x 30	450
18	Photographer	15 x 25	375
19	Cosmetics	15 x 25	375
20	Children's Shoes	30 x 25	670
21	Men's Wear	15 x 25	375
22		15 x 25	375
23	Maternity Wear	15 x 25	375
24	Cotton Shop	15 x 25	375
25	Weaving Shop	20 x 25	370
26	Books	15 x 30	450
27	Gifts	15 x 30	450
28	Power House	30 x 10	236
29	Post Office	30 x 15	450
30	Silverware	60 x 15	900
31	Administration	25 x 8	200
32	Florist	30 x 15	375
33	Nuts	10 x 8	80
34	Grocery	75 x 60	4,400
35	Frozen Food Lockers	30 x 145	4,600
36	Liquor	15 x 60	900
37	Men's Wear	30 x 60	1,800
38	Cleaners	15 x 45	675
39	Barber	15 x 35	525
40	Men's Shoes	15 x 35	525
41	Doctor's Office	30 x 35	950
	Professional Offices above stores 38-41	80 x 35	
42	Steak House	45 x 65	2,925
43	Coffee Shop	35 x 65	2,275
44	Delicatessen	15 x 60	850

RUSTIC FOR ECONOMY
— AND FOR CHARM TOO

	TYPE OF STORE	WIDTH, DEPTH	SQ. FT. AREA
45	Bakery	30 x 60	1,800
46		15 x 60	900
47		30 x 30	900
48	Toys	30 x 30	900
49	Stationery	15 x 30	450
50	Fabrics	15 x 30	450
51	Beauty Shop	30 x 30	900
52	Sporting Goods	30 x 30	800
53	Electrical Appliances	15 x 30	450
54	Pet Shop	30 x 30	900
55		30 x 30	900
56	Women's Shoes	60 x 30	1,800
57	Hardware	30 x 60	1,800
58	Garden Furniture	30 x 30	900
59	Fabrics	30 x 60	1,800
60	Variety	30 x 60	1,800
61	Appliances	30 x 60	1,800
62	Ice Cream	30 x 50	1,500
63	Lingerie	30 x 50	1,500
64	Women's Wear	30 x 55	1,600
65	Warehouses	250 x 15	
TOTAL STORE AREA			**70,095**

CONTINUED ON NEXT TWO PAGES

SMALL SCALE, USED MATERIALS, FOR CHARM THAT PAYS

TOWN & COUNTRY Village Shops, Sacramento, Calif., is one of the most successful shopping centers in the U.S. In design it is a sophisticated step-sister of the Farmers Markets shown on preceding pages: a group of congested, small-scale stores, threaded by picturesque pedestrian alleys, surrounded by a wide belt of parking *(plan on page 98)*. Great stress has been laid upon the charm of irregularity, which, incidentally, was imposed by the limitations and shortages during and immediately after World War II. Jere Strizek, a man of action and ingenuity, born in California but raised in Alaska, and educated in Europe and America, first bought 25 bridges from an abandoned railroad. To these he added a number of telephone poles and some obsolete Navy lanterns.

PLENTY OF SPACE FOR PARKING AROUND THE OUTSIDE

All these and a good deal more he fitted together to form a series of tight, informal, picturesque little shopping courts. As a result the original investment in buildings was comparatively low, yet gross sales are high.

As the stores themselves are very small, and have no basement or mezzanine, there is a warehouse building for reserve stocks at the edge of the parking area.

Designer & Owner: Jere Strizek.

NO LARGER THAN YOUR OWN RANCH HOUSE PORCH

EVEN THE SIGNS ARE SMALL

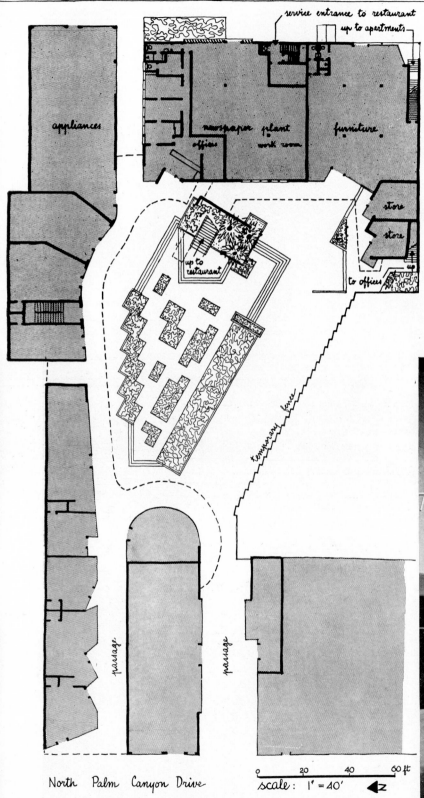

service entrance to restaurant

up to apartments

appliances

newspaper plant

offices

work room

furniture

store

store

up to restaurant

to offices

up

temporary fence

passage

passage

North Palm Canyon Drive

scale: 1" = 40'

0   20   40   60 ft

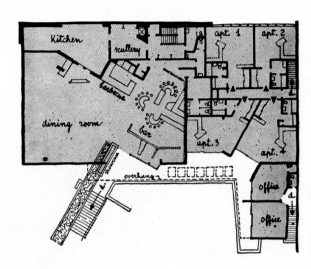

Kitchen

scullery

barbecue

apt. 1

apt. 2

dining room

bar

apt. 3

apt. 4

overhang

office

office

SECOND FLOOR PLAN

SHALLOW STEPS IN ANGLED GROUPS FOR AN EASIER-LOOKING CLIMB

IN A CLOSED COURT, SHOPS SURROUND A GARDEN

TOWN & COUNTRY, Palm Springs, Calif., is an extremely specialized type of shopping center, in the downtown section of a small resort town. It has almost no street frontage, and relies for parking space upon the bordering streets. But the beautifully effective charm created here does show the possibilities, at least as regards appearance, in the central pedestrian malls now being so widely advocated. Particularly suggestive is the skillful use of irregular angles and off-center balance.

At the focal point of the courtyard, emphasized by a group of three palm trees, approached by shallow steps between carefully ordered beds, is a second-floor restaurant. Combined in this main building are three stores, a newspaper plant and some offices on the first floor, four apartments, the restaurant, and two offices on the second floor. This probably sets some sort of a record for an assortment of uses. Each of the four major tenants insisted upon a special layout; and to add to these problems the building had to be set on old foundations.

Owner: Palm Springs Corporation
Architect: A. Quincy Jones, Jr.

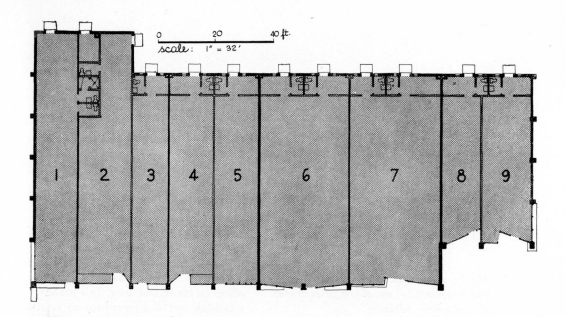

scale: 1" = 32'

1 2 3 4 5 6 7 8 9

FAIRLAWN SHOPS, Stamford, Conn., is on a site of less than an acre at one corner of a garden apartment development. It fronts on the Boston Post Road, a highway used by long-distance trucks and local passenger traffic. There is parking space at the rear of the stores.

The materials used for the stores are the same as those used in the neighboring apartments — white-painted wood and brick. Uniform sign lettering and built-in plant boxes add to the quality, and the variety of store depths to the practicality of this design.

Owner & Developer: First Stamford Corp. *Architect:* Paul Sternbach.

	TYPE OF STORE	WIDTH, DEPTH	SQ. FT. AREA
1	Rental Office	15 x 85	1,275
2	Bakery	19 x 85	1,615
3	Barber	13 x 70	910
4	Delicatessen	16 x 70	1,120
5	Stationery	16 x 70	1,120
6	Supermarket	32 x 70	2,240
7	Drugs	32 x 70	2,240
8	Household Appliances	13 x 58	755
9	Self Service Laundry	17 x 58	990
TOTAL STORE AREA			29,785

TWO SMALL CENTERS
ONE MODERN, ONE COLONIAL

	TYPE OF STORE	WIDTH, DEPTH	SQ. FT. AREA
1	China, Glass	32 x 90	2,980
2	Tailor	15 x 75	1,125
3	Children's Shoes	15 x 75	1,125
4	Women's Wear	30 x 75	2,250
5	Restaurant	30 x 100	3,000
	TOTAL STORE AREA		10,480

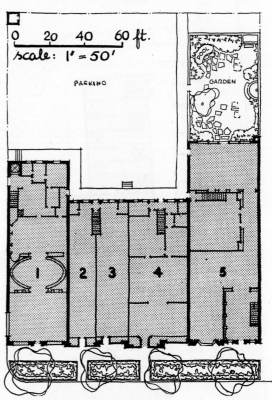

COLONIAL SHOPS, Evanston, Ill. This red-brick store group, crisp and neatly detailed, is a better than usual example of a common type of small shopping center. Behind a traditionally symmetrical facade there is a variety of store sizes. A line of parallel front parking on the street is supplemented by a large parking area in the rear. This has been made vastly more attractive by a small garden at one end, overlooked by the large rear windows of the restaurant. Forethought has been shown in planning for future second-floor offices.

On the street front an extra wide sidewalk allows space for a line of trees and flower beds between the street and the stores. These windows are all shaded by uniform, gaily striped awnings, with the store name along the front edge. This detail is typical of the thought and good taste which informs this whole design.

Architects: Maher and McGrew.

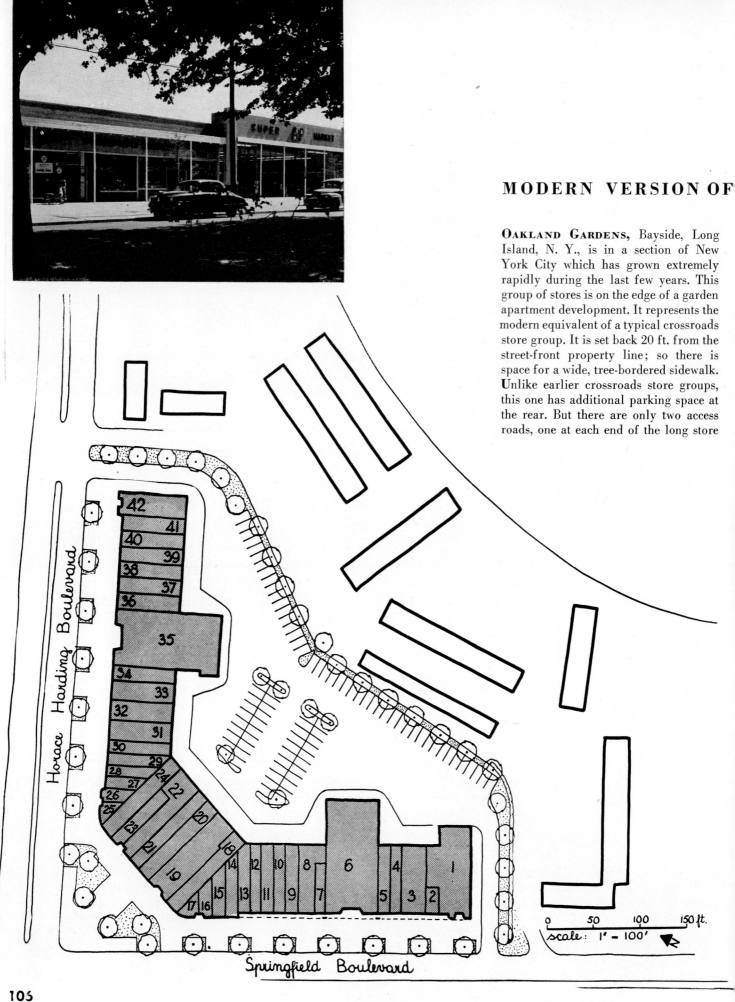

MODERN VERSION OF

OAKLAND GARDENS, Bayside, Long
Island, N. Y., is in a section of New
York City which has grown extremely
rapidly during the last few years. This
group of stores is on the edge of a garden
apartment development. It represents the
modern equivalent of a typical crossroads
store group. It is set back 20 ft. from the
street-front property line; so there is
space for a wide, tree-bordered sidewalk.
Unlike earlier crossroads store groups,
this one has additional parking space at
the rear. But there are only two access
roads, one at each end of the long store

scale: 1" = 100'

Horace Harding Boulevard

Springfield Boulevard

CROSSROADS STORE GROUP

block. So customers who park in the rear prefer to use the rear entrances of the stores. Unfortunately these are drably utilitarian freight entrances. In the case of the two supermarkets (which project into the rear parking area to gain increased store depth) there is not even a closed hiding place for the crates and vegetable garbage which such stores inevitably collect there. This merely emphasizes the obvious: split parking necessitates two-front stores, or frequent arcades joining front and rear.

The store signs on the street front are not restricted in style, but they are confined to a strip between the top of the show windows and the underside of the canopy. The latter exists primarily to hold the lights which illuminate these signs. It is not wide enough to protect the shoppers adequately; but the two supermarkets do have recessed lobbies where mothers may chat and leave their baby carriages under cover.

Owners & Developers: Oakland Gardens Inc.; Park & Shop Inc. *Architect:* B. Braunstein.

	TYPE OF STORE	WIDTH, DEPTH	SQ. FT. AREA
1	Post Office	38 x 97	4,120
2	Shoe Repair	13 x 33	430
3	Restaurant	27 x 70	1,900
4	Optometrist	10 x 70	700
5	Cleaners, & Tailor	14 x 70	950
6	Supermarket	60 x 117	7,020
7	Barber	12 x 53	630
8	Hardware	17 x 70	1,380
9	Shoes	14 x 70	980
10	Delicatessen	13 x 70	910
11	Stationery	14 x 70	980
12	Children's Wear	12 x 70	840
13	Meat	14 x 70	950
14	Dairy	14 x 58	810
15	Candy	14 x 48	670
16	Fabrics	14 x 35	490
17	Lingerie	26 x 18	390
18	Bakery	16 x 104	1,730
19	Drugs	30 x 104	3,120
20	Children's Furniture	14 x 104	1,460
21		15 x 105	1,575
22	Interior Decorator	15 x 105	2,025

	TYPE OF STORE	WIDTH, DEPTH	SQ. FT. AREA
23	Haberdashery	15 x 75	1,125
24	Radio	15 x 105	1,575
25	Lingerie	26 x 18	390
26	Liquor	14 x 35	490
27	Women's Wear	14 x 48	670
28	Children's Wear	14 x 58	810
29	Luncheonette	14 x 72	960
30	Drugs	14 x 72	1,000
31	Shoes	14 x 72	1,000
32	Bakery	14 x 72	1,000
33	Hardware	14 x 72	1,000
34	Cleaners	10 x 72	720
35	Supermarket	60 x 117	7,020
36	Meat & Fish	14 x 72	1,000
37	Delicatessen	14 x 72	1,000
38	Gifts	14 x 72	1,000
39	Radio	14 x 72	1,000
40	Vegetables	14 x 72	1,000
41	Beauty Shop	14 x 72	1,000
42	Rental Office	25 x 97	2,425
TOTAL STORE AREA			60,245

	TYPE OF STORE	WIDTH, DEPTH	SQ. FT. AREA
1	Drugs	40 x 120	4,800
2	Electrical Appliances	17 x 100	1,700
3	Laundry, Cleaners & Shoe Repair	17 x 100	1,700
4	Variety	80 x 100	8,000
5	Children's Furnishings	40 x 100	4,000
6	Women's Wear	17 x 100	1,700
7	Shoes	17 x 100	1,700
8	Radio	17 x 100	1,700
9	Children's Wear	17 x 100	1,700
10	Candy	17 x 100	1,700
11	Bakery	17 x 100	1,700
12	Supermarket	60 x 120	7,200
13	Bank	35 x 60	2,100
14	Poultry	15 x 60	900
15	Dairy	15 x 60	900
16	Florist	15 x 60	900
17		15 x 60	900
18	Barber Shop	15 x 60	900
19	Gifts	15 x 60	900
20	Drive-In Restaurant	120 x 50	6,000
21	Amusement Center		
22	Filling Station		
	TOTAL STORE AREA		51,100

ENTRANCE TO REAR PARKING AT NORTH END OF STORE BLOCK

STREET-FRONT STORES SURROUND REAR PARKING SPACE

PARK LANE shopping center, Baltimore, Md., lies between two main highways running northwest from Baltimore to a residential area. At one corner of the development is a Howard Johnson restaurant; this forms part of the shopping center, though it has its own parking space.

Land now occupied by an amusement area is available for future expansion. However, if more stores are built, as at present intended, the parking area, unless it is expensively increased by the acquisition of more land, will be entirely insufficient for the anticipated traffic.

The main front at this time is on Park Heights Avenue. Here the center section of the store block is recessed so that the fronts are 20 ft. back from the roadway. Such a wide sidewalk seems a little excessive for stores that are at least as de-

MAIN FRONT ON PARK HEIGHTS AVENUE

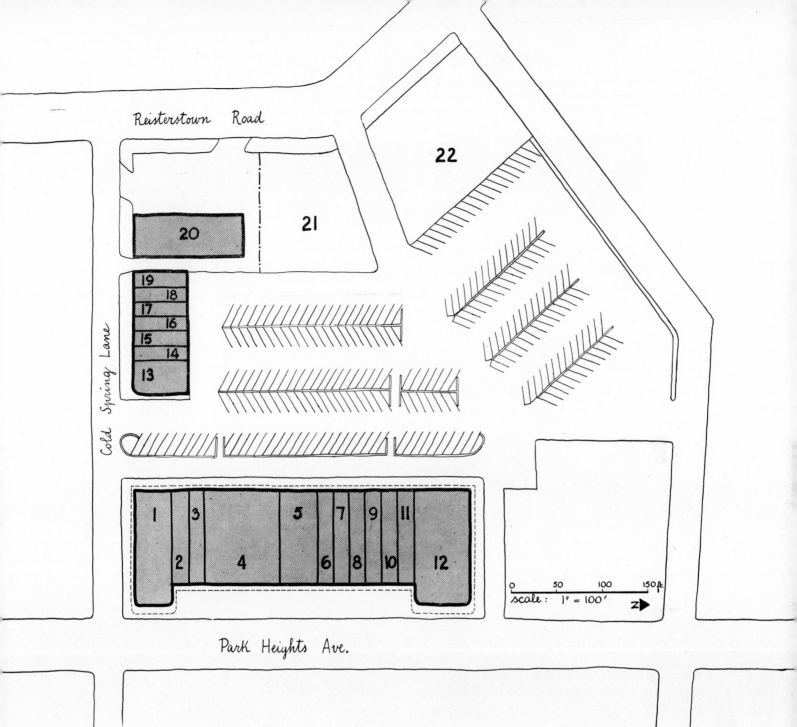

Reisterstown Road

Cold Spring Lane

20

21

22

19
18
17
16
15
14
13

1
3
5
7
9
11
2
4
6
8
10
12

scale: 1" = 100'

0   50   100   150 ft

Park Heights Ave.

pendent on automobile as on walk-in customers. The wide expanse of glass in the show windows, running uninterruptedly from the sidewalk baseboard to the canopy, gives a particularly airy, large-scale feeling to the front.

The canopy itself, of red and white porcelain enamel, extends not only along this front but also around the sides and back, for protection of customers coming from the rear parking area. Store signs are set on the front edge of this canopy, with a red brick parapet for background. Stores are grouped according to type. At one end of the line is a supermarket, with bakery and candy stores adjacent. Projecting at the crossroads corner is a big drug store. At the center of the line is a variety store. On Cold Spring Lane, a less heavily-traveled cross street, are smaller service stores and a bank. Lights in all stores must, under the lease, be kept burning until 10 p.m. A Merchants' Association, financed in part by the merchants (by a sq. ft. assessment), and in part by the owner, organizes and pays for co-operative promotion schemes, newspaper advertising, etc., to make this known as a convenient one-stop center.

Owner: Park Lane Shopping Center, Inc. *Developer:* Service Realty Co., Inc. *Architect:* D. Harrison.

Allison Street

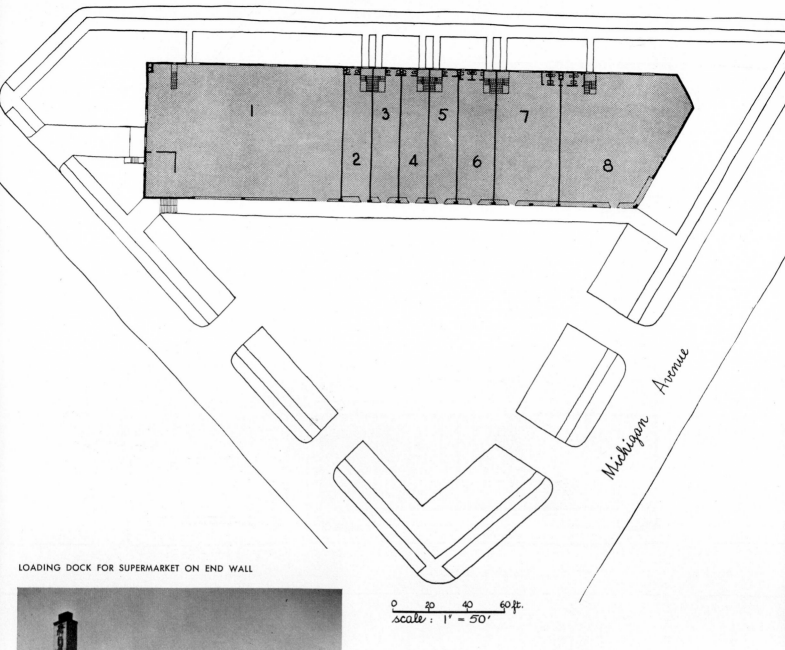

Michigan Avenue

LOADING DOCK FOR SUPERMARKET ON END WALL

0   20   40   60 ft.
scale : 1" = 50'

	TYPE OF STORE	WIDTH, DEPTH	SQ. FT. AREA
1	Supermarket	110 x 71	7,810
2	Beauty Shop	17 x 71	1,207
3	Laundry & Cleaners	17 x 71	1,207
4	Florist	17 x 71	1,207
5	Gifts	17 x 71	1,207
6	Bakery	20 x 71	1,420
7	Hardware	35 x 71	2,485
8	Drugs	35 x 71	3,900
9	Liquor (in basement)		
TOTAL STORE AREA			20,443

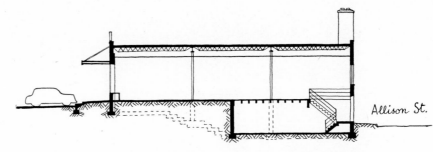

SECTION THROUGH STORES. MAIN FRONT AT LEFT

◀ LOW, WIDE CANOPY FOR SHOPPERS' PROTECTION

TRIANGULAR ISLAND SITE AT ROAD JUNCTION

MICHIGAN AVENUE shopping center, on the edge of Washington, D. C., makes ingenious use of a triangular, sloping plot at the junction of two important roads. The store block has been turned almost at right angles to the road (compare this with centers shown on preceding pages where the store fronts are almost always parallel to the highway). At the rear is a service street; the slope of the land allows direct entry from here to the storage basement below each store. This is definitely a neighborhood shopping center. There are only nine stores, and these are typical of the sort that can be supported by around-the-corner needs. At one end of the line is a big supermarket; at the other end is a drug store. The supermarket has a loading dock on the end wall, back up a steep slope from the road. This may seem a slightly extravagant use for land that might in some other center be profitably developed as rentable store space on two levels.

Store signs are set on the edge of the roof against the sky. This gives the otherwise clean outline of the block a ragged appearance, and does nothing to cure the basic difficulty of these signs being concealed from pedestrians by the canopy. And only at night do these neon signs stand out strongly enough to be read from afar. The supermarket has sensibly used the incinerator chimney as a pylon sign to be seen from a distance.

Owner & Developer: Steuart Brothers, Inc. *Architect:* Leon Chatelain, Jr.

SMALL SIGNS ON ROOF ARE ALMOST ALL UNSUITED FOR DISTANT READING BY DAY

BUS STOP WITH SEAT PROVIDED BY SUPERMARKET

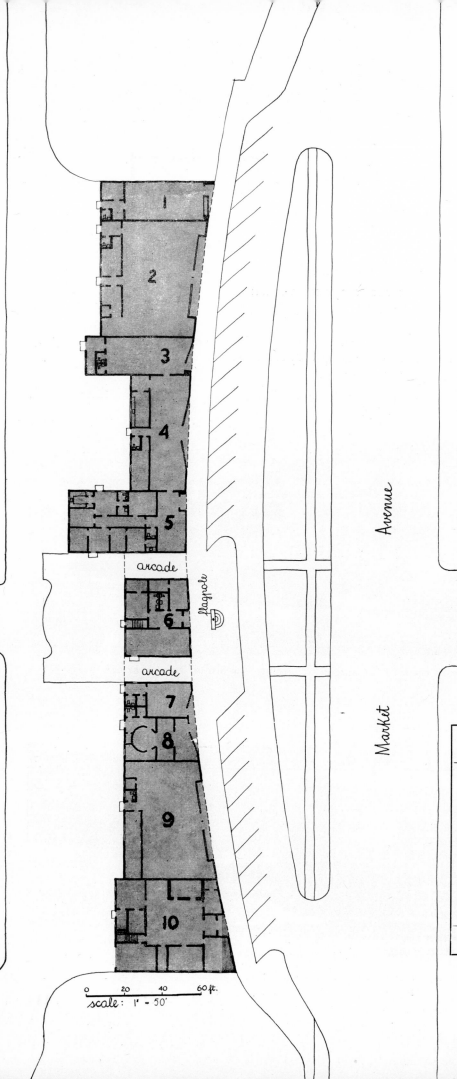

Avenue

Market

arcade

flagpole

arcade

scale: 1" = 50'

0   20   40   60 ft.

	TYPE OF STORE	WIDTH, DEPTH	SQ. FT. AREA
1	Bank	52 x 64	3,125
2	Supermarket	61 x 48	2,700
3	Beauty Shop	20 x 38	700
4	Barber	20 x 36	700
5	Municipal Building	40 x 35	1,375
6	Doctor's Offices	32 x 62	1,984
7	Drugs	58 x 32	1,800
8	Coffee Shop	20 x 55	1,140
9	Supermarket	60 x 57	3,200
10	Hardware	20 x 61	1,175
TOTAL STORE AREA			17,899

SHOPPING AND CIVIC CENTER IN MIDWEST
FOR SMALL INDUSTRIAL TOWN

PORT EDWARDS, WIS. This center is the nub of an ambitious plan for the improvement of a small town which depends for prosperity upon the paper industry. The slightly curved block closes off the end of Second Street, creating a classic type of axial vista. At the focal point of this vista, in the center of the new store group, is the Town Hall. An alley is left open on each side for pedestrian traffic. In front is a War memorial flagpole. This is a consciously created town center serving a symbolic purpose. The architectural character of the new block is restrained and stately, in keeping with its civic character. The stone facing is respectably solid, and even the aluminum lettering used for the signs is simple and uniform. Included in the group are a medical building and a bank. Although the center has a uniform front line, the architect has provided a variety of different store depths by irregular projections in the rear. There is a line of angle parking in the front, and additional parking space in the rear. The rear service court is large because of the many shoppers who want to load heavy packages directly into a car or truck.

Owner & Developer: Nekoosa-Edwards Paper Co. *Architect:* Donn Hougen.

113

UPPER LEVEL STORAGE SPACE ON SLOPING SITE

NAYLOR ROAD, Washington, D. C., is a small L-shaped neighborhood shopping center on the edge of a large group of garden apartments. The taller apartment houses are placed next to the center and act as a buffer between the stores and the smaller, walk-up apartments in the rear. There are doctors' offices on the first floor of the large apartment house alongside the stores; these may be a more convenient equivalent of the separate medical building which is so often attached to a shopping center.

The line of stores is set at the bottom of a steep slope. This slope, which might have been considered an awkward feature of the site, has been turned to advantage by building a second floor in the rear for storage. This storage space is on the same level as the rear service road, beyond which are apartments. In the projecting arm of the L are the supermarket and drug store, next door to each other (the two stepbacks give variation in store depth). A variety store anchors the other end of the line.

The fast turnover of shoppers which is so typical of a neighborhood center such as this, mostly used for quick in-and-out errands, and with considerable walk-in traffic from the neighboring apartment houses, means that the ratio of parking area to store area need not be so large as in a fashion goods store group. But the parking here has proved insufficient.

Designer & Developer: Waverly Taylor, Inc.

APARTMENTS AT REAR INCLUDE DOCTORS' OFFICES

	TYPE OF STORE	WIDTH, DEPTH	SQ. FT. AREA
1	Supermarket	50 x 150	7,500
2	Drugs	30 x 100	3,000
3	Liquor	20 x 70	1,400
4	Gifts	15 x 70	1,050
5	Beauty Shop	15 x 70	1,050
6	Laundry & Cleaners	15 x 70	1,050
7	Bakery	15 x 70	1,050
8	Restaurant	40 x 70	2,800
9	Children's Wear	12 x 70	840
10	Variety	30 x 70	2,100
TOTAL STORE AREA			21,840

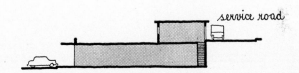

REAR SERVICE ROAD AT UPPER LEVEL

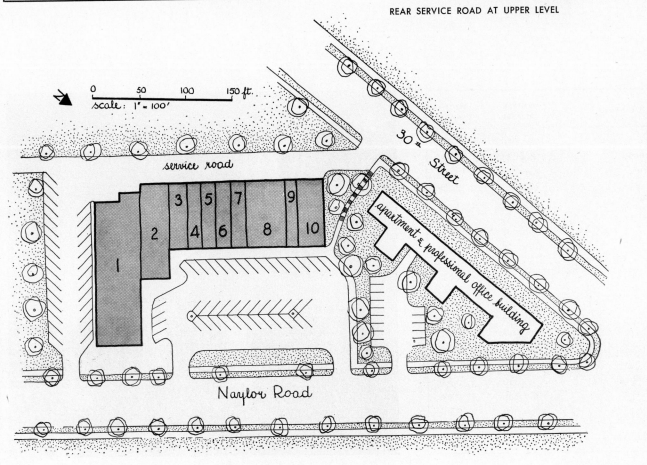

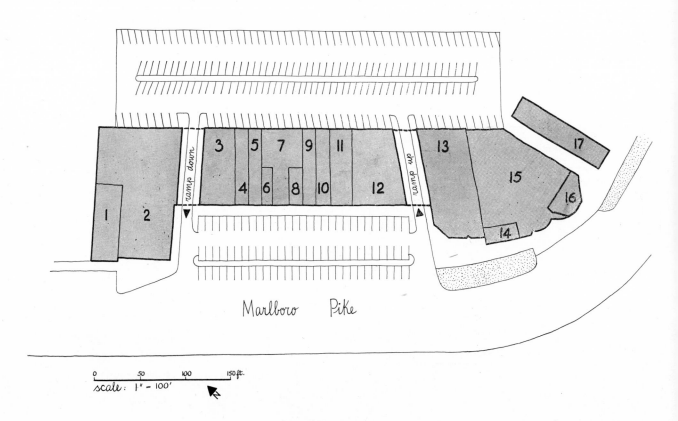

Marlboro Pike

scale: 1" = 100'

0   50   100   150 ft.

	TYPE OF STORE	WIDTH, DEPTH	SQ. FT. AREA
1	Cleaners	32 x 80	2,560
2	Supermarket	55 x 134	8,960
3	Hardware	41 x 82	3,200
4	Shoes	15 x 82	1,230
5	Men's Wear	15 x 82	1,230
6	Shoe Repair	12 x 42	508
7	Liquor	18 x 82	2,900
8	Barber	15 x 42	640
9	Children's Wear	15 x 82	1,230
10	Beauty Shop	15 x 82	1,230
11	Drugs	25 x 82	2,050
12	Variety	58 x 82	4,100
13	Drugs	50 x 115	5,500
	Dance and		
	Banquet Hall Above		
14	Bank	35 x 16	600
15	Theater (1050 seats)	50 x 110	8,000
16	Gifts	45 x 25	800
17	Restaurant	25 x 100	2,500
TOTAL STORE AREA			47,238

EXIT RAMP (LEFT) FROM REAR ROOF PARKING, AT END OF SHELTERED SIDEWALK

ADDITIONAL REAR PARKING OVER A BORROWED ROOF

CORAL HILLS is one of a number of similar shopping centers scattered around Washington, D. C. These centers are usually sited on the home-going side of the

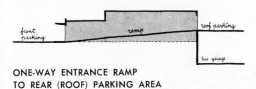

ONE-WAY ENTRANCE RAMP
TO REAR (ROOF) PARKING AREA

road so that government workers (very often both husband and wife are employed) can do their shopping on the way home in the evening.

This one is on the Marlboro Pike leading toward the northern suburbs. It is of the typical L shape, with the L turned to receive home-going traffic. As usual the supermarket is in the projecting wing of the L. In another projecting block at the opposite end is a theatre and restaurant. This center has become quite a community gathering place. A banquet hall above the drug store is used for various local events—dances, meetings, dinners and private parties. The center publishes a bi-monthly newspaper; a listing of baby sitters is one of its most popular features. As one might perhaps expect in a center with such strong local feeling, all the merchants are independents. This group of stores has grown beyond the limits of a neighborhood center. In addition to convenience goods stores, it includes several specialty shops.

All the buildings are of fireproof, reinforced concrete construction (for section showing details of construction *see page 66*). The store signs are set on the front edge of the canopy. As a result they are visible from the parking area, but they give a somewhat ragged and broken look to the otherwise neat horizontal line of the stores as can be clearly seen in the photograph above.

The small amount of front parking (primarily to take care of the quick in-and-out shopper) is supplemented by a somewhat larger parking area on the roof of a garage building in the rear. An entrance ramp is at one end of the recessed store block, an exit ramp at the other end. This roof parking is used only at peak shopping periods, and in the evening by theater patrons and those attending social functions in the banquet hall above the drug stores.

Owner & Developer: Kaufman-Steiner Properties. *Architects:* Ross and Walton.

SPLIT-LEVEL PARKING ON A SLOPING SITE INCREASES SHOPPING FRONTAG

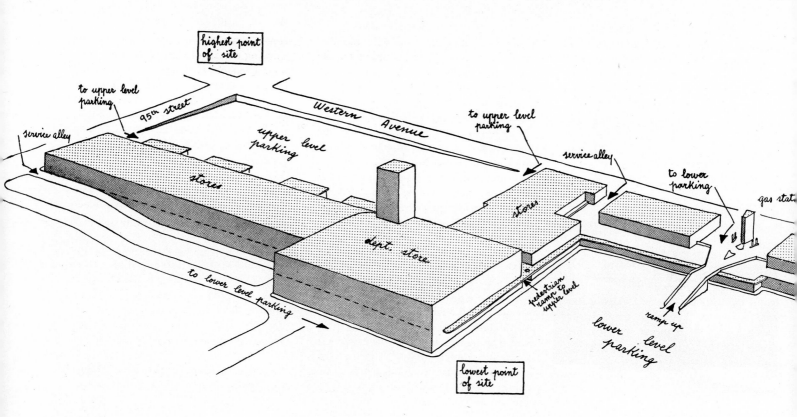

highest point
of site

to upper level
parking

95th street

service alley

upper level
parking

Western Avenue

to upper level
parking

service alley

to lower
parking

gas stat

stores

stores

dept. store

to lower level parking

pedestrian
ramp to
upper level

ramp up

lower level
parking

lowest point
of site

BIRDS-EYE VIEW OF THE UPPER LEVEL SHOPPING COURT FROM THE NORTHEAST.
IN THE FOREGROUND IS THE INTERSECTION OF WESTERN AVENUE AND 95TH STREET

EVERGREEN PARK Shopping Plaza is on the outskirts of Chicago, Ill. Very often in an already developed area it becomes exceedingly difficult to assemble a site of both the size and shape required for a modern shopping center. This explains the somewhat awkward shape of this site. A further complication was the steep slope which runs diagonally across the site (see drawing opposite) from a high point at the intersection of Western Avenue and 95th Street.

Western Avenue is a main highway leading into Chicago from the South. 95th Street is a main east-west highway with an equally large traffic flow, according to a survey made for this project. This particular intersection is more than ten miles from downtown Chicago. The Buying Power upon which the center will depend, starting from an area immediately encircling the center, extends far to the west, is restricted on the east by competing store groups.

The shape and slope of the site suggested a division of the center into two shopping courts, each with its own parking area, but connected by a covered pedestrian ramp. In the upper court, the slope of the ground has been used to advantage by sinking the parking area in one corner below road level; thus the stores can be clearly seen from the highway intersection.

All the large stores in this L have service courts in the rear. There are two large supermarkets, one in each wing of the L, and both have parcel pickup booths at the outer edge of the sidewalk, (see plan on following two pages). Each booth is connected by conveyor belt through a tunnel to the store basement. The shopper leaves her package of groceries at the check-out gate, and is given an index number. Having finished her shopping she fetches her car from the parking area, drives alongside the pickup booth, presents the index number, and

an attendant then brings out her groceries and loads them into the car.

On the very wide sidewalk in the upper shopping court are a number of small sales pavilions. These give the whole area a more intimate feeling and satisfy the constantly recurring demand for smaller stores on busy traffic lanes.

A department store, in the corner of the L, is on three levels, with entrances from both upper and lower parking areas. The lower parking area is reached either by a road at the rear of the department store, or down a ramp from Western Avenue through a wide opening cut in the line of stores which face that highway. There is a gas station in the center of this ramp access road. All the service stores open on to the lower shopping court.

Owner: Evergreen Park Shopping Plaza. *Architects & Engineers:* Howard T. Fisher & Associates, Inc., and Holabird & Root & Burgee.

PLANS OF EVERGREEN PARK ON THE FOLLOWING PAGES

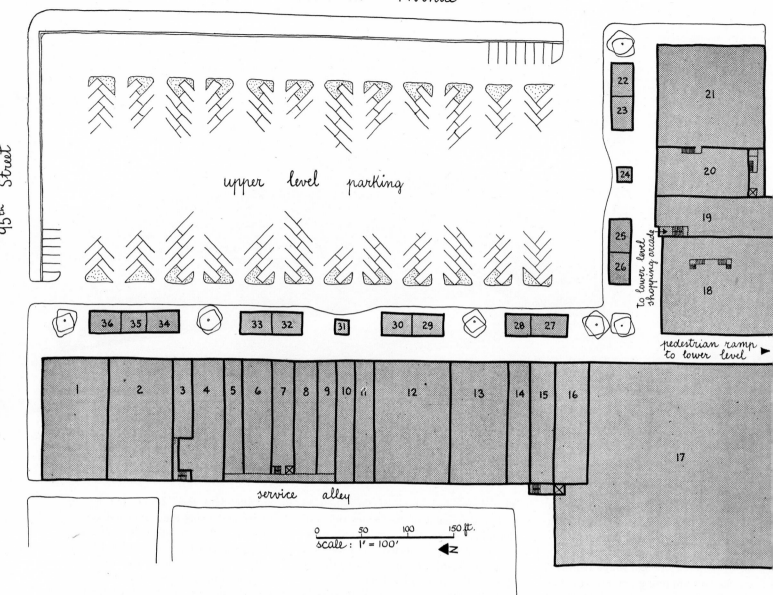

UPPER LEVEL SHOPPING COURT

	TYPE OF STORE	WIDTH, DEPTH	SQ. FT. AREA
1	Drugs	70 x 124	8,680
2	Supermarket	70 x 124	8,680
3	Bakery	20 x 80	1,600
4	Hardware	35 x 124	4,865
5	Fabrics	20 x 116	2,335
6	Children's Wear	30 x 116	3,583
7		25 x 108	2,708
8	Needlework	25 x 116	2,920
9	Sportswear	20 x 116	2,335
10	Luggage	20 x 124	2,480
11	Sewing Machines	20 x 124	2,480

	TYPE OF STORE	WIDTH, DEPTH	SQ. FT. AREA
12	Variety	83 x 148	12,358
13	Women's Wear	60 x 148	8,880
14	Furrier	25 x 116	2,920
15	Women's Wear	28 x 116	3,350
16	Shoes	35 x 124	4,360
17	Department Store	200 x 209	44,860
18	Family Clothing	100 x 124	12,400
19	Shoes	30 x 124	4,745
20	Radio, Household Appliances	50 x 99	4,950
21	Supermarket	105 x 116	12,180

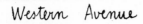

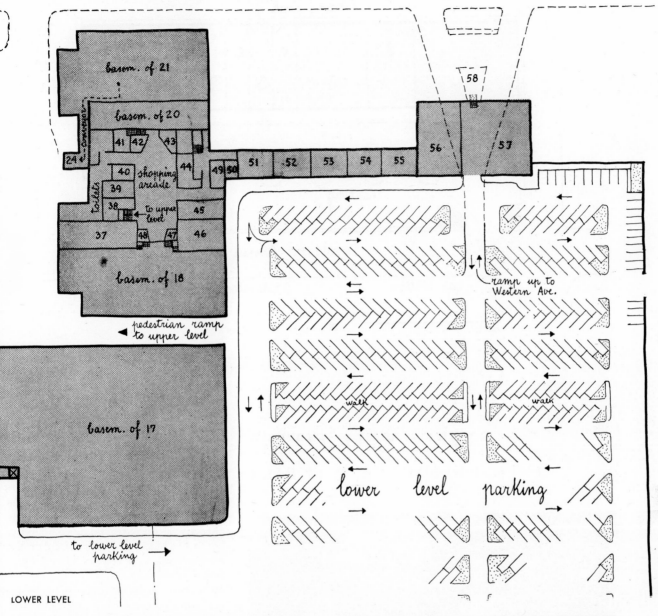

Western Avenue

LOWER LEVEL

	TYPE OF STORE	WIDTH, DEPTH	SQ. FT. AREA
22		34 x 24	816
23		34 x 24	816
24	Package Pick-up	16 x 16	256
25		34 x 24	816
26		34 x 24	816
27	Gifts	40 x 24	960
28	Tobacco	28 x 24	672
29	Millinery	34 x 24	816
30	Lingerie	34 x 24	816
31	Package Pick-up	16 x 16	256
32	Candy	34 x 24	816

	TYPE OF STORE	WIDTH, DEPTH	SQ. FT. AREA
33	Florist	34 x 24	816
34	Cutlery	35 x 24	840
35	Books	28 x 24	672
36	Jewelry	35 x 24	672
37-55	Service Stores at lower level		
56	Auto Accessories	55 x 80	4,400
57	Auto Repairs	70 x 80	5,600
58	Gas Station		
TOTAL STORE AREA IS OMITTED FROM THIS LIST.			

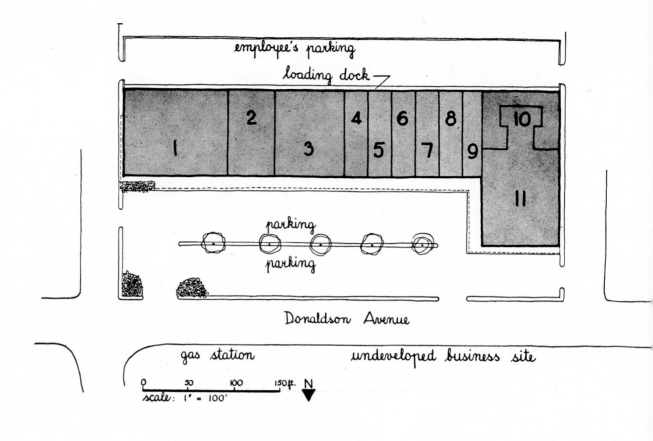

employee's parking
loading dock

parking
parking

Donaldson Avenue

gas station   undeveloped business site

scale: 1" = 100'   N

STORES WELL FITTED
INTO RESIDENCE DISTRICT

JEFFERSON VILLAGE, San Antonio, Texas. This neighborhood center, with more land reserved for expansion across Donaldson Avenue, is entirely surrounded by a residential area. Care has been taken to make the center look as attractive as the surrounding community. Large live oaks have been set out in the parking area, and beds of low planting at the entrances.

Most prominent of the stores in the group is the drug store, in the projecting arm of the L. At the rear of this store is the "Arcade," containing a barber shop, a book store with rental library, and a dining room for community and club affairs. The super market is at the other end of the store block, near the intersection.

All tenants have 10-year leases. A maintenance tax of 1 cent per sq. ft. is levied by the Merchants' Association. This fund is used for lighting and maintenance of the exterior.

Owner & Developer: L. E. Fite & Co.
Architect: Bartlett Cocke.

	TYPE OF STORE	WIDTH, DEPTH	SQ. FT. AREA
1	Supermarket	113 x 90	10,170
2	Hardware	50 x 90	4,500
3	Variety	75 x 90	6,750
4	Gifts	25 x 90	2,250
5	Beauty Shop	25 x 90	2,250
6	Bakery	25 x 90	2,250
7	Jewelry	25 x 90	2,250
8	Fabrics	25 x 90	2 250
9	Leather Goods	25 x 90	2,250
10	Arcade, containing Music Store, Florist, Book Store, Barber Shop, Post Office	85 x 60	5,100
11	Drugs	85 x 100	8,500
	TOTAL STORE AREA		48,520

SLANTED L FOR BETTER VISIBILITY

HACKENSACK, N. J. This projected center on Route 4 is of the same L formation as many of the centers on preceding pages, but it is on a much larger scale. To increase its visibility from passing cars it has been set at an angle to this important New Jersey traffic artery.

A restaurant and theater are at the near end, a department store at the far corner. The supermarket is set at the apex of the L furthest from the highway, to draw customers far into the parking area.

Six arcades, cutting through the line of stores, enable those parking in the rear to reach the front of the stores without long detours. And this concentration of traffic in the arcades will provide high-profit locations for the small stores.

Architects: Kelly & Gruzen.

PLANNED FOR A COMMUTER TOWN

NORTH SHORE MART, at Great Neck, Long Island, N. Y., is designed to take advantage of traffic created by a suburban railroad station and two bus lines. There is a group of apartment houses behind the stores. Only because it had been a private estate was a seven-acre site available in such a built-up section. For the same reason there were a number of fine old trees on the property, and many of these will be left standing in the front parking area. The space allotted for parking will undoubtedly prove insufficient, but is probably all that could be afforded in an already developed downtown section such as this. At the left end of the center is a drug store, at the other end a supermarket (with additional parking space at the rear, on the far side of Brompton Road). Along the rear of the stores is a service court for freight deliveries and employee parking. Eventually there will be 65,000 sq. ft. of second-floor office space.

In addition to the usual variety and apparel stores there is a branch of Wanamaker's department store which juts out across the sidewalk, inviting pedestrians to pass through.

Owner: Sol G. Atlas. *Architect:* Lathrop Douglass. *Site Engineer:* W. Lee Moore.

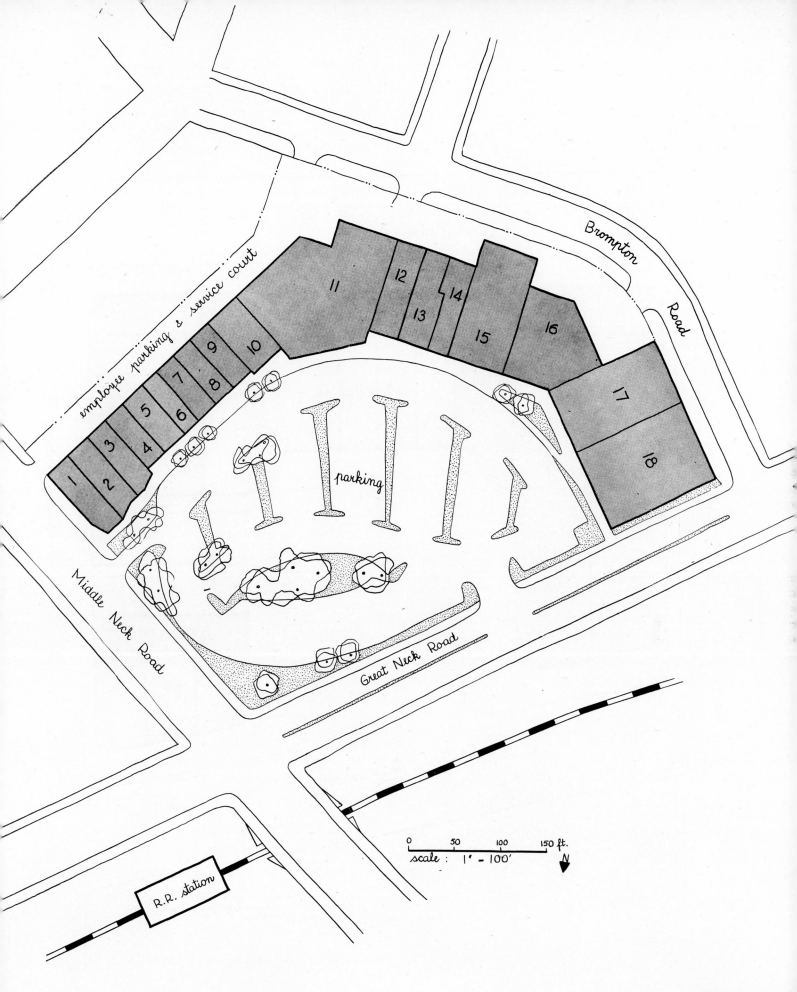

employee parking & service court

11 12 13 14 15 16

1 2 3 4 5 6 7 8 9 10

17 18

parking

Brompton Road

Middle Neck Road

Great Neck Road

R.R. station

0   50   100   150 ft.
scale : 1' - 100'
N

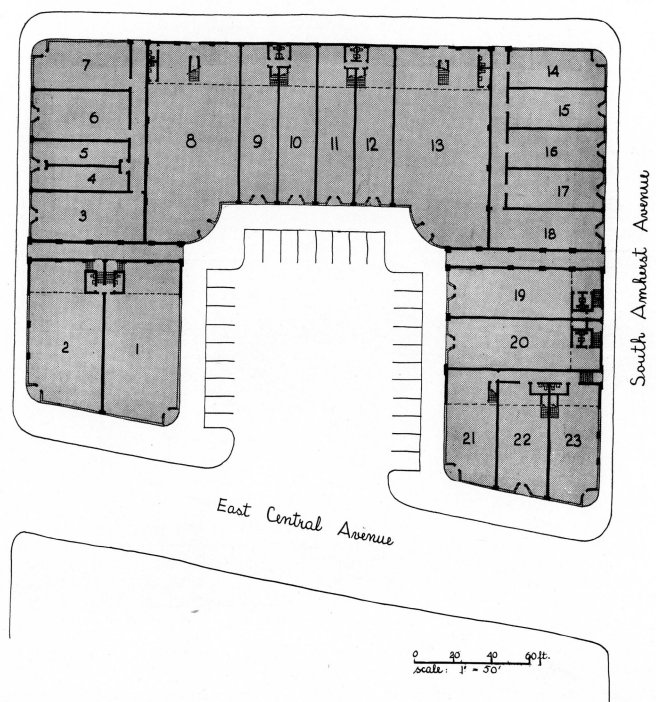

East Silver Avenue

South Carlisle Avenue

South Amherst Avenue

East Central Avenue

scale: 1' = 50'

	TYPE OF STORE	WIDTH, DEPTH	SQ. FT. AREA
1	Drugs	40 x 83	3,320
2	Children's Wear	40 x 77	3,080
3	Self-Service Laundry	26 x 62	1,612
4	Barber	13 x 53	689
5	Office	13 x 53	689
6	Office	26 x 53	1,378
7	Shoe Repair	26 x 53	1,378
8	Variety	51 x 105	4,900
9	Office Supplies	20 x 85	1,700
10	Photo Studio	20 x 85	1,700
11	Paint	20 x 85	1,700
12	Books	20 x 85	1,700
13	Grocery	51 x 105	4,900
14	Dentist	21 x 53	1,113
15	Office	21 x 53	1,113
16	Office	21 x 53	1,113
17	Notions	21 x 53	1,113
18	Beauty Shop	21 x 62	1,302
19	Bakery	26 x 83	2,158
20	Shoes	26 x 83	2,158
21	Men's Wear	22 x 60	1,320
22	Women's Wear	22 x 58	1,276
23	Gifts	22 x 63	1,386
TOTAL STORE AREA			42,798

NOB HILL Business Center, at Albuquerque, N. M., is of an almost square U form, with the inside of the U serving as a parking court. As we have shown elsewhere *(see page 38)*, with a plan of this shape it is impossible to provide an adequate ratio of parking space to store area. It is also difficult to use this parking space economically and still have the store fronts facing on this courtyard easily accessible. The parking area becomes congested and pedestrians are hindered by close-parked automobiles.

A number of the stores in this center face on the side streets. Whether for this reason, or because the number of stores is too large for the current needs of this neighborhood, many of these stores on the side streets are now rented as offices. The cumulative pulling power of any center will necessarily be reduced by scattering store frontage on different streets; and with the conversion of first-floor stores into offices, a center's effective power may be reduced still further.

There is a mezzanine at the rear of all but the smallest stores. Service access to many of the stores is by interior passages. No parking space has been reserved for freight; trucks must find space on the abutting streets.

Developer: R. B. Waggoman. *Architect:* Louis G. Hesselden.

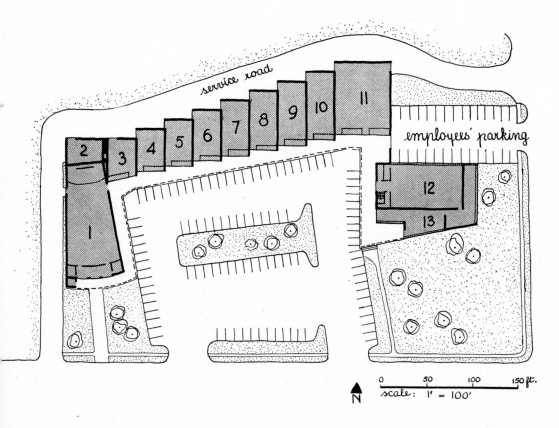

AERO ACRES, at Middle River, Md., was a community built during World War II for workers at the Glenn L. Martin aircraft plant. The buildings shown here formed the neighborhood shopping and recreation center for 2,000 families living in prefabricated houses nearby.

The line of stores is set at right angles to the slope of the ground. A wide sheltering canopy steps down this slope in rhythm with the stores behind. The store fronts are of uniform type, each turned at an angle to the pavement line so that it can be seen from a distance along the length of the walk. Signs are confined to a small strip above each multi-paned show window.

The staggered arrangement of the stores results in a wide and useful variety of depths, from 84 ft. down to 48 ft. It also creates a recessed loading dock at the rear of each store. Trucks can load and unload at these docks without blocking other traffic on the service road.

The uses shown in the store list below are those for which the center was originally designed. Post-war changes in the character and size of the community have been reflected in some changed uses.

Developer: Glenn L. Martin Co. *Consulting Architects:* Skidmore, Owings & Merrill.

	TYPE OF STORE	WIDTH, DEPTH	SQ. FT. AREA
1	Theater	50 x 120	6,000
2	Heating Plant & Incinerator	25 x 40	
3	Beauty Shop	30 x 42	1,260
4	Barber	30 x 42	1,260
5	Liquor	30 x 48	1,440
6	Laundry, Cleaners	30 x 52	1,560
7	Men's Wear	30 x 56	1,680
8	Women's Wear	30 x 60	1,800
9	Bank	30 x 65	1,950
10	Drugs	30 x 70	2,100
11	Supermarket	60 x 75	4,500
12	Rrecreation Hall	45 x 95	4,275
13	Restaurant		2,950
TOTAL STORE AREA			30,775

one family houses

two and four family houses

community center

parking

school

shopping center

parking

EXPERIENCE CAUSES CHANGE IN PARKING LAYOUT

MAPLEWOOD, LA., is a community built during World War II in the Lake Charles industrial area. It provides housing for workers in the various oil refineries and chemical plants nearby.

The planning of this town was greatly influenced by that conception of the ideal dormitory town which had earlier taken shape in Greenbelt *(see page 232)*. It is a self-contained community of controlled size. There are one-family houses, also two- and four-family houses. The latter are placed near the community center, where churches, schools, shops and public parks are all situated. Unfortunately the original plan was not completed, so that this center is now at one edge of the community instead of being its heart, as the planning concept would demand. The illustration above shows the shopping center as originally designed, with two parking wings and a grassed pedes-

trian mall within the U. This has now been drastically changed. The parking areas were found to be too far from the road, and not sufficiently convenient to the stores. It was therefore decided to convert the central pedestrian mall into a parking area.

Built and managed by: John W. Harris Associates Inc.
Architects: Walker & Gillette.

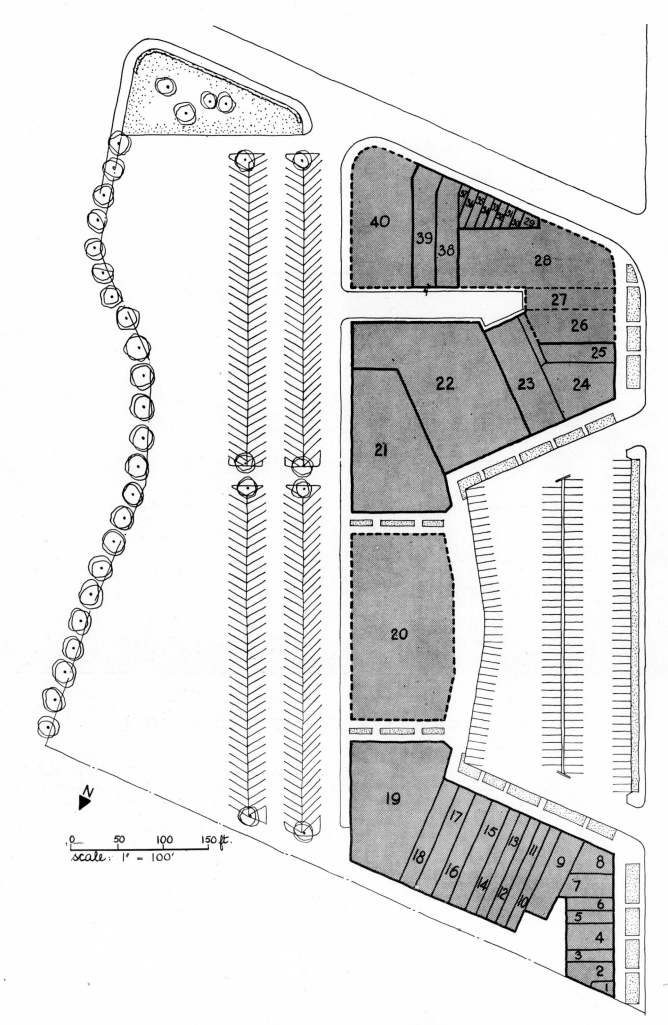

scale: 1" = 100'

MODERN DESIGN, WITH FIELDSTONE FACING, UNIFIED BY EFFECTIVE SIGN CONTROL

	TYPE OF STORE	WIDTH, DEPTH	SQ. FT. AREA
1	Self-Service Laundry	18 x 25	310
2	Beauty Shop	20 x 48	970
3	Florist	13 x 48	626
4	Women's Wear	28 x 48	1,350
5	Knitted Goods	14 x 48	675
6	Books	14 x 48	675
7	Children's Wear	25 x 48	1,258
8	Jewelry, Silverware	22 x 42	1,040
9	Electric Appliances	25 x 95	2,340
10	Women's Tailor & Furrier	12 x 120	1,440
11	Women's Wear	12 x 120	1,440
12		12 x 120	1,440
13		12 x 120	1,440
14		12 x 120	1,440
15	Bank	20 x 120	2,400
16	Linens & Gifts	20 x 120	2,400
17	Women's Wear	20 x 120	2,400
18	Men's & Boys' Wear	17 x 120	2,144
19	House Furnishings	100 x 140	11,900
20	Future Department Store		
21	Supermarket	100 x 150	12,590
22	Department Store (2 stories and basement)	100 x 160	16,250
23	Grocery	40 x 125	4,920
24	Drugs	57 x 50	3,360
25	Liquor	21 x 75	1,470
26	Restaurant	33 x 90	2,970
27	Bank	27 x 96	2,592
28	Variety	168 x 60	10,080
29	Entrance to Office Building		
30 through 37	8 Service Stores	10 x 30 each (average)	2,400
38		20 x 120	2,400
39	Post Office	20 x 128	2,560
40	Theater (1100 Seats)		9,500
TOTAL STORE AREA			108,800

RIDGEWAY shopping center at Stamford, Conn., was one of the earliest centers of modern design in the East. It has been carefully planned to mold all the stores into an integrated group of uniform appearance, using that cut fieldstone facing which has now become almost a cliché of suburban store design. The geometric impossibility of providing sufficient front parking in a U plan *(see page 38)* has been overcome in this case by the addition of a rear parking area. The two parking areas are connected by wide driveways. It is doubtful, however, if the total area at present allotted to parking will be sufficient when the center has been built up to its intended size. Double decking of the parking may then become essential.

Ridgeway is on the edge of a large, recently-constructed group of garden apartments. It is also on a main road leading north out of Stamford toward the Stamford Hills-Poundridge area, where live a growing number of high-income families who use the Stamford R.R. station for commuting to New York, and therefore normally pass the center daily.

Considering also how little parking space is available in the central shopping district of Stamford, there might be the opportunity here for an even larger center to be successful. It is perhaps significant that Sears, Roebuck has recently moved from downtown Stamford to Ridgeway. We already find here the standard elements of a neighborhood center —

CORNER OF NORTH WING WITH STORES ALONG THE HIGHWAY

CONTINUOUS CANOPY WITH FLUSH CEILING LIGHTS HAS UNDULATING EDGE

RIDGEWAY (continued)

supermarket, drug store, service stores. Eventually this will develop into a shopping-goods center with greater Trading Area and with another department store tenant; also more apparel and home-furnishing stores.

At present the stores have been divided on the two sides of the U according to type. The food stores, the drug store, and Sears Roebuck are on one side, the apparel, home furnishing and household appliance stores on the other. The result is lopsided use of the front parking area. Also the stores on the north side of the U receive little or no benefit from the traffic created by the supermarket. The service stores are grouped together with the Post Office and theater (and eventually second-floor offices) on the less heavily-traveled side street.

Control over store signs has been very effective. There is a pleasant uniformity in store fronts and lettering, but certainly no monotony. Particularly good is the lighted cove against which the store names (unlighted) are silhouetted.

A fine row of elms along the street front has been carefully preserved, to very good effect. The wide planted areas at the edge of the sidewalk have proved difficult to maintain.

All the stores have full basements. In some cases these are used for selling, in others for storage only. Eventually many, perhaps all, of the present buildings will have second stories added, part used for store space, part for offices. The new Sears Roebuck store on the south side of the U shows what flexibility this may give in space division. Its total space of 65,000 sq. ft. is divided as follows: 16,000 sq. ft. on the first floor, 16,000 sq. ft. in the basement, and 33,000 sq. ft. on the second floor, spreading over the neighboring stores.

Owner: Ridgeway Shopping Center, Inc.
Designer & Developer: Alfons Bach.

VARIETY IN STORE FRONTS
IN SPITE OF RIDGEWAY'S
SLEEK, UNIFORM CHARACTER ▶

FORMAL FRONT WITH SIMPLE
SIGN BACKLIGHTED

RECESSED FRONT FOR LEISURELY
WINDOW-SHOPPING

OPEN FRONT SCALED DOWN BY
DIVIDED WINDOW

OPEN FRONT CONTRASTED WITH
CLOSE-UP DISPLAY

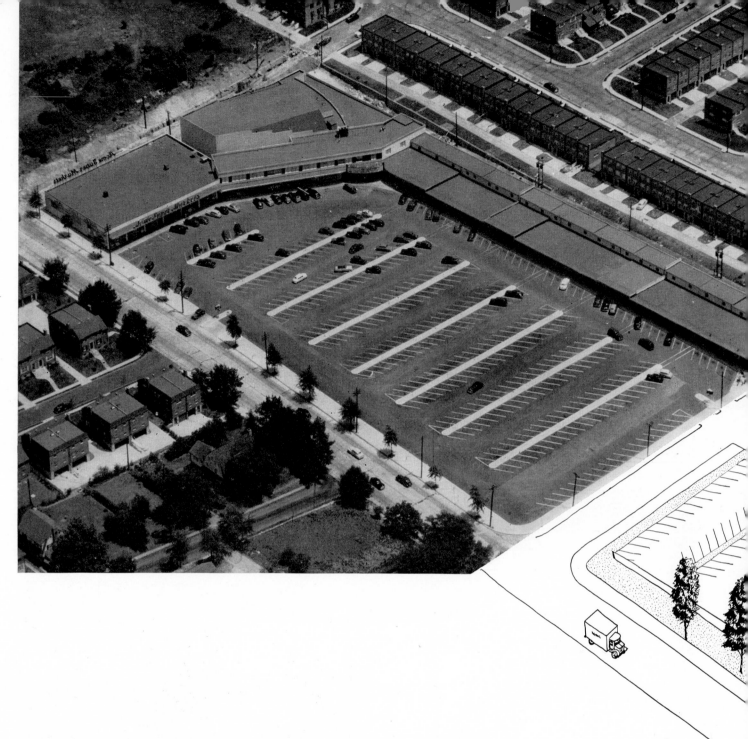

SMALL-CENTER PLAN WITH FRONT PARKING
STRETCHED OUT TO A 1,600 FT. FRONTAGE

CITY LINE CENTER, Philadelphia, Pa., is an example of the typical L-shaped neighborhood center plan stretched to what may be beyond the limits of success. Even in the half already built it is about 500 ft. from the theater at the apex to the hardware store at the southwestern end of the L. And present plans call for this existing store group to be doubled, as shown in the sketch opposite. All the parking space in this center is in front, between the stores and the highway. Most centers of L and U shape have found it more advisable to have split parking, some in front of, the rest behind the store group. In that way the stores are not set so far back from the road, beyond a large parking area which will

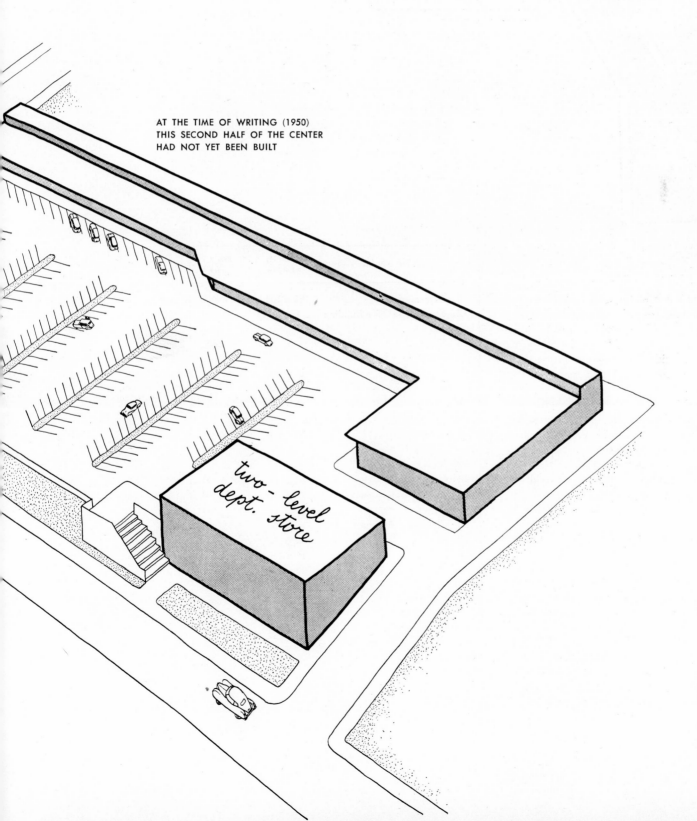

AT THE TIME OF WRITING (1950)
THIS SECOND HALF OF THE CENTER
HAD NOT YET BEEN BUILT

two - level
dept. store

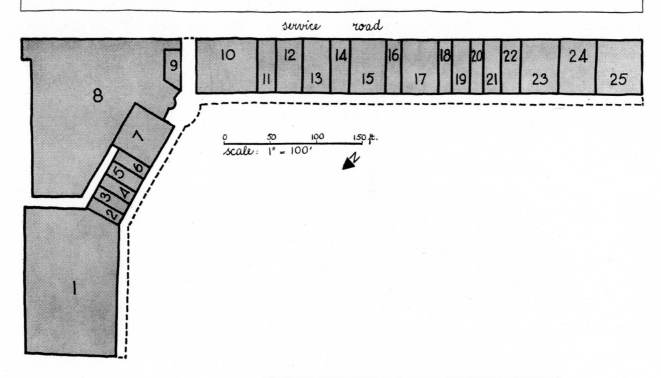

appear much of the time as half-empty, black and barren.

At one end of the section already built is a large supermarket, on the highway. Along the side of the theater (larger than usual in a center of this type), in the crotch of the L, is a row of smaller stores with offices above. A covered passage, cut through the line of stores by the theater entrance, is used by pedestrian shoppers from the apartments and two-family houses which are at the rear of the stores beyond the service road.

All the stores in the south wing of the L have a mezzanine at the rear. This is used for storage, also for air conditioning units, if these are installed.

At the far corner of the property, on the highway at the end of the proposed extension, is a separate two-story building intended as a department store. This uses the changing level of the ground to make the bottom floor accessible from the street. The upper floor will be entered from the parking area behind.

Developer: Harry Fried. *Architects:* Frederick W. Dreher & Son; W. H. Lee.

	TYPE OF STORE	WIDTH, DEPTH	SQ. FT. AREA
1	Supermarket	155 x 100	15,500
2	Entrance to Office Building		
3	Bakery	15 x 40	600
4	Florist	15 x 40	600
5	Candy	15 x 40	600
6	Photo Supplies	15 x 40	600
7	Furniture & Gifts	50 x 45	2,250
8	Theater	40 x 160	19,000
9	Post Office	40 x 12	480
10	Drugs	68 x 60	4,080
11	Children's Wear	20 x 60	1,200
12	Bank	30 x 60	1,800
13	Carpets	30 x 60	1,800
14	Radio & Television	20 x 60	1,200
15	Furniture	40 x 60	2,400
16	Children's Furniture	16 x 60	960
17	Shoes	40 x 60	2,400
18	Jewelry	15 x 60	900
19	Men's Wear	20 x 60	1,200
20	Cleaners	15 x 60	900
21	Lingerie	20 x 60	1,200
22	Women's Wear	20 x 60	1,200
23	Women's Wear	40 x 60	2,400
24	Stationery & Gifts	40 x 60	2,400
25	Hardware	55 x 60	3,300
TOTAL STORE AREA			68,970

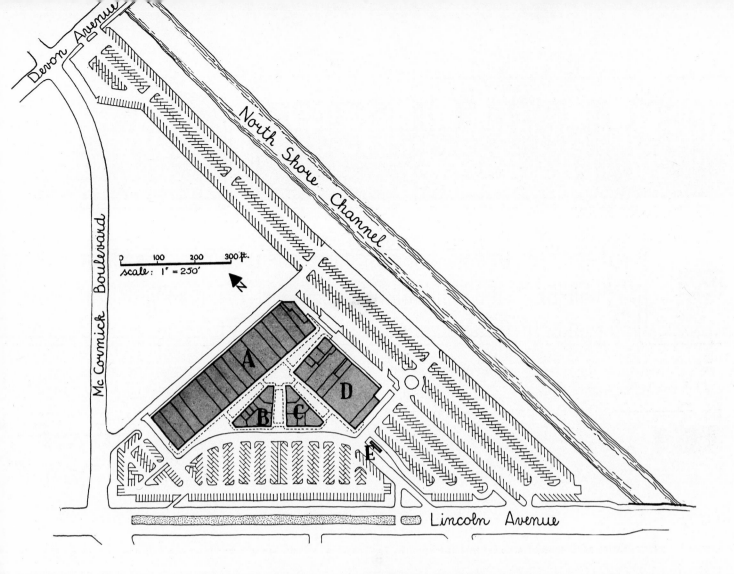

TYPE OF STORE	WIDTH, DEPTH	SQ. FT. AREA
BUILDING A Restaurants (2), Drugs, Variety, Children's Wear, Women's Wear (3), Shoes, Men's Wear, Sewing Machines, Furniture, Auto Supplies, Home Appliances, Self-Service Laundry	500 x 110	55,000
BUILDING B Ice Cream, Candy, Toys, Women's Accessories (3)	100 x 100	7,400
BUILDING C Liquor, Men's Wear, Millinery, Florist, Dairy	100 x 100	5,110
BUILDING D Floor Coverings, Bank, Service Stores (3), Hardware, Food (3)	220 x 120	27,400
BUILDING E Package Pick-up Station		
TOTAL STORE AREA		94,910

FITTED INTO AN AWKWARDLY SHAPED PLOT

LINCOLN VILLAGE, Chicago, Ill. This awkwardly-shaped plot has the advantage of connecting both with Lincoln Avenue, on the main south front, and also with the Devon and McCormick intersection north of the parking area.

The L-shaped block of stores is turned at an angle to Lincoln Avenue. Two low-roofed pavilions on the front sidewalk, in the crotch of the L, will house small specialty stores. By keeping these two pavilions low, the larger stores behind are not hidden from passers-by on the highway, yet small and busy shopping courts are created.

Owner & Developer: Lincoln Village Shopping Center, Inc.
Architects & Engineers: Howard T. Fisher & Associates, Inc.

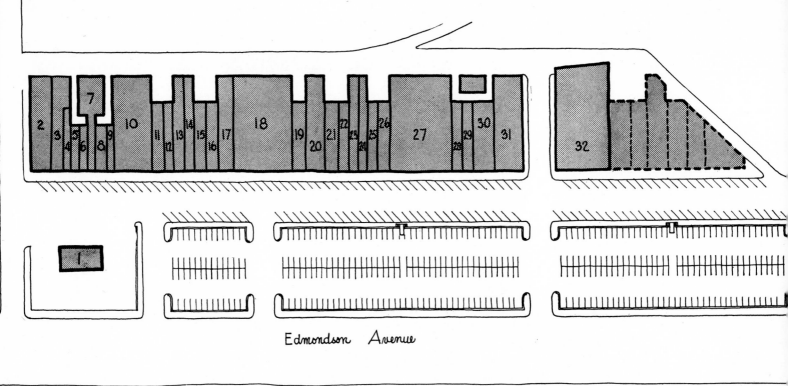

Edmondson Avenue

scale: 1" = 150'

N

ORIGINALLY ONLY PARALLEL PARKING WAS ALLOWED ON THE ROAD IN FRONT OF THE STORES. NOW, THERE IS ANGLE PARKING (SEE OPPOSITE PAGE)

TYPE OF STORE	WIDTH, DEPTH	SQ. FT. AREA
1 Gas Station		
2 Auto Supplies	33 x 150	4,950
3 Bank	21 x 150	3,750
4 Poultry & Dairy	12 x 100	1,200
5	13 x 70	910
6 Laundry	20 x 70	1,400
7 Hall	40 x 60	2,400
8 Sporting Goods	20 x 70	1,400
9 Jewelry	13 x 70	910
10 Variety	66 x 150	9,900
11 Ice Cream	17 x 110	1,870
12 Hardware	17 x 110	1,870
13 Restaurant	16 x 150	2,400
14 Women's Wear	20 x 150	3,000
15 Shoe Repair	20 x 110	2,200
16	16 x 110	1,760
17 Men's Wear	25 x 150	3,750
18 Department Store	100 x 150	15,000
19 Shoes	20 x 110	2,200
20 Women's Wear	33 x 150	4,950
21 Gifts	20 x 110	2,200
22 Sewing Center	16 x 110	1,760
23 Children's Wear	16 x 150	2,400
24 Lingerie	16 x 150	2,400
25 Candy	13 x 110	1,430
26 Fabrics	20 x 110	2,200
27 Supermarket	100 x 150	15,000
28 Bakery	17 x 110	1,870
29 Photo Supplies	17 x 110	1,870
30 Music Shop	33 x 110	3,630
31 Drugs	50 x 150	7,500
32 Theater & Bowling	90 x 170	15,000
TOTAL STORE AREA		123,080

BREAK IN LEVELS ALSO BREAKS MONOTONOUS EXPANSE OF PARKING

STORES ON TERRACE ABOVE PARKING AREA

EDMONDSON VILLAGE, Baltimore, Md. Masquerading behind these Colonial fronts with their small-paned windows and steep pitched roofs, is a one-sided street of modern stores, more than 1,000 ft. in length. The changing levels of the site have been used advantageously to set the stores on a terrace behind the parking area; so parking is on a level with the highway, but does not block the motorists' view of the stores spread out along the terrace behind. Originally, parallel parking only was allowed on the road directly in front of the stores. Now it is congested by diagonal parking. Varying projections at the rear are used to vary store depths to suit the individual needs of each tenant. This has the incidental advantage of providing a number of small service courts. The main pullers are scattered regularly throughout the line of stores. A two-story department store is in the middle, the supermarket and drug store are toward the right end. A theater (building 32 in plan opposite page), and a number of smaller stores, is in a small block at the right, slightly separated from the rest of the stores by a service access road.

Owner & Developer: Edmondson Village, Inc.
Architect: Kenneth Cameron Miller.

TYPE OF STORE	WIDTH, DEPTH	SQ. FT. AREA
BUILDING A		
Gas Station		
BUILDING B		
Future Warehouse	50 x 70	3,500
Future Stores	60 x 60	3,600
BUILDING C		
Pet Shop	16 x 20	320
Veg. Prep for Supermarket	60 x 20	1,200
BUILDING D		
Supermarket	110 x 145	16,000
Liquor	30 x 60	1,800
Men's Wear	17 x 60	1,020
Beauty Shop	17 x 60	1,020
Children's Wear	21 x 60	1,260
Variety	28 x 60	1,680
Cleaners	25 x 60	1,500
Barber	12 x 60	720
Photo Supplies	18 x 60	1,080
Drugs	40 x 75	3,000
BUILDING E		
Hardware	35 x 50	1,750
Sporting Goods	25 x 50	1,250
Women's Wear	15 x 50	750
Slenderizing Salon	15 x 50	750
Shoe Repair	13 x 50	650
Knit Shop	12 x 50	600
Jewelry	10 x 50	500
Florist	10 x 50	500
Radios	20 x 50	1,000
2nd floor offices over entire building E		
BUILDING F		
Future Theater		35,600
TOTAL STORE AREA		81,050

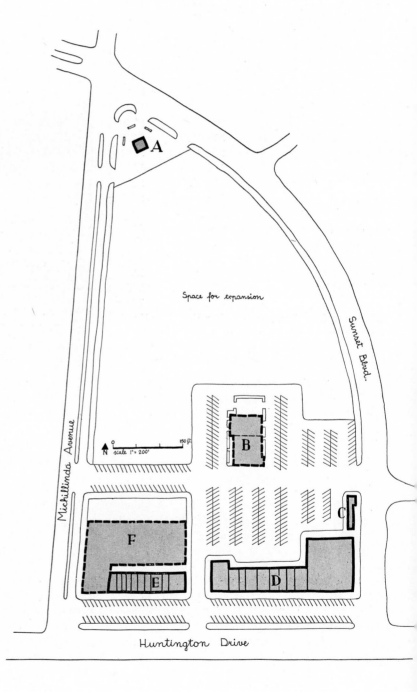

THE REAR FRONT OF THE SUPERMARKET. SERVICE WING AT LEFT

DRUG STORE AT CORNER, ON ROAD CONNECTING FRONT AND REAR PARKING

TWO-FRONT STORES WITH SPLIT PARKING

EL RANCHO SANTA ANITA shopping center in Arcadia, Calif., a growing suburb of Los Angeles, has a typically Californian plan: store blocks parallel to the main highway, a small amount of front parking space for quick in-and-out shoppers, supplemented by a considerably larger parking area in the rear. Access to the latter is through a wide gap in the center of the line of stores, also from the roads on each side of the block.

Very ample space has been allowed for future expansion. One of the buildings planned is a large common warehouse in rear of the store blocks. The need for such outside storage space becomes acute in the case of stores which have two entrance fronts and no basement.

For the same reason, the supermarket cannot be furnished with a separate freight entrance on a rear service road. But here, instead, a low building set at right angles to the rear wall of the supermarket is used effectively to conceal stock storage, garbage etc., behind large sliding doors. This little extension also marks off, to some extent, a loading bay. The design of the buildings in this shopping center might be described as Californian Commercial. Particularly striking are the two high and outward sloping glass fronts of the supermarket and the side wall of the drug store, with its rippling corrugated surface.

Owner & Developer: Rancho Santa Anita Inc. *Architects:* Roland Crawford, E. L. E. Co., Barnett Hopen & Smith.

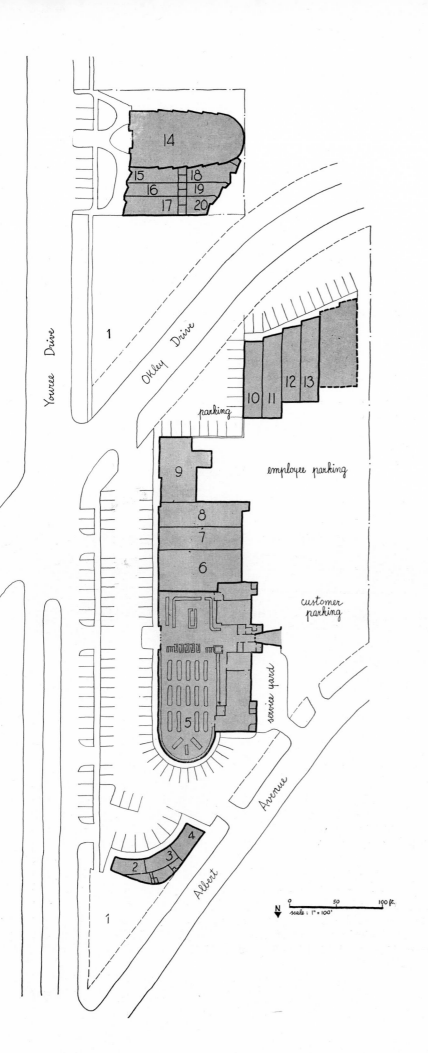

FOUR SEPARATE STORE

	TYPE OF STORE	WIDTH, DEPTH	SQ. FT. AREA
1	Filling Station		
2	Barber	30 x 20	750
3	Shoe Repair	30 x 20	800
4	Jewelry	30 x 20	750
5	Supermarket	175 x 100	16,500
6	Variety	40 x 90	3,400
7	Beauty Shop	24 x 90	2,160
8	Cleaners	24 x 90	2,160
9	Drugs	70 x 40	2,960
10	Self-Service Laundry	20 x 78	1,560
11	Seed Store	20 x 83	1,660
12	Floor Coverings	20 x 78	1,560
13	Fabrics	20 x 83	1,660
14	Theater	58 x 124	7,000
15	Misses' Wear	16 x 60	960
16	Women's Wear	14 x 60	840
17	Shoes	18 x 60	1,080
18	Household Appliances	20 x 56	1,120
19	Real Estate	14 x 40	560
20	Candy	18 x 30	540
21	Filling Station		
TOTAL STORE AREA			48,020

GROUPS COMBINED TO FORM ONE CENTER

BROADMOOR COMMERCIAL CENTER, Shreveport, La. Because various sections of the site are held in different ownership, and also because of variation in zoning restrictions, this center has been split up into four groups of stores, each group having its own parking area close by. All the groups are, however, tied together by a certain harmony of design and material.

The largest and most important group is that dominated by the supermarket. Here extensive display windows were considered unnecessary and replaced by a plain brick wall. A long ribbon of glass tops this wall, lighting the store interior during the daytime, and at night allowing the store illumination to overflow and help to light the parking lot.

Large chunky letters, set at the edge of a thrusting overhang to emphasize the supermarket entrance, are characteristic of this particular grocery chain. The 60-foot-wide clear span within the store is of particular value for the flexibility which it gives in the arrangement of fixtures and displays. Between the line of check-out gates and the bakery, lunch, and drug counters in the supermarket pedestrian shopping traffic is funneled through a covered passage connecting front and rear parking areas.

The small building at the north end has an interesting boomerang shape. This gives a pleasant look of softness to the group, but is of course more costly to build than the ordinary rectangular store block.

Developer: Big Chain Stores, Inc.
Architects: Samuel G. & William B. Wiener.

AT NIGHT A RIBBON OF GLASS BLOCK ALLOWS LIGHT TO ESCAPE FROM THE SUPERMARKET AND ILLUMINATE THE PARKING AREA

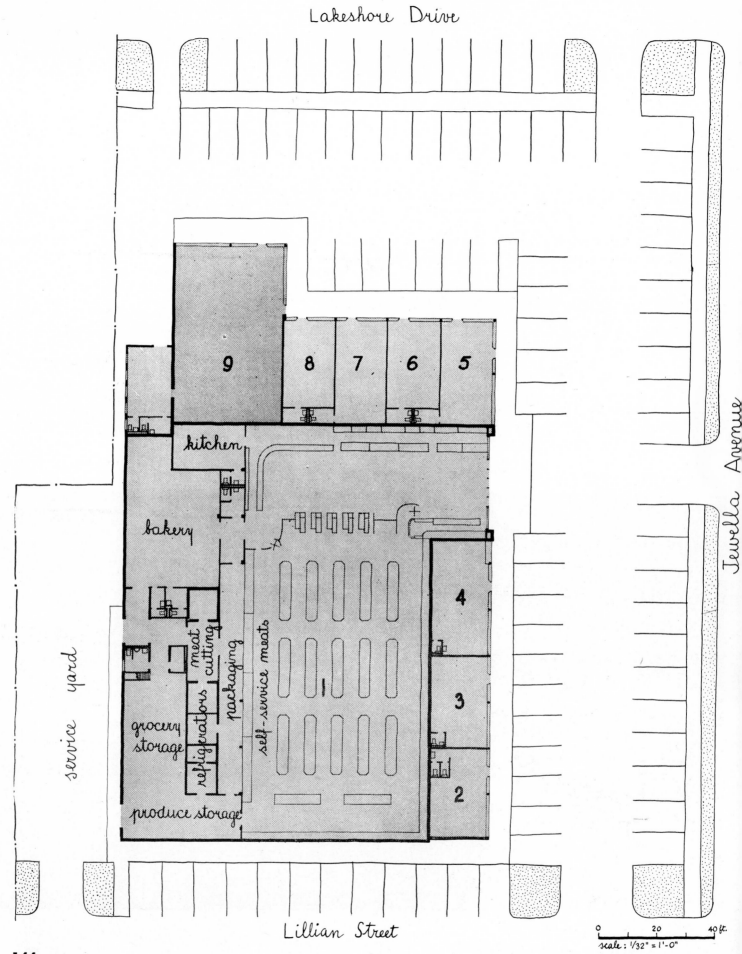

Lakeshore Drive

9 8 7 6 5

kitchen

bakery

service yard

meat cutting

packaging

self-service meats

refrigerators

grocery storage

produce storage

4

3

2

Jewella Avenue

Lillian Street

scale: 1/32" = 1'-0"

0   20   40 ft.

144

	TYPE OF STORE	WIDTH, DEPTH	SQ. FT. AREA
1	Supermarket	142 x 107	15,200
2	Barber	31 x 20	620
3	Shoes	31 x 20	620
4	Jewelry	30 x 20	780
5	Ice Cream	35 x 18	630
6	Children's Wear	18 x 35	630
7	Cleaners	18 x 35	630
8	Shoe Repair	18 x 55	630
9	Variety	39 x 60	2,820
	TOTAL STORE AREA		22,560

SMALL STORES CLING TO BLANK WALLS OF SUPERMARKET

LAKE SHORE DRIVE shopping center, at Shreveport, La., is basically a single large supermarket surrounded by a number of small stores; so that the whole group forms a neighborhood center. The supermarket (as shown in the section drawing) is larger and higher than the small stores, so that it can be lit by a clerestory strip of glass block.

The owners of the supermarket feel that the rentals gained from the small stores more than outweigh any disadvantages the market itself may suffer, from being deprived of display window space. Moreover the entrance of the supermarket, as the pictures show, dominates the whole center both in height and width.

The smaller stores face outward from the periphery of a rectangle. Probably in a small neighborhood center of this kind it is not so vitally desirable that they face each other as well as the public. The variety store at the rear corner, projecting from the rectangle for greater depth, helps to boost the traffic of those stores which do not benefit directly from the traffic generated at the supermarket entrance.

Owner & Developer: Big Chain Stores, Inc. *Architects:* Samuel G. & William B. Wiener.

ENTRANCE TO SUPERMARKET, MARKED BY HIGH CANOPY, IS FLANKED BY SMALLER STORES

IN THE SHOPPING CENTER AT
LAKE SHORE DRIVE, SHREVEPORT, LA.

STAGGERED STORE FRONTS AND OVERHANGS

BROADMOOR AND LAKE SHORE. One of the most striking points of design in both of these centers *(see previous pages)* is the detail of the overhangs to protect the pedestrian shopper from rain and sun. It is not to be expected, however, that an overhang can have anything but a minor effect upon the reflections that mar the transparency of large show windows *(see page 60)*. But these overhangs do carry through the ceiling line unbroken from inside to out. As a result the interior of the store gains greatly in apparent spaciousness.

The illustration at right shows clearly the interesting saw-tooth arrangement of one store block in Broadmoor Center *(see plan on page 142)*. This plan has the advantage of separating one store front from its neighbor, while keeping the whole line of stores visible from the street, and within the purview of shoppers on the sidewalk.

STAGGERED FRONTS IN ONE OF THE BROADMOOR STORE GROUPS

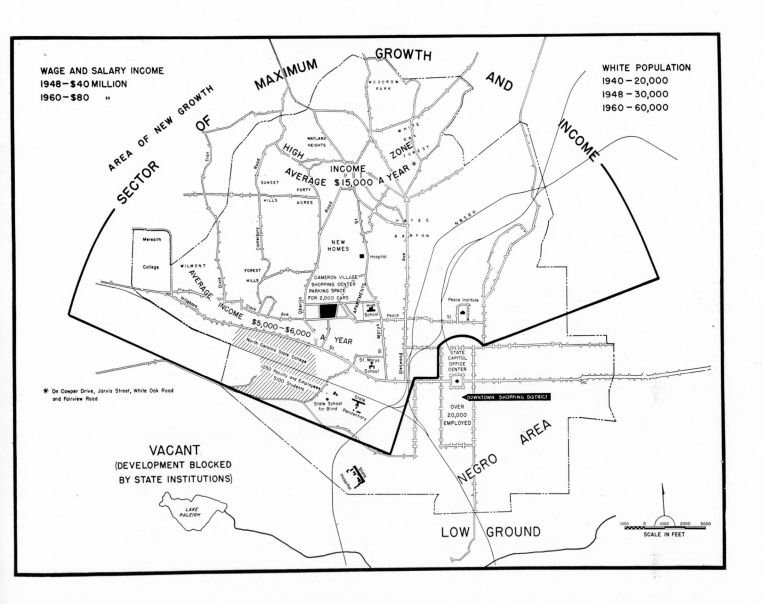

GROWTH

MAXIMUM

AND

SECTOR   OF

AREA OF NEW GROWTH

INCOME

HIGH   INCOME   ZONE

AVERAGE $15,000 A YEAR ✳

WOODROW PARK

WHITE OAK FOREST

WAYLAND HEIGHTS

SUNSET HILLS

FORTY ACRES

HAYES BARTON

N & S R R

NEW HOMES

Hospital

CAMERON VILLAGE SHOPPING CENTER PARKING SPACE FOR 2,000 CARS

AVERAGE   INCOME

$5,000 - $6,000   A   YEAR

Meredith College

WILMONT

FOREST HILLS

Canterbury

Clark   Ave

Oberlin

APARTMENTS

High School

Peace   St

Peace Institute

St. Marys School

Glenwood

State School for Blind

State Penitentiary

North Carolina State College

1250 Faculty and Employees
5100 Students

STATE CAPITOL OFFICE CENTER

DOWNTOWN SHOPPING DISTRICT

OVER 20,000 EMPLOYED

NEGRO   AREA

✳ On Cowper Drive, Jarvis Street, White Oak Road and Fairview Road

Hillsboro

Dixie Trail

Road

VACANT
(DEVELOPMENT BLOCKED
BY STATE INSTITUTIONS)

State Hospital

LAKE RALEIGH

LOW   GROUND

1000 0 1000 2000 3000
SCALE IN FEET

EXPANDING SOUTHERN TOWN GETS NEW VILLAGE GREEN

No city expands equally in all directions. The natural growth of every community has a predictable lopsidedness. In Raleigh, N. C., suburban growth is pushing out strongly and fast to the north-west. Between 1940 and 1948, 2,680 dwelling units were built in this section, whereas in all the other perimetal areas together only 525 units were built, and 267 of those by public funds.

Moreover the physical barriers which channeled growth to the north and west will continue to exist. In the south-west sector of the town there is a band of universities, schools, hospitals and an insane asylum, lying square across the natural lines of growth.

To the south the land is in general low and damp. On the edge of the town toward the east and south is the negro section, which has acted as a barrier to high-grade new building on that side.

In contrast to this, in the north-west section the white population has increased from 22,300 to more than 30,000 between 1940 and 1948. Now most of Raleigh's wealthiest families live in this section of the city.

The small farms which were once scattered across this rolling countryside were early turned over to builders for speculative development. The remaining negro families are gradually being edged out by increasingly large offers for their few, but now desirable acres.

But until 1948 the old Cameron property remained almost untouched, as it had for more than 100 years, only 1½ miles from downtown Raleigh and square across this surging residential boom. The Cameron estate had been 200 acres originally; but as the value of those acres on the tax books rose from $50 to $1,000 per acre, as the tide of suburban growth pushed around and beyond it, some small parcels were nibbled off, sold for a hospital, a school, a group of apartment houses.

The timber was sold, the towering pines were cut. Squatters pitched their shacks for as long as they could get away with it. One managed to stay so long that he claimed the land, and was eventually evicted only after long legal process.

It was not, however, until 1948 that Mrs. Smallwood (née Annie Cameron Graham, a direct descendant of the original Duncan Cameron) decided to accept the offer made by J. W. York, a Raleigh builder, and his partner R. A. Bryan, a contractor from Goldsboro, for the remaining 158 acres. By that time this huge vacant lot was almost surrounded by a superior residential neighborhood. Willie York and his partner had bought themselves a village green.

30 acres for Shopping Center

The new owners realized immediately that this was the ideal site for a large shopping center. No less than 30 acres, alongside Clark Avenue, the main through-traffic road, was immediately allotted to stores. Application was made for a zoning change to convert this acreage from residential to retail. Also requested was an increase in density from the existing limit of 6 families per acre to as high as 30 in rental apartments immediately adjacent to the proposed shopping center. In this way it was possible to boost the Buying Power available to the new stores.

Both neighbors and town officials have now approved these zoning changes, convinced that, under the careful planning and landscaping which Willie York promised, such a development would actually become an asset to the neighborhood. And the developers, in turn, have a shopping center isolated from competitors by a belt of residential property, almost all of which they own.

In each one of these moves advantage was being taken of experience gained by other developers throughout the country. Originally forward-looking builders had provided shopping centers as a service to householders which would make the new houses more saleable, the new apartments more rentable. Later it was realized that the shopping center, by its continuing and increasing returns, might often turn out to be the most profitable part of the whole investment. In Cameron Village it has been considered as such from the start, with the residential part of the development planned to make the stores more rentable.

Economic analyst hired

To confirm their own belief in the potentialities of a shopping center of this large size in this location, and to convince the bankers and merchants upon whom they would have to depend for support, the two promoters agreed to hire Homer Hoyt as economic analyst. He was asked first to make a survey of Raleigh's growth from 1940 to 1950, and then to project his estimates ten years further into the future to 1960.

Within this framework he also produced a detailed estimate of the special potentialities of the Cameron Village area for retail selling. For this estimate available statistics were keyed into a sample canvass of 100 residents in the area, to show the average family income and the ways in which it was spent.

Hoyt's estimates were extremely optimistic (although in at least one of the anchor stores his predictions have proved to be almost 25% too low), so optimistic, in fact, that Willie York now smilingly claims that he keeps the report hidden in the safe, secure from the eyes of prospective tenants. For York's novel percentage leases provide that the minimum rental shall have an increasingly large percentage added as gross sales reach above a certain high point.

To many merchants the advantages of the site have been so obvious as to need no statistical proof. But in other cases—particularly the first key stores—Hoyt's report undoubtedly gave added authority to York's proposals.

As in every other shopping center the first steps were the hardest. The number and type of stores and their speed of building must be continually modified to fit available capital and the demands of prospective tenants. Inevitably the design and layout of the stores becomes subject to all sorts of compromises, though they seem to have been fewer here than in almost any other center of comparable size.

But undoubtedly there have been occasions when Willie York, like many another thoughtful developer, was stirred to doubt; when he set the cost of Seward Mott's somewhat academic, grand-plan layout, with solidly-built, brick store blocks separated from each other by wide belts of perimetal parking and public streets, against the closely-packed huddle of market stalls and tiny, ramshackle stores, which give such a profit-making atmosphere to many shopping centers of the Farmers Market type in California (see pages 94-101).

Don't shoppers spend more money when they are crowded? But don't they prefer a center where they won't be jostled? Aren't we putting too much capital into the buildings, considering the possible return on this investment? But will the regulations allow us to build much more cheaply here in the East?

The store list

Cameron Village was fortunate enough, very early in its development, to attract a Sears Roebuck B class store. This should be the new center's trump card in attracting customers from beyond the immediate neighborhood.

As a condition of entering Cameron Village, Sears insisted upon the developers finding these eight tenants to be their neighbors in the new center: a grocery store, variety store, restaurant, drug store, and at least three service shops, also a theater.

All of these, plus furniture and jewelry stores, women's apparel stores, gift shop, laundry, a drive-in bank and a gas station, should be installed by the end of 1950. Most of them are already in operation, but little publicity has attended their opening. This has not prevented them developing into a thriving neighborhood center, and some of the stores —Colonial Stores' supermarket in particular—have attracted trade from way beyond the immediate neighborhood.

Willie York, however, has more ambitious plans for Cameron Village. He hopes eventually to make this a center with regional appeal. There would be a department store here, and a group of

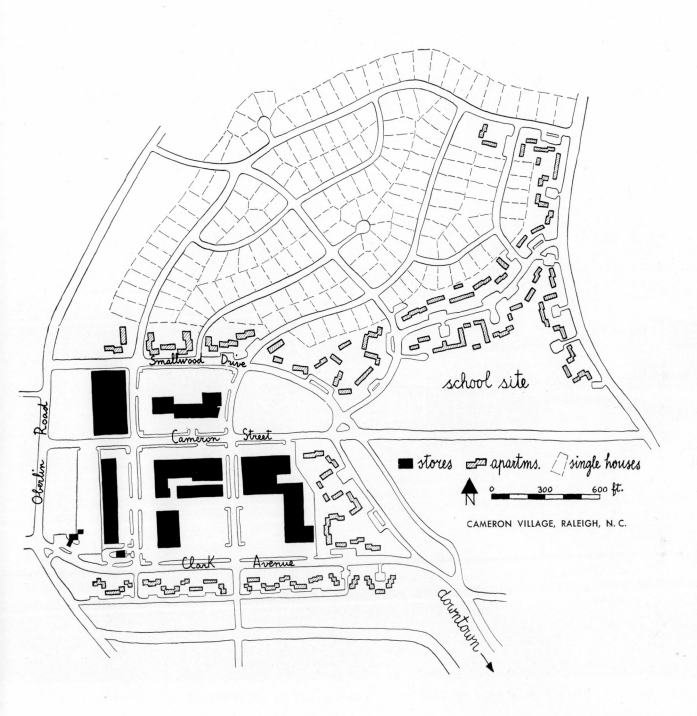

Smallwood Drive

Oberlin Road

Cameron Street

Clark Avenue

school site

■ stores ◰ apartms. ▱ single houses

0   300   600 ft.

N

CAMERON VILLAGE, RALEIGH, N. C.

downtown →

first-grade fashion goods stores, including branches of New York stores.

The stores in downtown Raleigh are already established as a fashion goods center for the surrounding countryside; but there is almost no parking space adjacent to these stores. If Cameron Village, with its ample parking facilities, can attract the number and type of fash-

ion goods stores for which it hopes, then it should draw trade from as far away as the eastern part of North Carolina and the southern part of Virginia, areas which are now almost forced to depend upon Richmond for fashion goods.

Homer Hoyt emphasizes in his report on future prospects that were Cameron Village to develop in this way with a branch

department store, the business of the present tenants would also be greatly increased. For success produces its own momentum; in women's fashion goods especially, doubling the number of stores, so that there is better opportunity for comparison shopping, may well triple the total business done by the shopping center.

THE SUPERMARKET, AT THE CORNER OF ONE STORE BLOCK, IS TYPICAL OF CAMERON VILLAGE ARCHITECTURE AND PARKING LAYOUT

ECONOMIC SURVEY SHOWS GROWTH OF RALEIGH AND

REGIONAL TRADE VITAL FOR SUCCESS OF CAMERON VILLAGE

THE GROWTH OF RALEIGH is one of the two factors upon which the successful growth of Cameron Village will depend (the other is the attraction of trade from the eastern section of North Carolina beyond the city limits), according to the economic survey by Homer Hoyt Associates prepared in 1948 and summarized here.

Raleigh has had a sustained and rapid growth from 1900 (pop. 13,643) to the present (estimated 1948 pop.: 67,000. Preliminary 1950 census figures: 65,-123). Never, during this period, has the population increased less than 25% every ten years; and from 1940 to 1948 the increase was 42.6% (estimate based on a 44% increase in electric light meters over this eight-year period). This 1940-48 population increase was almost entirely among the whites. The natural increase in the negro population was drained off by a greater emigration to the northern cities.

There have been three building booms: 1925-29, 1937-41, 1945-47. But building has still not caught up with population growth. There are thousands of families doubled up, so that there is an average of two wage-earners in every household, a most unusual situation.

More than 85% of all new residential building during the 1940-48 period was in the north-west section of the city,

which is synonymous with the Cameron Village section. Moreover it seems probable that the future growth of the city (estimated 1960 population: 100,000) will also be concentrated in this section.

THE ECONOMIC BASE, upon which the recent and future growth of Raleigh depends, is diversified. Much of the town's

income is drawn from services and goods bought by those living outside the city limits, in the eastern part of North Carolina and even beyond.

Being the State capital, Raleigh gives employment to a large number of civil servants: 1,000 Federal Government employees, and 4,450 State employees, including 1,250 at North Carolina State

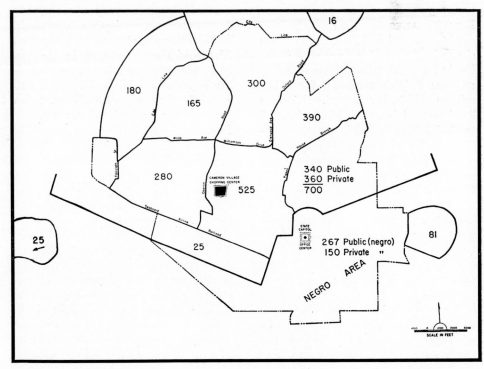

NUMBER OF NEW DWELLING UNITS BUILT FROM 1937 TO 1948 IN EACH SECTION OF RALEIGH

151

College. Five other colleges employ 268 faculty members in all. During term time there are about 7,500 students added to the normal population of the city.

Next door to Wake County, in which Raleigh is situated, is a belt of fertile land with a 45-50 inch annual rainfall. Here is produced 70% of North Carolina's tobacco crop. In 1947 this tobacco belt had an income of one billion dollars. Raleigh is the commercial and professional center of this region, in fact of the whole northeastern part of the state. Doctors, dentists and professional men draw much of their income from those living outside the narrow limits of Wake County. Two railroads and two big U.S. highways pass through the town, so that it is an important regional transportation center. As the chief distributive and branch office center for the eastern part of the state, Raleigh's demand for office space has far outstripped the available buildings. The 420,000 sq. ft. of office space available is 100% rented and there is a long waiting list.

Wholesale trade employs 1,700 workers, manufacturing 4,500. Retail stores, particularly women's ready-to-wear, clothes, shoes, automobiles and machinery, draw $50 million annually from beyond the limits of Wake Co. Raleigh is a shopping magnet which exerts a strong pull through all of eastern North Carolina.

RETAIL SALES for Wake Co. in 1947 can be estimated as follows: In 1939 (as shown by the retail trade census) Wake Co. had a retail sales volume of $31½ million; Raleigh accounted for $25½ million of this. But as national income has increased from $71 billion in 1939 to $200 billion in 1947, so national retail sales have increased from $55.3 billion to $118 billion during the same period of expansion.

However, Wake Co. sales increased even more than sales in the nation as a whole (as shown by the retail sales tax, which can be assumed to indicate about 15% less than the actual gain). Moreover retail sales in Wake Co. increased more rapidly than in other parts of North Carolina.

In 1946-47 this one county chalked up 4.95% of North Carolina's total retail sales, but it has only 3.19% of the population and 3.90% of the buying power

of the state. This gives a clear indication of Raleigh's power to draw sales from beyond the boundaries of Wake Co.

Retail sales in the county for 1947 (based on a special tabulation with allowances made for under-enumeration) were judged to be $125 million, of which Raleigh accounted for $100 million.

About half of the city's total was drawn from beyond its boundaries. And what drew these retail sales were just three blocks on Fayetteville Street, in which apparel stores (and primarily women's apparel) occupy more than half the total frontage. A secondary attraction was the jewelry stores, of which there are seven in this district. Altogether this three-block area on Fayetteville Street accounted for 30% of the retail sales in the city in 1947, in spite of there being parking space in that district for less than 400 cars.

THE NET INCOME of those living in Raleigh and surrounding Wake Co. will depend primarily on the total number and average income of wage earners. For wages and salaries constitute 60% or more of the income in any state or town, just as they do in the nation as a whole. In 1940 there were 42,726 wage earners in Wake Co. (almost 40% of the population). Of these, 22,033 were employed in Raleigh (47% of the city's population). If these same proportions were in force today — 1947 — then there would be 55,000 wage earners in Wake Co., 31,450 of them employed in Raleigh. State unemployment insurance records are of little help in checking such estimates, for they omit all small firms, also domestic and professional workers.

However, by taking the average weekly earnings shown in those types of business covered by insurance, and then filling this out with estimates made on the basis of income-tax returns and other data, the average earnings of a wage earner in this area appear to be slightly over $2,000 per year.

The 7,500 college students in Raleigh each spend an average of $667 per year, in addition to their tuition and college fees. This contributes another $5 million to Raleigh's income. Then there is income from rents, profits, interest and dividends, which is estimated at $35 million for Wake Co. as a whole; Raleigh

accounts for $27 million of this.

Adding all these items together the total 1947 income of Wake Co. appears to be approximately $142 million, of which Raleigh contributes $100 million.

Individual incomes are more difficult to estimate. State income tax returns show clearly only those above $10,000 per year. And the latest complete records are for 1945. 1946 incomes, according to the State Income Tax Division, were half as much again; and 1947 incomes are expected to be half as much again higher than 1946. So the number earning more than $10,000 per year should have increased from 275 in 1945 to at least 550 in 1947.

The income of those employed in several colleges and State institutions is known, and it is known that of those employed at the State Capitol over 100 had in 1947 an income of more than $5,000 per year. Income distribution in many other lower-paid groups can only be estimated from the figures of average earnings, correlated with State income tax returns and surveys of the higher income groups.

From these calculations and estimates it is possible to set up a table showing the number of wage earners to be found in each of eleven income groups ranging from "Under $1,000" to "$25,000 and over", both in Wake Co. as a whole and in Raleigh.

INCOMES IN THE CAMERON VILLAGE TRADE AREA. The higher incomes of Wake Co., it appears from the table of income distribution, are to be found mostly in Raleigh. And the high incomes of Raleigh are mostly concentrated in the northwestern section of the city, in the immediate vicinity of Cameron Village. Here there are none of the low-paid agricultural workers found in other sections of Wake Co., and there are almost none of the low-paid colored workers found elsewhere in the city.

A sample enumeration of 100 families in the Cameron Village area on February 3rd and 4th, 1948, showed an average family income in the preceding year of $5,333. Applying the income distribution found in this survey to the 7,500 families in the Cameron Village trading area: in the year 1947, 2,700 families should have had an income of more than $5,000, 760 families one of more than $10,000.

Bearing in mind that in the city as a whole, there is an average of slightly more than two wage-earners in every household, it is probable that at least 20% of the families in the Cameron Village trading area contained two wage-earners and it is evident that quite a number of them had three.

The anticipated doubling of population in the Cameron Village area by 1960 will also double the wage and salary income, bringing it to $80 million, added to which will be an estimated $20 million from property.

ANTICIPATED SALES in Cameron Village shopping center. The exceptional advantages of this new center will probably draw trade from a wider area than would normally be anticipated. There will be parking space for 2,000 cars, as compared with less than 400 spaces in the present downtown shopping area on Fayetteville Street. There will be added conveniences such as covered sidewalks, amenities such as garden areas, and a freedom from through traffic.

The new center is surrounded by residential development, and main highways connect it with all the high-income residential areas. Within a 1½ mile radius there is a high-income population of 30,000. Seldom is it possible to develop such a large center in the middle of such a rapidly-developing residential area. Almost never is enough land available.

If a high-grade department store is established in Cameron Village it should be capable of drawing trade from all parts of eastern North Carolina, and even from Greensboro and Winston-Salem. It could become not only Raleigh's largest shopping center, but also one of the largest regional centers in the South.

Food. It is estimated that 2,500 of the 7,500 families in the Cameron Village area will buy 80% of their food in the center. If they conform to the 1948 national average they will spend 24% of their average $6,000 per year income on food. This would mean gross sales of $3 million for these food stores.

The remaining 5,000 families in the trading area will buy from 25% to 75% of their food in Cameron Village, contributing $3,411,000 more to the general prosperity. Customers coming from outside the immediate trading area may be expected to spend $590,000 in the center's food stores and restaurant, to round out a total of $7 million. $1 million of this total would be spent in the restaurant, $6 million in groceries and meat markets. These sales should double by 1960 with the anticipated doubling of population in the trading area.

To cope with this demand for food there should be at least four groceries and meat markets: two self-service supermarkets, two groceries with delivery service. Two or more restaurants would have gross annual sales of $1 million (average of 4,000 meals daily), and this volume could be expected to double by 1960.

Sears, Roebuck, drawing upon the $40 million of wages and salaries in the immediate Cameron Village area, in addition to the spending of those coming to town from the rich tobacco belt to the east, should have an initial sales volume of $5 million. This would be doubled by 1960.

Filling Stations. Over 1 million gallons of gasoline should be sold each year. Together with services and sale of accessories, this should represent total annual sales of $500,000, enough to support two or three filling stations.

Apparel. The average family spends 5% of its income on apparel. So the 7,500 families in the Cameron Village area should spend at least $2 million on this item. Moreover, as was noted earlier in describing the present downtown shopping area at Fayetteville Street, Raleigh is already established as the fashion goods center for this part of the state. It is estimated therefore that Cameron Village could support four women's ready-to-wear stores with a total annual sales volume of $2 million. $1 million of this would be spent by local customers, $1 million by those from out of town. Then there would also be opportunity for two menswear stores with an annual sales volume of $1 million. Three-quarters of this would come from the immediate neighborhood, one-quarter from out of town customers.

Shoes. Approximately 90,000 pairs of shoes are bought each year by those living in the Cameron Village area. A single store for men's and women's shoes should have an annual sales volume of at least $500,000.

Stationery and Gifts. Stores of this type in Raleigh had sales of over $3 million in 1947. Two such stores in Cameron Village should easily realize an annual volume of $500,000.

Variety stores, 5 & 10. A single variety store should have an annual sales volume of more than $1 million.

Drug Stores. In communities with purchasing power equal to that of Cameron Village, drug store sales have amounted to more than $50 per head. On this basis the 30,000 residents of Cameron Village would spend $1½ million. So it may be safely estimated that two drug stores will have an annual sales total of $1 million between them.

Jewelry. Since Cameron Village is in the midst of the highest income area of Raleigh, and since Raleigh is already established as the jewelry center for this part of the state, it is not unreasonable to estimate that two jewelry stores, dealing also in silverware and watches, would have sales of $500,000.

Total sales of all stores in Cameron Village, as estimated above, would amount to $20 million in 1950. Actually the 7,500 families in the Cameron Village trade area spend $24 million annually in retail stores, so that these estimates assume that Cameron Village, in spite of its excellent amenities, will corral only 80% of the local trade.

If we also take into account the $6-8 million which this center could expect to draw from outside the immediate trade area, and still hold to our $20 million estimate of total sales, we are assuming that those in the immediate Cameron Village trade area will make only about *half* their purchases in the new stores. This is a very conservative assumption. If, in addition to the stores suggested above, there were a high-grade department store in the new shopping center, it would attract trade from a very much wider area. Such a store would have an annual sales volume of $5 million itself and would also add $5 million to the sales volume of its companion stores.

As the advantages of Cameron Village become more widely known, and if the population doubles, as anticipated, by 1960, sales volume will steadily increase from a total of $20 million in 1950 to $40 million by 1960. If a department store is added the increase will be from $30 million to $60 million by 1960.

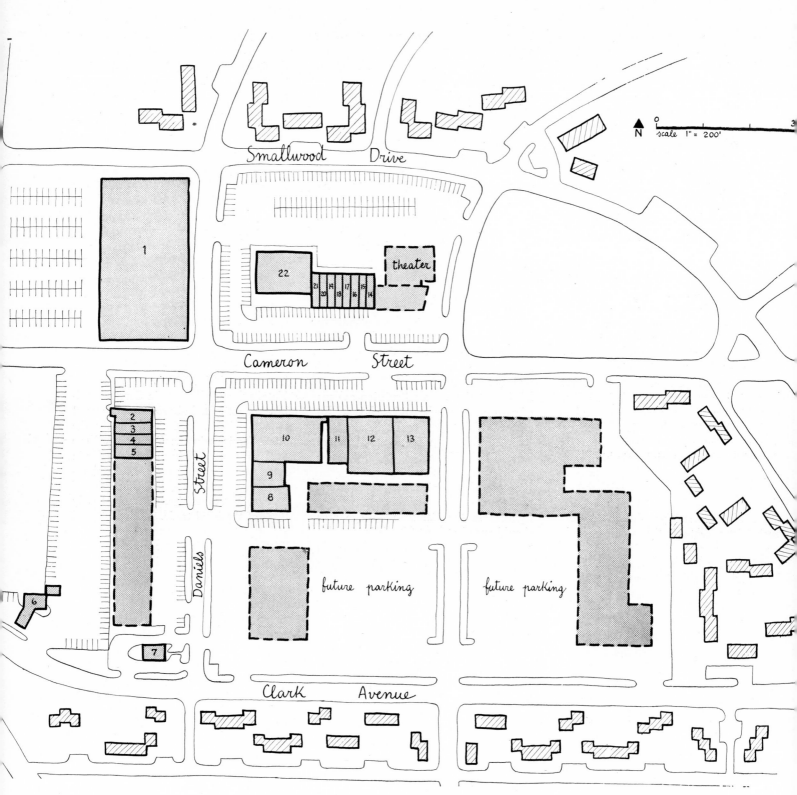

Smallwood Drive

theater

22

21 20 19 18 17 16 15 14

1

Cameron Street

Street

2
3
4
5

10

11 12 13

9

8

6

7

Daniels

future parking

future parking

Clark Avenue

N scale 1" = 200'

ARCHITECT: LEIF VALAND. SITE PLANNER: SEWARD H. MOTT

ADJOINING THE RESTAURANT IS A ROW OF SMALL SERVICE STORES

THE 16,000 SQ. FT. SUPERMARKET HAS A DOMINATING CORNER SITE

	TYPE OF STORE	WIDTH, DEPTH	SQ. FT. AREA
1	Department Store	350 x 200	75,000
2	Drugs	34 x 76	2,540
3	Jewelry	17 x 76	1,290
4	Gifts	17 x 76	1,290
5	Women's Wear	34 x 76	2,540
6	Gas Station		
7	Drive-in Bank	53 x 38	2,080
8	Variety	68 x 100	6,800
9	Children's Wear	34 x 64	2,180
10	Supermarket	103 x 153	15,750
11	Laundry	36 x 100	3,600
12	Furniture	100 x 120	12,000
13	Music	50 x 120	6,000
14	Bakery	17 x 76	1,290
15	Self-Service Laundry	17 x 76	1,290
16	Meat	17 x 76	1,290
17	Seafood	17 x 76	1,290
18	Cleaners	17 x 76	1,290
19	Beauty Shop	17 x 76	1,290
20	Barber	17 x 76	1,290
21	Real Estate	17 x 76	1,290
22	Restaurant	70 x 85	5,950
TOTAL STORE AREA			147,340

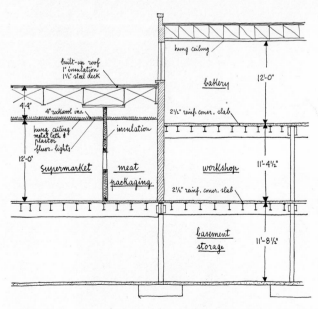

SECTION THROUGH REAR OF SUPERMARKET. PLANS ON PAGE 158

ENCIRCLING CANOPY IS FREE-STANDING IN FRONT OF RESTAURANT, WHICH IS RECESSED BEHIND A SMALL GARDEN

OPEN STORE FRONTS UNDER CANOPY ARE AT THEIR MOST IMPRESSIVE WHEN ILLUMINATED IN THE EVENING

BACKLIT NAME SIGN, NEON TRADEMARK, AND HIGH-LEVEL ILLUMINATION WITHIN MAKE THE SUPERMARKET A NIGHT LANDMARK

FREE-STANDING PLATFORMS IN AISLE FOR BULK PRODUCE

DAY AND NIGHT DISPLAYS
ENLIVEN CAMERON VILLAGE

REFRIGERATED FOR FRESHNESS, MIRROR-BACKED FOR DISPLAY

The standard canopy (13 ft. wide), which runs unbroken along the front of the stores, was originally designed as a cantilever. It turned out to be less striking in appearance, but far less expensive in its present form, supported by thin lally columns at the outer edge (for construction, see section on page 67).

The standard red brick facing of the stores is relieved by sections of Roman brick and Crab Orchard stone, which add considerably to the character and variety of the building front. The landscaping will also contribute much to the charm of this center, once the flowering shrubs and trees have become established.

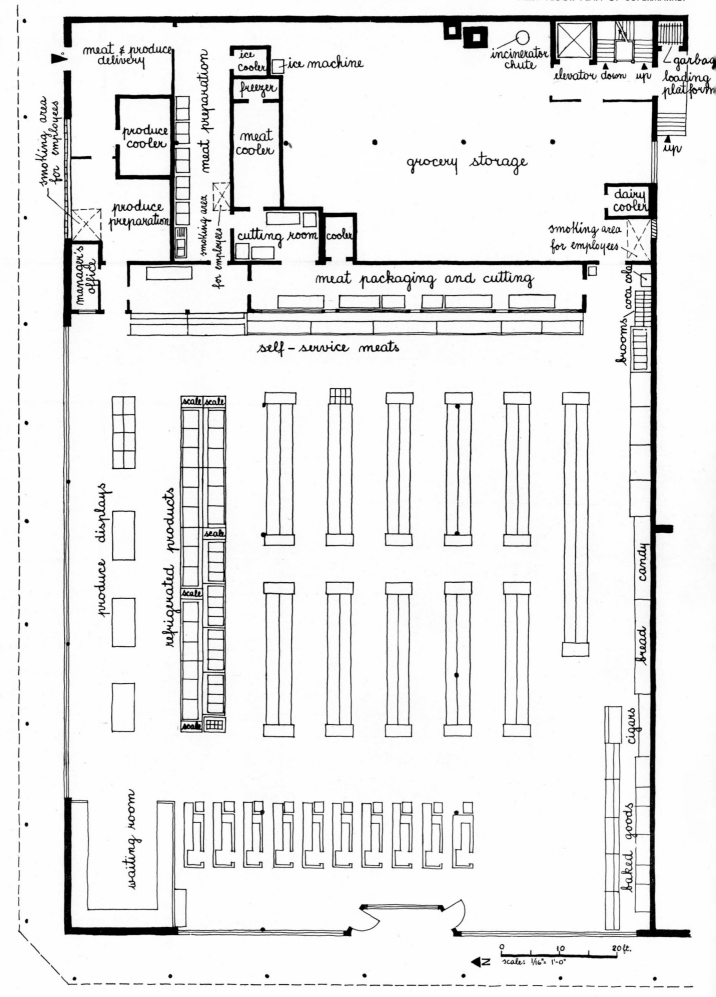

meat & produce delivery

smoking area for employees

meat preparation

ice cooler

ice machine

freezer

produce cooler

meat cooler

grocery storage

incinerator chute

elevator down up

garbage loading platform

up

produce preparation

smoking area for employees

dairy cooler

cutting room cooler

smoking area for employees

manager's office

meat packaging and cutting

brooms coca cola

self-service meats

scale scale

scale

scale

scale

produce displays

refrigerated products

candy

bread

cigars

baked goods

waiting room

N   scale: 1/16" = 1'-0"

0   10   20 ft.

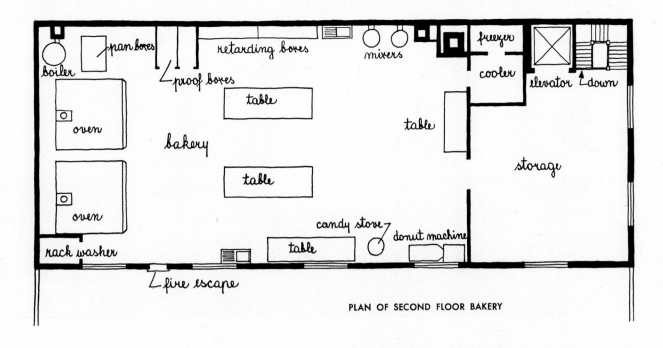

PLAN OF SECOND FLOOR BAKERY

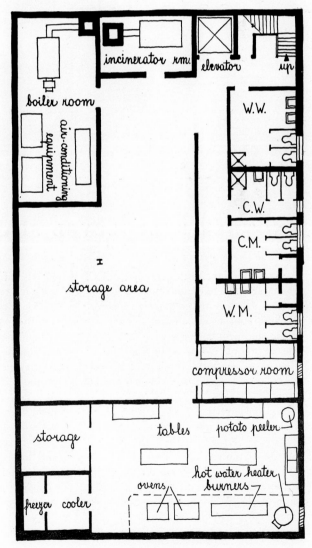

THE SUPERMARKET IN CAMERON VILLAGE, Raleigh, N.C., is one of the most up-to-date units in a chain that is spreading through the South. Typical of the trend in supermarket design, even the meat department here is self-service. The bakery, on the top floor of the three given over to food preparation and storage, is large enough to serve more than this one unit of the chain. An elevator in the corner by the loading dock moves incoming bulk shipments to whichever level is required, except for meat and vegetables which are unloaded on the north side of the building directly into refrigerated storage. All garbage is removed in a closed container *(see page 54)* or burnt in the basement incinerator.

Architects: William G. Bursnall, in association with Leif Valand.

THE LOWER LEVEL FRONT FACES INTO THE SHOPPING CENTER ON DANIELS STREET
THE ESCALATOR CONNECTING UPPER AND LOWER FLOORS IS IN TOWER AT LEFT

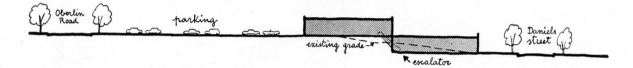

ANOTHER SPLIT-LEVEL SEARS

CAMERON VILLAGE, Raleigh, N.C. The Sears, Roebuck building *(see plan on page 154)*, is on the outside corner of the shopping center. Making good use of the sloping site, Sears have developed one of their favorite split-level plans. This gives ground-level entry to both floors. It also makes for economical construction, because it requires less excavation and leveling.

The large upper-level parking area abuts on Oberlin Road, a main highway leading out of the city. The lower-level section of the store faces into the shopping center. The restaurant is opposite, the supermarket diagonally across the street. On the other corner is a drug store. Sears' stone facing, and the continuous canopy supported on lally columns, are both in keeping with the other buildings.

Sears, Roebuck, having no downtown tradition or investment, were naturally among the first department stores to set up outside the downtown shopping area. After some experience of being entirely on their own, Sears have recently tended to settle in a more controlled environment such as a shopping center. In this case they own the land upon which their store is set, as well as the store itself; and they came into Cameron Village only on the condition that the promoters had signed up eight other specified and complementary merchants *(see page 148)*.

Architects: Shutze & Armistead.

DEPT. STORES GO SUBURBAN — BY STAGES

Stores follow the customer. The customer has moved to the suburbs and prefers to go shopping by automobile. The city department store can expand neither its building nor its parking facilities downtown, except at unwarranted expense. In the suburbs land is still comparatively cheap, and taxes are lower than in town. Department store owners are often prone to hedge. Once a single department store has moved to the suburbs, others must almost inevitably follow. We are now in the evolutionary stage. Newly-created shopping centers are still growing, new ones are being planned and built. The pattern is still not fixed.

In the suburban areas of smaller cities, where shoppers are accustomed to find only one or two major department stores, even in the downtown area, a single branch in a suburban shopping center (when supported by a comprehensive group of other fashion stores) may succeed. But in the suburbs of a city like New York or Chicago, the time may have arrived when suburban housewives will no longer be content with a single department store branch, but will demand comparison shopping in at least two, and possibly more, in the same center.

The success of any suburban branch store will always depend, to some extent at least, on its ability to give a deep selection in a few lines rather than token stocks in many; also on the store management's ability to win the goodwill of the community. The latter becomes especially important in the small suburban town jealous of its individuality.

Stage 1   **Macy's White Plains** shows the New York dept. store invading a suburban Main Street.

Stage 2   **Macy's Jamaica** is just off Main Street; has a token amount of parking on the roof.

SERVICE ROAD, HANDSOME LANDSCAPING,
BETWEEN HIGHWAY AND STORES

B. Altman & Co.

Munsey Park

B. ALTMAN HAS GROUND LEVEL ENTRY TO BOTH FLOORS
FROM REAR PARKING AREA

MUNSEY PARK'S 30-YEAR-OLD NEIGHBORHOOD
CENTER, COLONIAL STYLE, FRONT PARKING

DEPT. STORES GO SUBURBAN. Stage 3

THE MIRACLE MILE, Manhasset, Long Island, N. Y., is developer Sol Atlas' ambitious title for this section of the North Hempstead Turnpike. Here a group of New York department stores, and a number of other apparel, furniture, and convenience goods stores, have set up shop in what may be the automobile equivalent of a developing Main Street, strung out horizontally far beyond the historic limits of pedestrian shopping. This is a motorist's Main Street; yet none of these stores except Lord & Taylor's at one end (one of the earliest arrivals), and B. Altman's at the other, have allowed sufficient parking space. In almost every case the stores are set directly on the street, possibly due in large measure to the tradi-

Black, Starr & Gorham

Best & Co.

Peck & Peck

W. & J. Sloane

James McCutcheon & Co.

Lord & Taylor

Louis Sherry

Lane Bryant, inc.

ONE OF THE FIRST ARRIVALS. DESIGNED
TO FIT A RESIDENTIAL NEIGHBORHOOD

tional thinking of most store owners.
As a result of lining the buildings up
along the sidewalk, most stores have rear
parking. Where there is a general insufficiency of parking, as here, this may
help to prevent pirating.

THIS STREET FRONT
AT NIGHT IS LIT
BY FLOODLIGHTS
SET BETWEEN THE FLOWER BOXES

DEPT. STORES GO SUBURBAN. Stage 4

BULLOCK'S-PASADENA, Calif. has escaped from the Main Street pattern entirely, established itself on an independent block among residences and schools. Such an innovation is well suited, of course, to Los Angeles, where there is an average of one car per family, and shopping districts are seldom within walking distance. The street front here is completely without importance. The tall windows are curtained against the sun glare like those of a private house, and this pedestrian entrance is a mere side door. Automobile shoppers, on the other hand, having parked their cars among luxuriant flower beds, are welcomed by a large and shady portico, furnished with comfortable chairs. Here there are a few small display boxes, but the main display remains the building itself and its landscaping.

Architects: Walter Wurdeman, Welton Becket.

A WIDE AND SHADY ENTRANCE PORTICO, FURNISHED WITH EASY CHAIRS, OPENS ON TO THE UPPER PARKING AREA

AIR VIEW OF BULLOCK'S-PASADENA. FOR DETAILED PLAN OF PARKING LAYOUT SEE PAGE 46

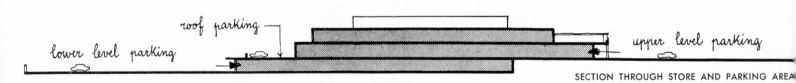

lower level parking   *roof parking*   *upper level parking*

SECTION THROUGH STORE AND PARKING AREA

DEPT. STORES GO SUBURBAN. Stage 4 (continued)

LORD & TAYLOR'S WESTCHESTER STORE, *DESIGNED BY RAYMOND LOEWY ASSOCIATES*

THE SPLIT-LEVEL STORE has become an established cliché of the suburban department store. The shopper can drive in and park right outside the entrance of the floor she wants to visit. Even in a store with two or three floors, she may never have to go up or down stairs. Every floor is a first floor; each has its own parking area right outside. Customers are brought into the store from a number of different directions. And a few cases *(see Bullock's-Pasadena, opposite page)* on a sloping site some added roof parking may be gained without costly and space-wasting ramps. And in big expanses of barren parking can be split up into smaller and more attractive units, at varying levels, with landscaped banks between the parking fields.

Originally split-level stores were evolved to make economical use of sloping sites. Now they have become so popular that even flat sites are being made hilly in order to accommodate them (e.g. Northgate, Seattle, Wash.; *see page 214).*

DISPLAY PAVILIONS PROJECT ALONG THE SEPULVEDA BOULEVARD FRONT

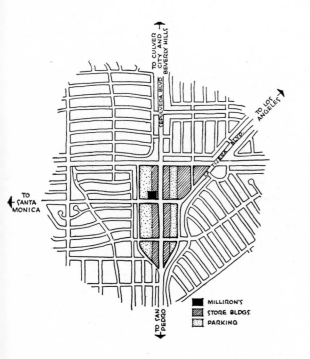

MILLIRON'S
STORE BLDGS.
PARKING

DEPT. STORES GO SUBURBAN

MILLIRON'S, Westchester, Los Angeles, Calif., is the case of a department store which moved into a shopping center already somewhat rigidly planned in a city gridiron pattern. This group of stores is in a 72-acre shopping center at the heart of a suburban residential development southwest of Los Angeles.

In the middle of this store group, at the intersection of two main highways, Sepulveda Boulevard and La Tijera Boulevard, is Milliron's. Their lease

originally called for a three-story building; but the architects were persuaded that a single-story one would be more efficient. They claimed that a single-story building would have certain economic advantages, notably the elimination of expensive elevators and their accompanying operators. They also felt that a store all on one floor would require fewer supervisors.

The layout of this Westchester shopping center is planned for lots 500 ft. deep.

Stage 5

150 ft. of this is used for building, the remaining 350 ft. at the rear for parking. To provide the selling space which Milliron's needed, a single-story building would have had to be 300 ft. square; so it would cover much of the established parking area at the rear. However, the architects pointed out that if the roof were to be reinforced, at a cost of $10,000, and if two 20 ft. wide ramps were built, at a cost of $40,000, the roof area could then be used for parking 220 cars.

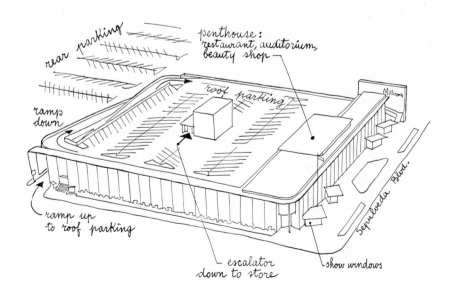

rear parking

penthouse:
restaurant, auditorium,
beauty shop

roof parking

ramps down

ramp up to roof parking

escalator down to store

show windows

Sepulveda Blvd.

Milliron's

DEPARTMENTS RADIATE IN COLORED QUADRANTS FROM CENTRAL ESCALATOR LEADING TO ROOF

Not only would this offset the loss of ground parking space, but it would be a positive economy when compared with the $300,000 it would cost to install elevators in a multi-storied building.

At present the ground level parking directly behind the store is supplemented by an area allotted to the use of a proposed new store block to the north. If and when that block is built, it seems probable that Milliron's total parking space will be insufficient.

The change in circulation patterns produced by this roof parking (see page 48) has had a profound influence on the layout of the store itself. There are now three principal entrances; one from Sepulveda Boulevard, one from the rear parking area, and one from the roof parking area.

The architects believe (and experience so far seems to prove them right) that a majority of customers will prefer to park on the roof, and then enter the store down the central escalator. Consequently, the departments have been laid out as the quadrants of a circle, with the escalator as its center. Each department has been designated by a color. There is the Rose Store (containing women's apparel), the Green Store (for men's, boy's, and children's wear), the Blue Store (with furniture and household appliances), and the Yellow Store (containing household goods).

Separating these quadrants are enclosed, two-story spaces for offices, fitting rooms, stock rooms, etc. Mechanical equipment is also hidden in these separators. The result of this unconventional planning is that the net selling area totals 66.5% of the gross floor area. This compares most favorably with the 50% that up to now has been considered normal.

Opening on to the roof is a penthouse story containing a restaurant, an auditorium (widely used by local clubs), and a beauty shop; also a supervised nursery, where customers may check their children while shopping in the store below. This added penthouse is valuable also in creating an imposing two-story front on Sepulveda Boulevard; and being independent from the main body of the store, it can be kept open in the evenings and on Sunday if required. Pedestrians may reach the penthouse by an outside stairway at the north end of the store.

The main front on Sepulveda Boulevard has been set back 25 ft. from the curb; some of this pavement space is used for planting. Although there are no store windows, in the traditional sense of the word, there are four display pavilions spaced out at regular intervals along this front. They project at an angle to the street line, for better visibility by both pedestrians and motorists. In the center there is a wide, glass-fronted entrance through which passers-by can see into the very heart of the store.

Storage space is concentrated along the west side of the building, in the basement, on the first floor, and on a mezzanine. A freight elevator connects with a loading dock at the northwest corner.

Architects: Gruen and Krummeck.

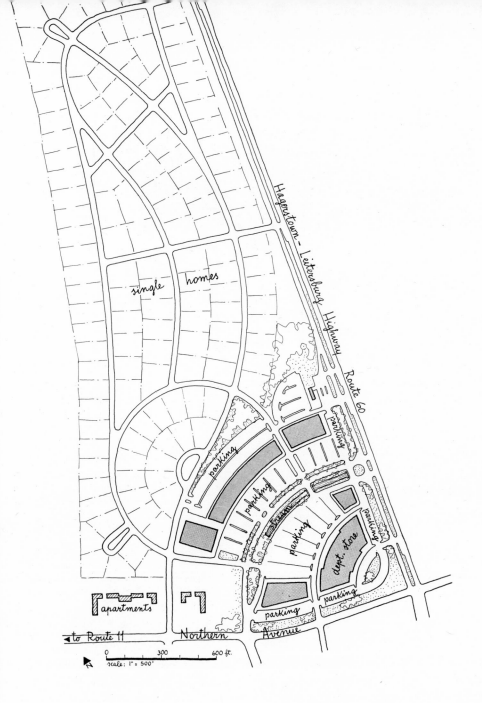

single homes

Hagerstown - Leitersburg Highway Route 60

parking

parking

parking

parking

dept. store

parking

parking

parking

parking

apartments

to Route 11   Northern   Avenue

0   300   600 ft.
scale: 1" = 500'

CROSSROADS LOCATION FOR DEPT. STORE

LONG MEADOW SHOPPING CENTER. In this tentative plan for a housing development and shopping center on the outskirts of Hagerstown, Md., a branch of Hecht Bros., well-known Washington department store, holds a dominant position at the intersection of two well-travelled roads. That going west connects with Route 11, an important highway running the length of the Appalachians, from Roanoke in the South to Harrisburg in the North. The road leading south becomes one of Hagerstown's main shopping streets.

From the department store at this crossroads the land slopes down to a canalized stream, then rises again to a wide-curving line of stores. Beyond these is a development of one-family houses under the same ownership as the shopping center. Due to the sloping site, the department store has a split-level plan, one-story high in front, two stories high at the rear, facing the main parking area.

The general plan of this center is original and interesting, but it may be questioned whether there is not too wide an area of parking between the department store and the line of stores at the rear. The latter are so far back from the road, and from the traffic generated by the department store, that the cumulative pull of the center will almost inevitably be dissipated. The housing development, including the group of apartment houses, has only 300 families, so that it could not support a neighborhood center if it included a large modern supermarket.

Developer: Antietam Realty Co. *Architect:* M. Duncan. *Landscape Architect:* W. L. Moore.

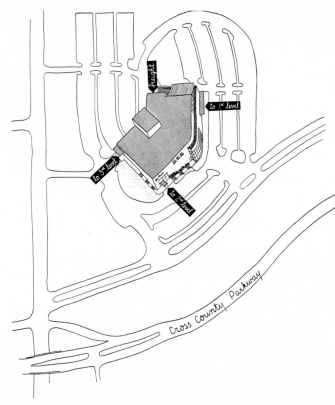

NOT JUST TWO LEVELS, BUT THREE;
EACH A FIRST FLOOR WITH SEPARATE ENTRANCE AND PARKING AREA.
WANAMAKER'S CROSS COUNTY

WHERE THE CITY MEETS THE SUBURBS

CROSS COUNTY CENTER, Yonkers, N. Y., is on the narrow neck of land where Manhattan and the Bronx spread out into the suburbs of Westchester Co. and Connecticut. At the intersection of the Cross County Parkway and Grand Central Avenue (an extension of the Bronx's busy Grand Concourse), it is enmeshed in a net of parkways and expressways. Within a short bus ride are the densely populated areas of the Bronx and Yonkers. Within easy driving distance by parkway are most of the rich New York suburbs. The 60-acre site has been specially rezoned

for business use. This is one of the most potentially successful sites for a shopping center in the New York region.

The birdseye perspective (opposite), shows a tentatively proposed arrangement of buildings on the site. This layout has been dictated in large part by the difficulty and expense of sinking foundations in many parts of this land owing to the spongey subsoil conditions.

Also influential in controlling the design are entrances from Central Park Avenue along the west, Kimball Avenue to the east, and Vredenberg Avenue on the

south. Two roads, connecting these entrances, cut the site into quarters. One, dedicated to the city, with center and curb parking, goes right through the middle of the store group from Central Park Avenue directly up to Wanamaker's department store. A narrow mall, interrupted by a parking area next to the supermarket, parallels this road. Entry direct from the parkway is forbidden.

Developer: Cross Properties Inc., Sol Atlas, Pres. *Architect:* Lathrop Douglass. *Site Engineer:* W. Lee Moore.

WANAMAKER'S DEPARTMENT STORE IS AT TOP LEFT, ON A SEPARATELY OWNED SITE

service tunnel in

service tunnel out

BROADWAY-CRENSHAW SEEN FROM BEYOND THE REAR PARKING AREA. AT LEFT, ACROSS FROM THE BROADWAY, IS THE RIVAL MAY CO. DEPARTMENT STORE

TWO-FRONT STORES, FREIGHT IN TUNNEL

BROADWAY-CRENSHAW, Los Angeles, Calif. In the widespreading development so characteristic of Los Angeles' growth, this shopping center has created a commercial nucleus at the intersection of Crenshaw Boulevard and Santa Barbara Avenue. With a May Co. department store dominating the opposite corner, and a number of smaller stores lined along the boulevard, this is already the major shopping center in this part of the city. The combination of two major department stores, The Broadway and the May Co., provides that element of comparison shopping which is so important in attracting customers, for fashion goods particularly. Unlike some recent suburban centers, which contain only one department store, this store group is in much better position to compete with older-established "downtown" centers which have already been built in other sections of Los Angeles.

Within a 20-minute drive are more than 160,000 families, more than 15% of the total population of Los Angeles County. 40% of these families either own, or are buying, their homes.

The Broadway-Crenshaw center is on a 35-acre corner of the old Sunset Fields golf course (this accounts for such a large parcel of land being available in such a promising commercial area). On the open hills at the rear of the stores new housing for more than 9,000 families is now under construction by the Prudential Insurance Co. and the Crenshaw La Brea Co.

The most striking feature of this center at first glance is the 10-acre parking field, with space for 2,000 cars. This occupies almost one-third of the total site area. Assuming a turnover of 3.5 cars per day (considered typical for a center of this type), the planners estimate that there should be space for 7,000 cars per day. The distance from the outer edge of this parking area to the stores is more than 400 ft., whereas 300 ft. is usually considered to be the allowable maximum. However, the most distant section here is reserved for employees' parking; and in normal times customers can usually find a parking stall not too far from the stores. The more distant stalls are in use only at peak shopping periods. But this condition will worsen when all the stores in the center are completed.

Assuming that the majority of customers would arrive by car, the architects have made the store fronts on the rear (parking) side just as attractive as those on the street front. In other words each store has two entrance fronts. To avoid that confusion between freight and shoppers which normally plagues the two-front store, all freight traffic is confined to a tunnel which runs along beneath the

STORE SIGNS UNDER CANOPY ON STREET FRONT

POINTING THE WAY TO 2,000-CAR REAR PARKING AREA

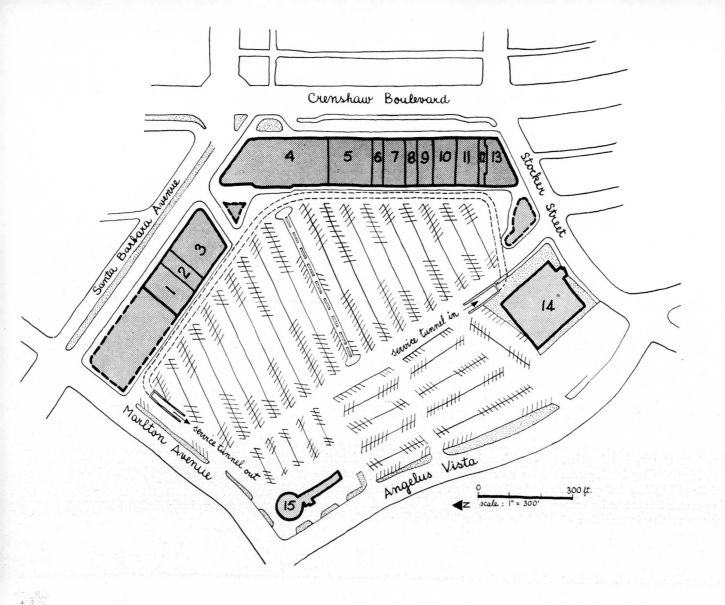

	TYPE OF STORE	WIDTH, DEPTH	SQ. FT. AREA
1	Drugs	75 x 150	11,250
2	Bank	50 x 150	7,500
3	Supermarket	175 x 150	22,000
4	Department	375 x 150	58,000
5	Variety	150 x 150	22,500
6	Children's Wear	35 x 150	5,250
7	Women's Wear	75 x 150	11,200
8	Shoes	40 x 150	6,000
9	Fabrics	55 x 150	8,250
10	Men's Wear	75 x 150	11,250
11	Cafeteria	75 x 150	11,250
12	Women's Accessories	20 x 150	3,500
13	Drugs	40 x 150	9,000
14	Utilities Office	180 x 200	36,000
15	Gas Station		
	TOTAL STORE AREA		222,950

rear service road. All stores have basements with loading docks which open on to this tunnel.

The Broadway department store, as owner and developer of the whole center, occupies the choice corner site.

The store blocks which wing out from this corner have a standard depth of 150 ft., which gives the smaller stores a rather awkward shape. At the far corner of the site, which is least suited for stores, there is a two-story office building for the Pacific Telephone & Telegraph Co.

A wide, continuous overhang extends all round each of the two large store blocks. Store signs for the pedestrian shopper (which includes the dismounted auto-shopper) are hung beneath this canopy at right angles to the store fronts.

Developer: The Broadway Department Store Inc. *Architect:* Albert B. Gardner.

REAR FRONT OF THE BROADWAY DEPT. STORE, OVERLOOKING PARKING AREA, IS IDEAL FOR LARGE ILLUMINATED DISPLAYS (SEE PAGE 73)

ACCESS ROAD SEPARATED FROM CRENSHAW BOULEVARD BY PLANTED STRIP

GAS STATION IN FAR CORNER OF PARKING LOT IS MARKED BY TALL, NEON-LIT PYLON

GAS STATION. In most shopping centers the gas station is placed at some main highway intersection, to catch passing trade. In Broadway-Crenshaw, however, it is set in the far corner of the parking area (in the airview on page 174 it appears in the bottom left corner). Presumably it is hoped to attract those who will live in the housing now being built on this side of the shopping center, in addition to serving customers who park here while shopping.

The circular, glass-walled section of the building contains an office and sales room. The gasoline pumps are set in clumps around the perimeter of this circular section. The wide, cantilevered roof overhang is lit on the underside by concentric lines of white neon. Projecting in a rectangular wing are stalls for servicing, lubrication, car-washing, etc.

Architect: Albert B. Gardner. Wolfe & Thormin, associates.

FREIGHT TUNNEL. All freight traffic in Broadway-Crenshaw is segregated in a one-way tunnel, 20 ft. wide and almost half a mile long, which runs along the rear of the stores. Entrance and exit ramps are on the outside edge of the rear parking area *(see airview, page 174).* Ventilation is by exhaust fans in the middle; they draw in fresh air through the two ends.

All stores have basements opening on to this tunnel, but only the department store and the supermarket have recessed loading docks. Where delivery trucks are docked at the curb, it has been found to cause some congestion. Experience has shown that it might have been better had all the stores been built with loading docks like that in the supermarket shown in the drawing at right.

Steel roller doors close off the loading dock from the storage space. A service elevator takes goods up to the selling floor as needed. There is a bin for trash and garbage in one corner of the dock.

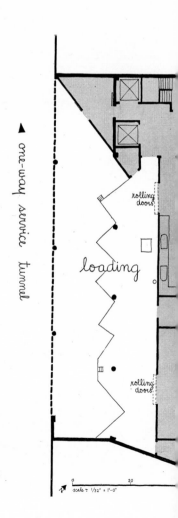

one-way service tunnel

rolling doors

loading

rolling doors

scale : 1/32" = 1'-0"

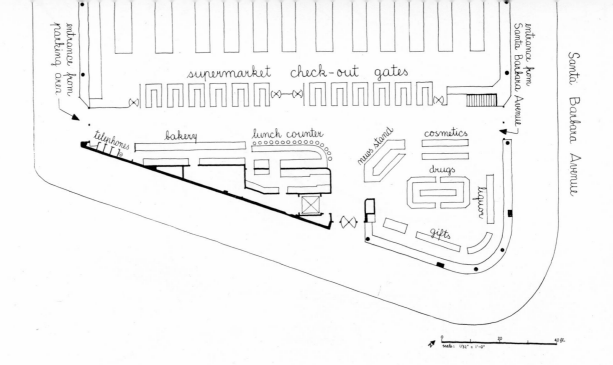

THE SUPERMARKET has been allotted an extremely important position *(see plan on page 176)* near the main highway intersection and at the entrance to the rear parking area. Being at one end of the store block this store could have had display windows on three sides: on Santa Barbara Avenue, on the rear parking area, and on the access road which leads to the parking area. It is surprising to find such an outstanding display position given to a supermarket, which depends so little upon window shoppers and impulse buying.

The plan of the store is one more commonly found in the West than in the East. An important feature is the intensive use of the area outside the line of check-out gates *(see plan above)*. This connects with two entrances, one to the rear parking area and one to Santa Barbara Avenue, so it funnels much of the traffic.

To take advantage of this there are a number of small counters for impulse goods: newspapers, cigarettes, candy, gifts, bakery goods and drug store items. There is also a quick-lunch counter.

These not only attract shoppers emerging from the supermarket with a load of groceries, but also draw in those who have been shopping elsewhere, and who would not come here for one or two small items if they feared having to wait in a queue before passing a check-out gate. The name signs on all these stores *(see picture, left below)* have large letters and are set at right angles to the highway, so they can be easily read by those

driving past at 30 m.p.h. It is particularly startling for conservative Easterners to find the bank sign as high and aggressive as that on Von's supermarket.

Due to the considerable traffic of pedestrian shoppers across Santa Barbara Avenue between the two rival department stores, The Broadway and the May Co., a fence has now been erected in the middle of the roadway, thus forcing pedestrians to cross only at the main intersection where their movements are controlled by traffic lights. This has the incidental benefit to the designer of channeling the customer traffic, and thus making it easier for him to site the various stores to advantage.

Architect: Stiles Clements.

SANTA BARBARA AVENUE FRONT OF SUPERMARKET

SUPERMARKET FRONT ON REAR PARKING AREA

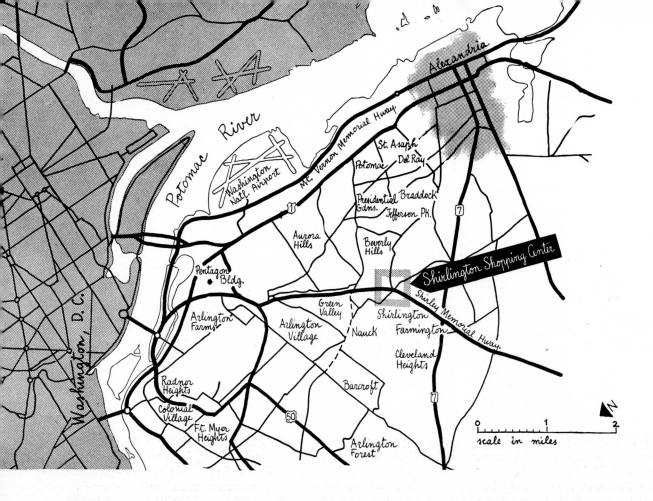

NEW DOWNTOWN FOR WASHINGTON SUBURBS

SHIRLINGTON is among the largest of the shopping centers which, like camp followers, have trailed the boom spread of Washington, D. C. during the last ten years. Across the Potomac River in Virginia the countryside is now peppered with housing developments of all types and sizes. The population of Arlington Co. has increased 114% since 1940. The housing groups are interspersed with store groups, but neither housing nor stores fit into the town pattern which existed before their coming. Instead they are loosely strung together along a few main highways *(see map above)*.

Shirlington Center, pictured on this and the three following pages, is at a main cloverleaf intersection on the Shirley Memorial Highway, a four-lane divided arterial road leading out of Washington into suburban Virginia. Southwest of this intersection is Fairlington, a 10,000-family housing development constructed by the Defense Homes Corporation during World War II. Just across the Shirley

Highway, to the east, is Parkfairfax, a group of apartment houses also erected during the war, by the Metropolitan Life Insurance Co. Here there are 1,684 families, most of them with young children. Economically these families lie in the medium to high income brackets.

The Shirlington business center itself is the brain child of Joseph Cherner. A successful automobile dealer, he found himself during the war with no cars to sell, so turned his energies to the development of this center. When he acquired the 23½-acre site, it was with the idea of developing it as an airport. It was then little more than a swamp, flanked by the county refuse dump. So he first spent $50,000 on a sewer to drain it, then put in 200,000 yards of fill to bring it up to its present level.

The shopping center which was finally developed on this site is closely akin to a section of downtown, but with the streets dead-ended and lots of parking space at the rear of each store block. In addition

there is some diagonal curb parking (mainly in front of the service stores in the northern wing) for the quick in-and-out shopper.

There is the usual difficulty here of rear parking combined with one-front stores. Having parked in the rear, the customer is faced by a line of unattractive service entrances, with the alternative of walking all around the end of the block in order to reach the store fronts. Only the department store has a sign at the rear inviting shoppers to walk through.

Facing down the main central street is the theater, flanked by two-story wings with professional offices on the upper floor. Between the store group and the Shirley Highway is a chain restaurant, a gas station, and the Cherner auto showroom. All of these can hope to draw a profitable trade from motorists passing by along the highway.

Developer: Shirlington Corp. *Architects:* William N. Denton, Joseph A. Parks.

SHIRLINGTON DURING CONSTRUCTION. BEYOND THE SHIRLEY HIGHWAY ARE THE PARKFAIRFAX GARDEN APARTMENTS

LOOKING DOWN THE CENTRAL STREET TOWARD THE THEATER

SHIRLINGTON'S CENTRAL SHOPPING STREET IS 110 FT. WIDE

	TYPE OF STORE	WIDTH, DEPTH	SQ. FT. AREA
1	Beauty Shop	20 x 70	1,400
2	Florist	20 x 70	1,400
3	Children's Shoes	22 x 70	1,540
4	Entrance to Offices above		
5	Photographer	16 x 44	704
6	Ice Cream	18 x 50	900
7	Theater	100 x 130	13,000
8	Gifts	18 x 50	900
9	Radio	16 x 44	704
10	Bank	40 x 80	3,200
11	Restaurant	22 x 70	1,540
	Professional Offices above stores 1 through 11		
12	Liquor	20 x 140	2,800
13	Hardware	40 x 140	5,600
14	Optician	20 x 80	1,600
15	Women's Wear	16 x 80	1,280
16	Notions	20 x 80	1,600
17	Lingerie	10 x 80	800
18	Candy	10 x 80	800
19	Fabrics, Upholstery	20 x 90	1,800
20	Department Store	100 x 140	16,500
21	Men's & Boy's Wear	20 x 125	2,500
22	Children's Wear	20 x 125	2,500
23	Children's Furnishing, Toys	20 x 80	1,600
24	Delicatessen	25 x 100	2,500
25	Bakery	20 x 80	1,600
26	Drugs	50 x 100	5,000

	TYPE OF STORE	WIDTH, DEPTH	SQ. FT. AREA
27	Beauty Shop	19 x 50	950
28	Barber	16 x 50	800
29	Hardware	16 x 50	800
30	Shoe Repair, Cleaners, Laundry	20 x 50	1,000
31	Gifts	20 x 50	1,000
32	Post Office	40 x 70	2,800
33	Cleaners	30 x 100	3,000
34	Auto Showroom		
35	Drive-in Restaurant		
36	Filling Station		
37	Supermarket	60 x 125	7,500
38	Supermarket	50 x 125	6,250
39	Women's & Children's Wear	60 x 120	7,200
40	Millinery	20 x 50	1,000
41	Jewelry	20 x 50	1,000
42	Variety	100 x 100	10,000
43	Women's Wear	25 x 100	2,500
44	Sewing Machines	35 x 100	3,500
45	Women's Wear	35 x 100	3,500
46	Mirrors & Frames	20 x 100	2,000
47	Women's Wear	30 x 100	3,000
48	Men's Wear	22 x 100	2,200
49	Shoes	40 x 100	4,000
50	Loan Office	15 x 30	450

TOTAL STORE AREA		138,218

S. Quincy Street

Mill Drive

Randolph Street

parking

parking

parking

parking

N scale : 1" = 100' 0 — 100 ft

BIRDSEYE VIEW OF SHAKER SQUARE AS ORIGINALLY PLANNED 25 YEARS AGO.
COMPARE THIS WITH PRESENT-DAY PHOTO, OPPOSITE PAGE

AN OLD-ESTABLISHED

SHAKER SQUARE, Cleveland, Ohio, is a shopping center started more than 20 years ago but still expanding. This formalized Colonial grouping was one of the earliest attempts to fit a crossroads store group into a high-class residential neighborhood. Mellowed by the years, its charm has grown, just like its trees.

On the other hand its basic mistakes have become more apparent. The store blocks were split by busy roads. The wide boulevard, with rapid transit tracks in

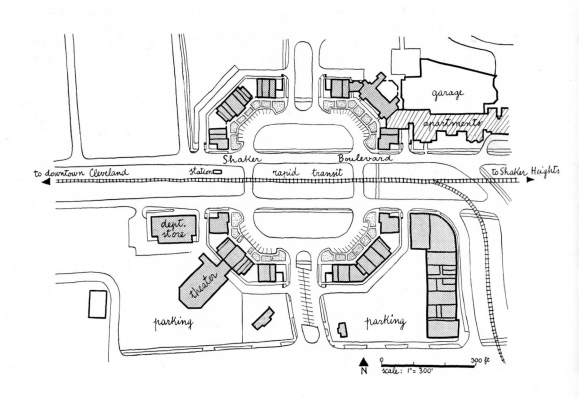

CENTER WITH USEFUL EXPERIENCE

the middle, clove the whole center in two. As a result development has been lopsided, to the south only; and the center of interest has shifted from the original crossroads store group to a block of new, larger stores on the corner of Shaker Blvd. and South Moreland Ave. The space allowed for parking has, of course, turned out to be insufficient. Unfortunately the symmetrical rigidity of the original plan gave no chance for hindsighted correction. Parking at the rear of the stores to the south was gained at the expense of the apartment houses originally planned (cf. birdseye view of original scheme on the opposite page). An even more important mistake was to underestimate the potential size of the center. For if land were available it might grow, as it is ideally placed between the city and the richest suburbs.

Owner & Developer: The Shaker Square Co. *Architect:* Philip L. Small & Assoc.

ONE OF THE ORIGINAL STORE BLOCKS

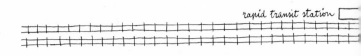

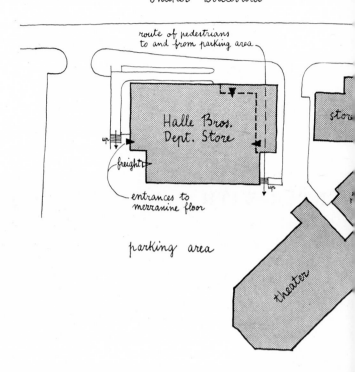

NEW STORE ADDED TO OLD SHOPPING CENTER

THE SHAKER BOULEVARD FRONT. IN FOREGROUND IS ACCESS ROAD TO REAR PARKING

HALLE BROS., famous Cleveland department store, have set their first suburban unit on one of the few remaining pieces of vacant land in the Shaker Square shopping center. Though far from the strict Colonial of the original buildings in this center *(see preceding page)*, the new store does hold to the same materials — red brick and white trim — as specified by the owners.

The parking area to the rear of the store is used by those patronizing the theater and drug store in an adjoining block, and by those commuting to Cleveland via rapid transit, as well as by Halle customers. To funnel all this pedestrian traffic past the Halle show windows, an attractive covered pathway has been laid out along the east end of the store.

As the parking area is at mezzanine level, the freight dock and an alternative shoppers' entrance is also at that level.

Owner: Halle Bros. Co. *Architects:* Conrad, Hays, Simpson & Ruth, and Robert A. Little.

FREIGHT DOCK, SHOPPERS' ENTRY, PARKING, ALL AT MEZZANINE LEVEL

STEPS UP FROM SHAKER BOULEVARD TO REAR
PARKING AREA AT MEZZANINE LEVEL.
AT WEST END OF STORE

TO LURE PEDESTRIANS: SHOW WINDOWS BENEATH OVERHANG AT EAST END OF STORE

	TYPE OF STORE	WIDTH, DEPTH	SQ. FT. AREA
1	Supermarket	200 x 150	30,000
2	Ice Cream	20 x 55	1,100
3	Household Appliances	20 x 55	1,100
4	Self-Service Laundry	20 x 55	1,100
5	Beauty Shop	20 x 55	1,100
6	Curtains	20 x 55	1,100
7	Paints	20 x 55	1,100
8	Floor Coverings	20 x 55	1,100
9	Music Shop	20 x 55	1,100
10	Florist	20 x 55	1,100
11	Cocktail Lounge	20 x 55	1,100
	Business Offices above stores 2-11		
12		20 x 55	1,100
13	Men's Wear	20 x 55	1,100
14	Shoes	20 x 55	1,100
15	Children's Wear	20 x 55	1,100
16	Cleaners	50 x 55	2,750
17	Toys	20 x 55	1,100
18	Shoes	20 x 55	1,100
19	Fabrics	20 x 55	1,100
20	Gifts	20 x 55	1,100
21	Drugs	60 x 115	6,900
22	Women's Wear	20 x 115	2,300
23	Women's Wear	20 x 115	2,300
24	Women's Wear	60 x 115	6,900
25	Women's Wear	20 x 115	2,300
26	Variety	100 x 115	11,500
	Doctors' Offices above stores 21-26		
27	Department Store	88 x 133	21,700
TOTAL STORE AREA			106,350

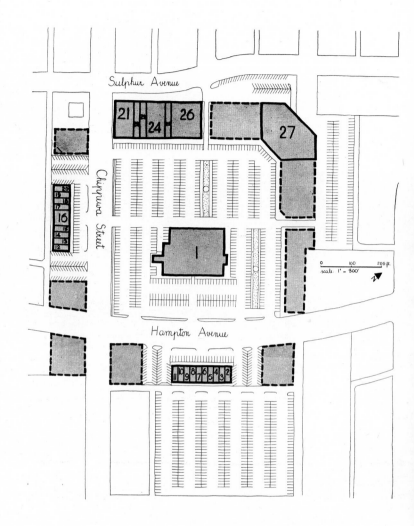

STRADDLING A BUSY HIGHWAY INTERSECTION

HAMPTON VILLAGE, St. Louis, Mo. The late Harry Brinkop started to assemble the land for this center back in 1930. The present 25-acre site straddles a main highway intersection (modern planners consider this of doubtful advantage) on the southwestern edge of the city, in the fastest growing suburbs. Between 1935 and 1940, 92% of the city building permits were issued for construction in this part of the city. Since World War II there has continued to be more building here than in any other section. New apartment houses are now springing up in the surrounding neighborhood and all the established, well-to-do suburbs are within ten minutes driving time along good highways.

Hampton Village at this time has 30 stores and 44 professional offices, but it is still in the early stages of development. After Harry Brinkop's death in 1949 it was bought by an aggressive group of investors, headed by William Zeckendorf of New York's Webb & Knapp, for close to $5,000,000. The new owners have plans for developing the center to handle a gross of more than $50,000,000.

To achieve this they have considered several major improvements. First, double-decking of the central parking area, with pedestrian overpasses crossing the main highways. Second, a new food market, of 50,000 sq. ft. or more, so that Bettendorf's can reach its full potential. (The present store, in the center of the square, is an outstanding puller. It is said to gross almost $5,000,000, and attracts

THE 25-ACRE SITE BEING DEVELOPED. HAMPTON AVENUE CUTS ACROSS PICTURE FROM TOP LEFT TO LOWER RIGHT

STORE BLOCK ON WEST SIDE OF HAMPTON AVENUE HAS TYPICAL "COLONIAL" STYLE, FRONT PARKING

BY UTILIZING LAND SLOPE, SECOND-STORY DOCTORS' OFFICES HAVE REAR ENTRY AT GROUND LEVEL

customers from far beyond the expected Trading Area of a supermarket.) Third, as a site for some major department store, the new owners have considered acquiring (possibly by some exchange agreement) a large plot on Hampton Avenue immediately beyond the southern boundary of the present site.

Hampton Village is at present the largest of several shopping centers dotted through the nearby suburbs of St. Louis. This is an area where shopping interest seems destined to remain somewhat scattered; for both Sears, Roebuck and Famous Barr have started on a program of suburban store building around St. Louis, and each one of their stores may form the nucleus of a new and independent group of smaller shops. It may be difficult for any one of these new store groups to obtain a dominant position, but Hampton Village already has more than a head start.

Owner: Webb & Knapp Inc. & Associates.
Architect: J. Preston Bradshaw.

SKILLED MANAGEMENT MAKES EVERY SQ. FT. PAY

SUBURBAN SQUARE, Ardmore, Pa., was started in 1927. As with many other of the centers started just before the Depression it has reached a full measure of success only after its plan has become outdated. The parking space has, of course, proved insufficient; so later expansion (as far as it was possible) has been in parking space rather than stores.

Cut off on one side by the railroad, and surrounded on the other sides by residential property which has still not deteriorated in character, the center is protected from immediate competition; but also, for the same reason, prevented from expanding as much as potential business at this time might seem to warrant.

On the "other side of the tracks" from Ardmore's Main Street, the center is immediately adjacent to the railroad station, which is heavily patronized by prosperous Main Line commuters on their way to and from Philadelphia. At the heart of Suburban Square, across from the 8-story office building, is a large branch of Strawbridge & Clothier, high-grade, old-established Philadelphia de-

TYPE OF STORE	WIDTH, DEPTH	SQ. FT. AREA
1 Specialty Shop (2 stories)	75 x 120	8,025
2 Telephone Business Office (2 stories)	45 x 80	3,200
3 Home Appliances	65 x 70	2,625
4 Maintenance Workshop	65 x 70	2,912
5 Supermarket	20 x 65	1,300
6 Cleaners	17 x 50	850
7 Toys	60 x 72	3,370
8 Office (Auto Club)	25 x 38	950
9 Department Store (3 stories and basement)	130 x 160	20,360
10 Warehouse	40 x 107	4,455
11 China & Glass	20 x 60	1,100
12 Women's Wear	45 x 60	2,975
13 Books & Stationery	25 x 45	1,125
14 Entrance to 8-story Office Building	60 x 66	
15 Candy	20 x 23	460
16 Men's Wear	60 x 67	3,860
17 Supermarket	47 x 54	2,544
18 Beauty Shop	21 x 41	861
19 Florist	15 x 41	615
20 Linen	15 x 41	615

TYPE OF STORE	WIDTH, DEPTH	SQ. FT. AREA
21 Leather Goods	15 x 41	615
22 Radio	25 x 56	1,400
23 Bakery	13 x 41	533
24 Jewelry	13 x 41	533
25 Millinery	13 x 41	533
26 Optician	13 x 41	533
27 Specialty Shop	35 x 58	2,088
28	33 x 58	1,921
29 Farm Produce	20 x 40	800
30 Theater (800 seats)	124 x 90	10,800
31 Women's & Children's Wear	45 x 55	1,815
32 Photo Supplies	40 x 55	1,660
33 Drugs & Lunch	40 x 55	2,200
34 Floor Coverings	20 x 71	1,420
35 Gifts	20 x 55	1,100
36 Women's Sportswear	20 x 55	1,100
37 Hardware	20 x 55	1,100
38 Mexican Ware	20 x 55	1,100
39 Service Station		
40 Supermarket	70 x 130	9,100
41 Specialty Shop	67 x 40	2,680
42 Shoes	40 x 57	2,920
43 Restaurant	70 x 70	3,450
TOTAL STORE AREA		111,603

partment store. Around these two tall buildings are gathered a great number of smaller specialty stores, so that the fashionable suburban matron can find here a choice of shopping goods almost as wide as that offered in downtown Philadelphia. The small stores are laid out in a grid pattern, with service alleys down the middle of each block, and streets wide enough to allow a line of curb parking on both sides. The supermarket is set off in a separate building, on the edge of the center but adjoining the largest parking area.

Unable to expand, the management have pulled out every trick in the book in order to do more business per sq. ft. Compared with those in other centers (except Sacramento's Town & Country; *see page 100)* the stores are extremely small; yet the sq. ft. gross on this 9-acre site tops that prevailing in almost any other similar fashion goods center.

As all leases are on a percentage basis the management realizes that it has a common interest with the merchant in the promotion of more volume. Sparked by Fred Dreher, the architect who car-

ried this center through its early years of struggle to its present success, the management adopts a paternal attitude toward the tenants. Rival shopping centers have been known to call this pampering. Maybe so; but it is pampering informed by sound business sense and well justified by results.

The merchant, it is argued here, should concentrate upon the job of increasing sales. He should not be worried and distracted by housekeeping chores. So heat and hot water is included in the rent. If the merchant wants summer air-conditioning, he pays just for the power consumed; the management will supply and install the equipment.

In winter the management cleans off the walks after a snowfall, in summer it raises and lowers the awnings in accordance with the weather. A special bureau collects and passes on ideas for more profitable merchandising. In times of labor shortage the management has set up an employment office to help the merchants find reliable help. Co-operative newspaper advertising was organized to save the tenants money. If a new tenant

has energy and business initiative but not much capital the management will help him to get started by providing the fixtures. In order that none of the valuable ground-level selling space shall be wasted on storage, the management supplements the small mezzanines with space in a common warehouse. To prevent sales clerks putting their time to less valuable use than selling, the management provides porter service for handling freight.

To increase the turnover of customers, and thus use the limited parking space to greatest advantage, "reminder tags" are attached to cars which park more than two hours. Employee parking is prohibited within the bounds of the center. This is made a provision of the lease and most strictly enforced, each tenant being compelled to put on record the license numbers of his employees' cars.

About $5,000,000 was the price paid for this center when it was sold in 1950. A large part of this value has been built up by efficient, farsighted management.

Owner: Suburban Square Corp. *Architect:* Frederick W. Dreher & Son.

REGIONAL CENTER FITTED INTO RESIDENTIAL AREA

CLEARVIEW, Princeton, N. J. This is one of the smaller regional centers now in the planning stage. It is designed by the same group of architects and analysts as National Suburban Centers *(see page 199)*, and it resembles those centers in plan, though on a smaller scale.

PLANTED STRIPS AND TREES SOFTEN PARKING AREA

The core of this layout is an open pedestrian mall. This is ringed by stores, and finally a band of parking surrounds the whole complex. As the site slopes from north to south, a split-level department store is planned for the north end of the mall. The upper floor of this store will be at the same level as the big parking area behind, the lower floor will be at ground level for those entering from the central pedestrian mall.

The site also slopes toward Harrison Street on the west. The majority of customers will approach by this highway, so an attempt has been made to open out the store group in this direction. The store blocks on this western side of the mall have been kept lower and more open. The four-story office building has been raised on stilts so that an approaching motorist can look right through into the central mall with its decorative off-center pool (which can double as cooling for the air-conditioning equipment). The two main pullers, the department store and the supermarket, have been set at opposite ends of the mall, to encourage the through flow of customer traffic. Actually the supermarket is, comparatively speaking, cut off from the northern end of the center by the office building on

ARCADE BETWEEN PARKING AND CENTRAL MALL

one side and the bank and post office on the other. The drug store, as might be expected, has been placed on the busy corner next to the office building. A series of roofed arcades, with clerestory lighting, join the parking areas and the central pedestrian mall. Such arcades, with their concentration of traffic, will provide an ideal setting for small shops dependent upon impulse buying.

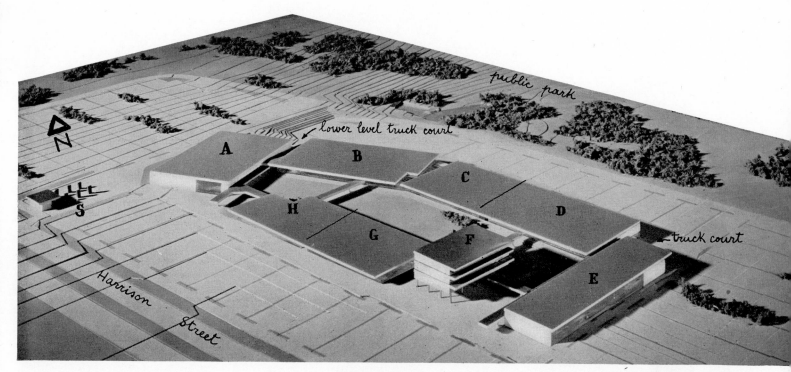

The image contains the following handwritten labels: public park, lower level truck court, N, S, A, B, C, D, E, F, G, H, Harrison Street, truck court

INFORMAL BUILDING GROUP ISOLATED BY PUBLIC PARK FROM SURROUNDING RESIDENCES

The two largest parking areas are at the north and south ends of the store group, close to the department store and the supermarket. The parking area to the east is intended mainly for employee parking; but it can be used for customer parking also, when needed at peak shopping periods. A service road, for freight traffic, borders the line of stores on the outside. At the two outer corners of the store group, where there will be the least conflict with customer traffic, there are loading docks for the supermarket and the department store, which together will account for most of the freight traffic.

The promoters of this new center were faced from the start with opposition from neighboring residents and local Princeton merchants. To placate the neighbors a 9-acre strip, which closes off the center on three sides, was given to the town as a public park. And the architects, with this chain of low buildings irregularly grouped, have made every effort to fit the center into its residential setting.

To placate the nervous merchants, the promoters demonstrated that there would be little overlapping between existing local stores and those proposed for the new center. In addition they claimed that much of the trade now drained off by larger shopping centers such as New York, Philadelphia, Trenton, and the Oranges, would henceforth come to this new center, and thus benefit Princeton. To accommodate this increased business, much of it drawn from outside the town, the promoters suggested widening Harrison Street to avoid congestion.

Developer: Clearview Associates. *Architects:* Ketchum, Giná & Sharp.

KEY LIST OF PROPOSED STORES	SQ. FT.
A. Department Store (2 stories)	60,000
B. Restaurant, Women's and Children's Wear, Men's Wear, Photographer (2 stories)	45,000
C. Home Furnishings and Gifts, Hardware, Electrical Appliances, Radio, Shoe Repair, Cleaners, Tobacconist, (partially 2 stories)	29,000
D. Beauty Shop, Variety, Bank, Post Office	25,000
E. Supermarket, Bakery, Delicatessen	21,200
F. Offices (4 stories)	22,600
G. Drugs, Newsstand, Books & Stationery, Candy, Florist, Photo Supplies, Cosmetics	13,500
H. Lingerie, Shoes, Jewelry, Millinery	11,325
S. Gas Station	

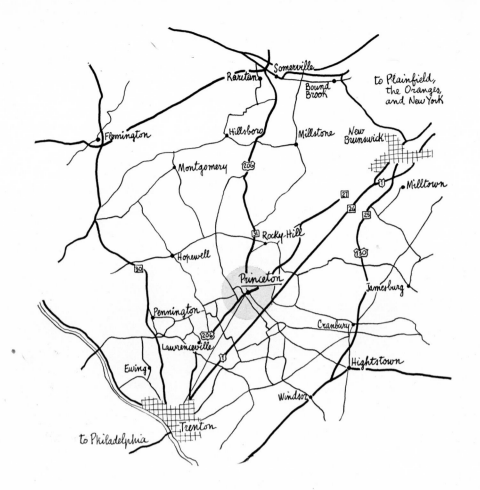

CLEARVIEW'S TRADE GAUGED BY ISOCHRONS

To delimit the Trading Area from which the new Clearview center at Princeton *(shown on the two preceding pages)* might anticipate drawing customers, Kenneth C. Welch, who prepared this market analysis, has used the time-distance method. Only the area lying within 30 minutes driving time of the center is taken into consideration. Its geographical limits are plotted on the ingeniously scaled map reproduced opposite.

How many minutes driving time is needed to reach the center? On the main highways where a high average driving speed is normal and safe, the minute dots are far apart. In the congested outskirts of a town, or on a winding narrow road, they draw closer together.

So it becomes dramatically clear that Montgomery township, for example, is 7½ miles from the new center, but only 13 minutes in time-distance. West Windsor township, on the other hand, though 1½ miles nearer, is 3 minutes further away in time-distance.

The glib concentric circles of earlier commercial surveys have been outdated by the special influence of the automobile shopper. Plotting the isochrons gives a succession of amoeba-like shapes which are both more complex and more accurate patterns of the time-distance areas.

Having established the boundaries of the Trading Area, the next step is to estimate how many of the potential shopping dollars within that area will be spent at the new Clearview center.

First consideration is given to the two basic items, food and clothing. All other retail expenditures will be considered as a proportion of these. Each locality (delimited according to the available census data of population and income), listed in order according to its time-distance from the new center, has its population classified by income into five groups. The "very low" group has an average annual income of only $769, the "low" group $2,000, the "medium" group $5,500, the "high" over $10,000, and the "very high" probably over $20,000, for this last group includes less than 3% of the total number of families classified. As an example of this classification, con-

sider Plainsboro township, 11 minutes driving time from the new center. Out of its 300 families, 155 are classified as "very low" income, 61 as "low", 50 as "medium", 21 as "high", and 3 as "very high".

Taking the average annual expenditures for food and clothing which are typical of each income group (these figures are available in Department of Commerce statistics), and then multiplying these by the number of families in the corresponding income group, it is easy enough to calculate the total expenditure for food and clothing by each income group either for the Trade Area as a whole, or locality by locality.

Thus, if we again take Plainsboro township for example, the 50 medium-income families there will each spend an average of $800 each year on clothing, an average of $1,450 on food. The total expenditure of all the medium-income families living in this particular locality will therefore be $40,000 for clothing and $72,500 for food.

However, the new Clearview center at Princeton cannot expect to capture more than a small fraction of such calculated totals. Various discounts must be applied. And so drastic are these that it is assumed in the final count that, of the total expenditure for food and clothing by all income groups in the Trading Area, only 2.7% in the case of clothing, and no more than 0.44% in the case of food will be spent at the new center.

The first discount is to disregard all expenditures by those families in the "very low" income group. This immediately eliminates entirely more than half the total population of the Trading Area. Next, graduated discounts are made according to time-distance. These vary from 12% for the 5-minute zone, through 46% for the 20-minute zone, up to 90% for those on the very edge of the Trading Area in the 29-minute zone.

The third discount is predicated on existing local shopping habits and facilities. It takes into account competition from local stores and from the large retail centers such as Philadelphia and New York. In fixing the amount of such discounts the economic analyst must rely upon an extensive knowledge of local conditions, which he can then measure against past experience in other areas.

In Princeton itself, for example, there are no good clothing stores, so that in that locality a discount of only 45% is applied to the total expenditure on clothing. In New Brunswick, on the other hand, there are a number of good apparel stores, so the analyst applies a 95% discount there. As the influence of such a complete shopping district spreads beyond its immediate boundaries, a high discount (80%) is also applied to the clothing expenditure of a locality such as Millstown. For those living in that area can reach New Brunswick more easily than they can reach the new Clearview center at Princeton. In Cranberry, on the other hand, this relative accessibility is exactly reversed, so a discount of only 60% is applied.

The discounts applied to food expenditures are invariably higher than those applied to clothing, because in almost every locality there already exist satisfactory food stores.

After applying all these various discounts the survey arrives at a net total of $3,060,000 for clothing and $2,190,800 for food, as sales to be anticipated at the new center. The volume of all other sales is figured as a proportion of the food and clothing sales. In the "Shopping Goods" category, General Merchandise, Apparel, and Furniture-Household-Radio (abbreviated to a category heading of GAF) are most significant in these calculations. Their principal outlet will be the department store.

In a regional center of this size the department store should have gross sales of $3,500,000. Experience shows that half of this business will be in clothing. The rest of the anticipated clothing sales —$1,310,000—will be absorbed by the smaller apparel stores. The other half of the department store sales—$1,750,000—will be in home furnishings and small wares. The remaining $250,000 in home furnishings will be spread over the other variety and GAF stores in the center. Total sales for the complete GAF group are estimated at $5,060,000.

Translating these various sales figures into store areas, the department store should have 60,000 sq. ft., assuming the well-tested figure of $58 per sq. ft. for gross sales in a store of this type. Smaller apparel stores need 37,810 sq. ft. to average the required $41 per sq. ft.

In order to create a balanced group of stores in the center for maximum convenience and therefore the maximum cumulative pull, tentative sales estimates in other store classifications have been patterned on the proportions shown by figures of New Jersey State sales. As these, like the GAF sales figures, had to be taken from the 1939 retail census, they have been increased (on the authority of Standard Rate and Data Service figures) to correspond with the realities of 1948.

If GAF sales in New Jersey are taken as 100, then the ratio for Drug Stores in the State is 14, for Restaurants and Bars it is 44, and for "Other Stores" (excluding Feed, Fuel and Office Supply stores) it is 20.6. This last category includes such stores as Jewelry, Florists, Optical, Camera, Luggage, Stationery, etc.

Applying these ratios to the previously determined GAF sales total of $5,060,000, we can forecast Drug Store sales of $710,000. Assuming gross sales of $40 per sq. ft. 18,000 sq. ft. of store area should be allotted to this use.

"Other Stores" with potential sales of $1,040,000, and business at the rate of $55 per sq. ft., would require an allocation of 18,900 sq. ft. of store area.

Restaurants and Bars, at the ratio of 44 to 100 GAF, should anticipate $2,220,000 in sales. However, since Princeton has more than its normal share of restaurants (because of the University), it is suggested that this figure of anticipated sales be cut in half. Assuming that part of these sales would be in a high-grade restaurant requiring comparatively large service areas, and partly in a cafeteria, an average gross of $40 per sq. ft. is used. The allocation for restaurants and bars is then 27,750 sq. ft.

For food sales at Clearview (in all types of store: supermarket, grocery, bakery, meat, candy, etc.) the survey had already arrived at a sales figure of $2,190,800, after all discounts had been made. Assuming gross sales of $100 per sq. ft.,

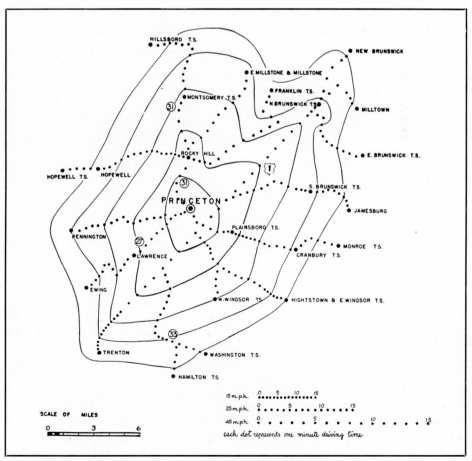

AMOEBA-SHAPED ISOCHRONS ARE THE CONTOUR LINES OF DRIVING TIME

this can be translated into 21,908 sq. ft. of store space required.

One further allocation of space is made to complete a balanced center: 20,657 sq. ft. for service stores, such as dry cleaning, laundry, barber, beauty shop, banks, post office, etc.

It is perhaps interesting to note that the total sales of slightly over $10,000,000, which this survey calculates the new center should be capable of drawing, represent only 2.7% of the present sales within the Trading Area set by the 30-minute isochron. This appears to be a conservative estimate indeed, and could easily represent no more than the needs of the anticipated population increase in this area. Such a future population increase has not been taken into account in this survey. It is also emphasized throughout that all store allocations are intended as a general framework only, and as a guide in the selection of proper tenants. It is realized that the latter would want to make more intensive studies of their own before signing a lease.

The survey does not consider allocation of space in the proposed office building, for this bears no relation to the retail sales figures being reviewed here.

CLASSIFICATION OF BUILDING	$ SALES	$ SALES PER GROSS SQ. FT.	GROSS AREA (SQ. FT.)
Department Store	3,500,000	58	60,000
Variety, Apparel and Home Furnishing Stores	1,560,000	41	37,810
Total General Merchandise, Apparel, and Home Furnishings (GAF)	5,060,000		97,810
Miscellaneous Stores (Dept. of Commerce "Other Stores", except Feed and Office Equipment): Jewelry, Stationery, Florists, Optical, Camera, Luggage, Etc.	1,040,000	55	18,900
Drug Stores	710,000	40	18,000
Restaurants, Cafeterias, Bars	1,110,000	40	27,750
Food Stores (Supermarket, Grocery, Meat, Bakery, Candy, Etc.)	2,190,800	100	21,908
Total Retail Stores	10,110,800		184,368
Services: Dry Cleaning, Laundry, Barber Shop, Beauty Parlor, Bank, Post Office			20,657
Total Store Area required			205,025
Approximate ground coverage for structures (second floor and basement 60,000 sq. ft. excluded)			151,500
Parking Spaces — 1,850 for customers — including access roads			809,000
Estimate for mall, landscaping, extra parking for employees, etc.			257,500
Total Ground Area (28 acres)			1,218,000

ANOTHER AND LARGER VERSION OF THE CENTRAL MALL SCHEME

MIDDLESEX CENTER, Framingham, Mass., is one of a chain of large regional shopping centers proposed by Suburban Centers Trust, and the first upon which construction has actually been started. Its design is by the architects of the Princeton center shown on the preceding pages, and the two are closely similar; but this center is double the size.

The site, on the heavily-traveled Worcester Turnpike about 15 miles out of Boston, has a comparatively narrow frontage. This will be dominated by

Jordan Marsh's circular department store, with four selling floors. Stretching back from this, at right angles to the highway, is a long, formally landscaped pedestrian mall surrounded by stores, which in turn are surrounded by an extensive belt of parking.

The store buildings are either 125 ft. or 85 ft. deep, except for a few shallower stores in front of the theater. A tentative directory lists a total of 45 stores, occupying 500,000 sq. ft. This includes a second department store at the opposite end

of the group to Jordan Marsh. There would be at least one supermarket, in the center of the store block.

The central mall is 8 ft. below the level of the parking areas. Both long store blocks are two stories high, and the shopper coming from her car may go up a ramp 4 ft. to the upper level stores, or down a ramp 8 ft. to the stores at mall level (see section at right). Freight loading docks, 4 ft. above roadway level, are on the parking side of the upper level stores, between the pedestrian arcades

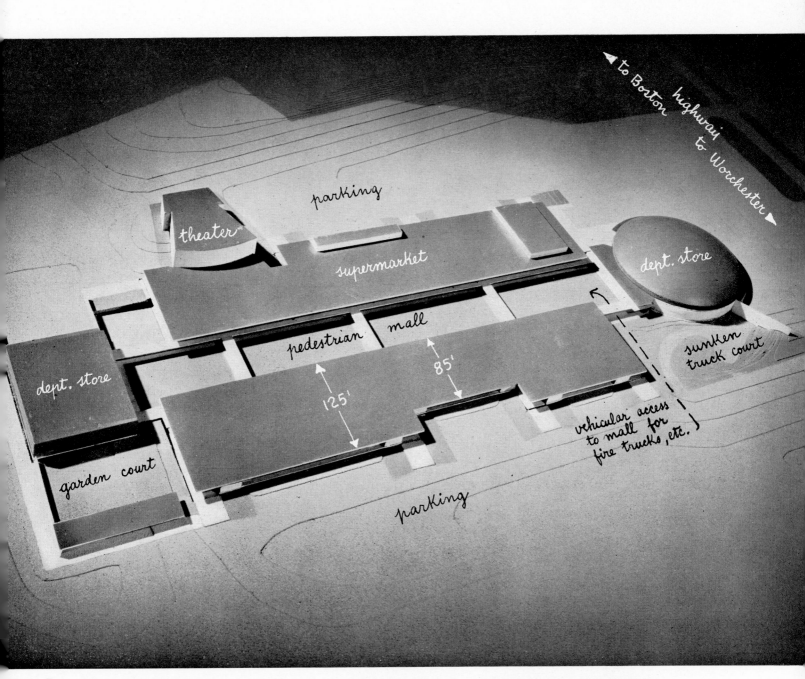

Labels within image:
parking
theater
supermarket
pedestrian mall
dept. store
garden court
parking
85'
125'
vehicular access to mall for fire trucks, etc.
dept. store
sunken truck court
to Boston highway to Worcester

IN MIDDLESEX CENTER STORES FRONT ON THE CENTRAL PEDESTRIAN MALL, SHELTERED FROM TRAFFIC AND NOISE

which pierce the store blocks at regular intervals. Freight elevators connect these docks with the lower level stores. All stores front on the pedestrian mall, which is crossed by several covered walkways, protecting shoppers from sun and rain.

Owner & Developer: Suburban Centers Trust. *Economic Survey:* Kenneth C. Welch. *Site Plan:* Adams, Howard & Greeley. *Architects:* Ketchum, Gina & Sharp. *Landscape Architects:* Arthur A. & Sydney N. Shurcliff.

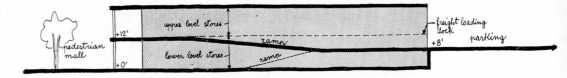

Labels within section image:
pedestrian mall
+12'
upper level stores
+0'
lower level stores
ramp
ramp
freight loading dock
parking
+8'

TEN MILES FROM DOWNTOWN DETROIT, HUDSON'S NEW CENTER
IS NEAR THE RICH LAKESIDE SUBURBS AROUND GROSSE POINTE

DEPARTMENT STORE PROMOTES
120-ACRE CENTER WITH FREIGHT TUNNEL

THE J. L. HUDSON CO. has long been noted in Detroit, Mich., for its conservatism (also for a gross that is reputed to be second only to Macy's in New York). Now, having decided at long last to follow its customers to the suburbs, it seems determined to do it bigger and better than the other stores throughout the U.S. who have long since made this move.

In this new 100-acre center, some 10 miles out from downtown Detroit, Hudson's will gather round its new circular store more than 100 other retail stores, probably including one or two other department stores. Hudson's intention seems to be that this vast new retail store group, which will cost more than $12 million, shall give that full measure of comparison shopping which formerly could be found only in the downtown shopping area.

The compelling reasons for Hudson's move are succinctly put forth in statistics such as the following. About 100,000 automobiles enter downtown Detroit every day; but there are only 15,029 legal parking spaces. Trade is being strangled by this insufficiency. Detroit's population has increased 14% during the last ten years; but in the suburbs the increase has been 45%. Hudson's trade has done better than the population; it has doubled during these ten years. Store executives believe that this new suburban store will cut into the volume of the downtown store, but that the total of Hudson's sales will be increased.

To appreciate the tremendous scale of this new center, it is only necessary to state a few figures. This oval of stores is more than 1300 ft. long and about 500 ft. across. There will be parking space for about 6,000 cars, yet no parking stall will be much more than 300 ft. from the nearest store, for cars are parked inside as well as outside the oval of stores. Unlike the two centers shown on the preceding six pages, there is here no pedestrian mall. All stores have parking front and rear; Hudson's has space for 200 on the roof also.

The tremendous scale of this center and its spreading plan would seem likely to put many stores beyond walking distance for the average shopper. It must be assumed, then, that shoppers will go by car from one store to another within the center. This will, of course, tend to destroy that cumulative pull which formerly was considered to be one of the shopping center's prime advantages, particularly for the small merchant. For the same reason some planners might question Hudson's roof parking (predicated, no doubt, on the success of Milliron's; *see page 169*), on the grounds that it will enable Hudson's customers to drive up a winding ramp to the roof, do all their shopping in the store below, and then drive away without once being exposed to any other store in the center. If this were so, then the other stores would not

be benefiting at all from the traffic generated by this outstanding puller. With such a widely scattered layout of stores the bustling intimacy of pedestrian traffic will have to be carefully encouraged. For this the little island pavilions between the main store blocks should be of help. The uniform arcade, running the length of the oval, on the inside face of the store blocks, could better be abandoned, however, in favor of greater variety in vista, proportion and ornament.

Extremely careful thought has been given to the traffic pattern, both for automobiles and trucks. Wide center islands

and deceleration lanes make it a simple matter for traffic to turn into the center from Eight Mile Road. Within the site all traffic flows clockwise in a unidirectional pattern around and through the store group. Whether shoppers will find this gigantic clover leaf too complex is open to question.

All freight traffic is carried in two tunnels which serve basement loading docks in all the principal stores. Freight and passenger traffic separate where the main entrance roadway dips down beneath a pedestrian bridge at the side of Hudson's. One of the tunnels merges with the road-

way again at the far side of the oval as it passes through the line of stores beneath another pedestrian bridge. The other tunnel, serving the stores in the foreground of the drawing above, emerges on Eight Mile Road. There is a continuous pedestrian walk the whole length of the stores. In addition there are pedestrian overpasses crossing Eight Mile Road *(see page 204)* and the road which bisects the huge parking area within the oval.

Developer: Sub Dev Corp. *Architects:* Gruen & Krummeck.

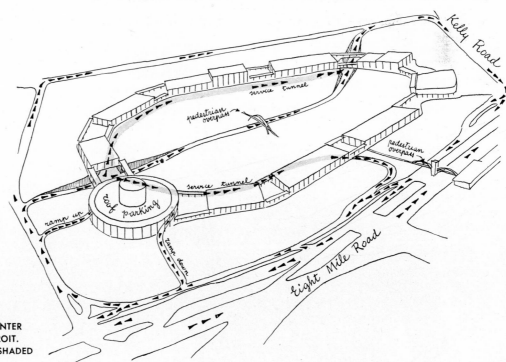

DIAGRAM OF
TRAFFIC CIRCULATION
IN HUDSON'S
VAST NEW SHOPPING CENTER
IN THE SUBURBS OF DETROIT.
THE SERVICE TUNNEL IS SHADED

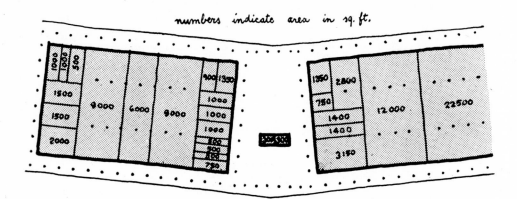

numbers indicate area in sq. ft.

VARIETY IN STORE SIZE in Hudson's new suburban center is achieved by short blocks separated one from the other by open courts with small pavilions. These standard blocks can be divided up into a wide variety of shapes, for there is no back nor front; all freight and service traffic is confined to a tunnel beneath. The small pavilions are valuable on two counts: they help to give a feeling of bustle and intimacy to this vast center, and accommodate those small specialty shops which can do a big volume of business in a very confined space.

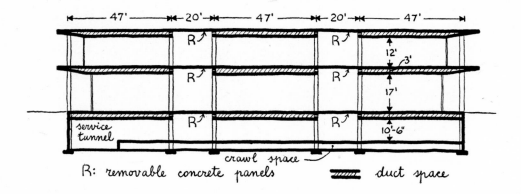

R: removable concrete panels ▦ duct space

THE STORE BUILDINGS, if they follow the architects' suggestions, will be of standard construction, yet still retain an ingenious flexibility. Of reinforced concrete construction, there will be two 20 ft. bays with removable panels, so that vertical connections between floors — stairs, elevators, or escalators — can be easily installed if a tenant wishes. The first-floor height of 17 ft. gives space enough for a mezzanine if required. The 3 ft. space between the two floors will accommodate all duct work.

Freight handling is confined to the service tunnel which connects with the basement of each store. Consequently all four sides of each store building may be selling fronts with large display windows.

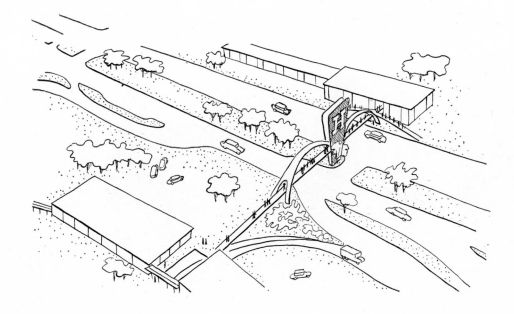

A PEDESTRIAN OVERPASS crosses Eight Mile Road to a proposed bus stop. With its flaring concrete arches and its tall central pylon, this bridge doubles as an impressive signboard, bringing J. L. Hudson's new center to the notice of motorists passing along the highway.

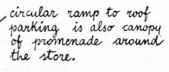

circular ramp to roof parking is also canopy of promenade around the store.

sales area has lower level, mezzanine and upper level connected by escalators.

central core extending through roof contains air conditioning equipment; restaurant, cafeteria and outdoor dining on top.

THE DEPARTMENT STORE, off on its own comparatively cheap land in the suburbs, is no longer hemmed into the stern rectangular shape imposed by downtown city blocks and high land values. It is perhaps significant that, given this new freedom of choice, several department stores have chosen a circular shape. If it is also made windowless, as this one for J. L. Hudson, all stock rooms and freight handling can be kept to the periphery, where two encircling one-way ramps lead to and from the roof parking.

THE CENTRAL TOWER of the J. L. Hudson department store contains all service ducts and air-conditioning equipment. In the section which extends above the roof, in addition to storage space, there is a restaurant and a beauty salon, which may be kept open in the evening and on Sundays when the main store is closed.

TRAFFIC CONTROL. Pedestrian and automobile traffic is kept separate, except where they encroach upon each other in the parking areas. Illustrated at left is the pedestrian overpass by the side of J. L. Hudson's circular store. In the background is that store's roof parking reached by circling ramps. In the foreground is the depressed roadway which carries automobile traffic entering the center. Trucks enter by this same road but are diverted at this point into one of two freight tunnels, which serve the major stores on each side of the oval. All traffic, except pedestrians, circulates in a one-way pattern.

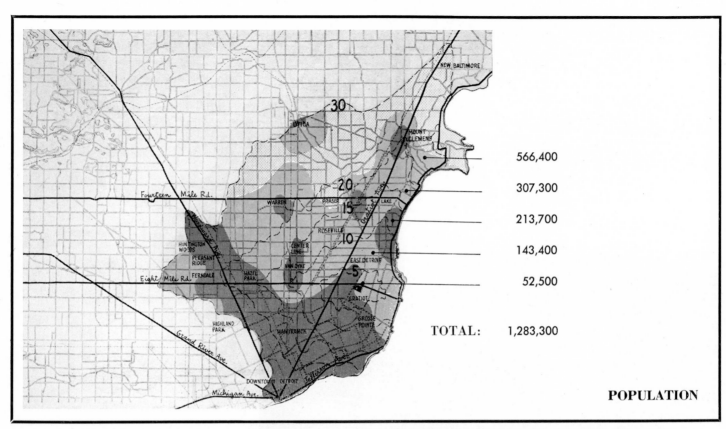

566,400
307,300
213,700
143,400
52,500

TOTAL: 1,283,300

POPULATION

FIGURES SHOW POPULATION IN EACH TIME-DISTANCE BELT. SHADING INDICATES POPULATION DENSITY—THE DARKER THE DENSER

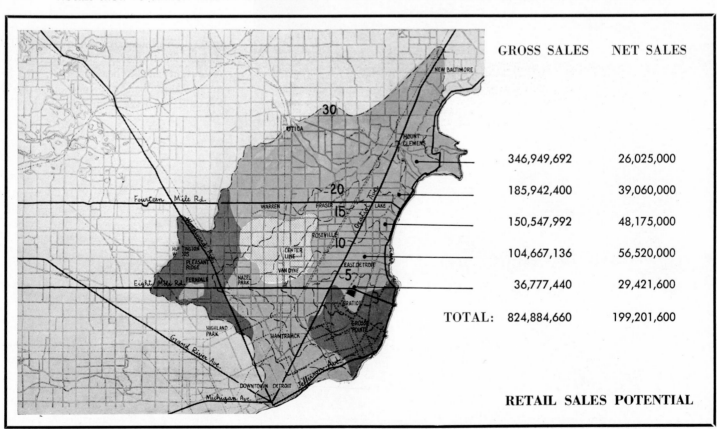

GROSS SALES	NET SALES
346,949,692	26,025,000
185,942,400	39,060,000
150,547,992	48,175,000
104,667,136	56,520,000
36,777,440	29,421,600
TOTAL: 824,884,660	199,201,600

RETAIL SALES POTENTIAL

FIGURES SHOW ANTICIPATED SALES FOR EACH TIME-DISTANCE BELT. SHADING INDICATES INCOME LEVEL — THE DARKER THE HIGHER

PRELIMINARY ECONOMIC SURVEY
FOR HUDSON'S NEW CENTER IN DETROIT SUBURBS

THE J. L. HUDSON CO. is Detroit's most famous department store. Detroiters buy three times as much from Hudson's as they do from any rival merchant. But as the traffic congestion worsened, these Detroiters (many of whom lived in the suburbs and preferred to shop by automobile) found it increasingly wearisome to reach the downtown store. Sears Roebuck, Montgomery Ward, and other smaller stores had already followed their customers to the suburbs. Now at last Hudson's felt it worthwhile to do likewise. Their architects, Gruen & Krummeck, had an economic survey made for the huge shopping center shown on the preceding pages.

LOCATION. The site for the suburban Hudson's had to be more accessible than the downtown store. For outsiders it must be mentioned that the highway pattern in Detroit is laid out like a series of spokes overlaid on the grid pattern of the city and converging in the downtown shopping district. Equally important for local traffic are the east-west roads of the grid. Bypassing the congested downtown streets, these roads connect the main highway spokes with the rich suburban communities along the shore of Lake Michigan.

The site finally selected for this new center is in Gratiot Township, at the intersection of Eight Mile Road and Kelly Road, both 200-ft. wide divided highways. Although not on any of the major highway spokes radiating from the city center, Hudson's new center is on the way downtown for a large number of suburbanites, and easily accessible to an even larger number living to the east and west of the new stores.

As driving-time-distance is considered one of the most important factors in the appeal of any shopping center such as this, the Trading Area was first delimited by a series of isochrons, at 5-minute intervals, up to 30 minutes driving-time-distance from the center.

It will be noticed that the fast-moving traffic on Gratiot Avenue brings Mount Clemens within 20 minutes of the center. Even New Baltimore (29 miles from the center of Detroit) is within 30 minutes. Grosse Pointe, Gratiot, and East Detroit are all within 10 minutes.

POPULATION. The total of 1,283,000 people living within the Trading Area (bounded by the 30-minute isochron) is broken down by time-distance belts. For example, within the 5-minute belt there are 52,500 people. Stretch the boundary line to the 15-minute isochron and the population enclosed is more than 400,000. Add another 5 minutes driving time and the population is 600,000.

There are recent industrial developments within the 15-20-minute belt, and these have created a demand for homes throughout the region. The area immediately surrounding the new center had already started growing fast as a middle-income neighborhood, and this growth is now spreading to the north. The Grosse Pointe area to the south-east has long since become the suburban hometown of Detroit's highest income families.

Population figures used in constructing the maps shown on the opposite page are based on census data, supplemented by data from the *Detroit News* Research Dept., and from the Detroit Regional Planning Commission. Income figures were obtained from the same sources.

SALES POTENTIALS. Income levels within the Trading Area have been graphically demonstrated by shading (the darker the higher). According to estimates made by the National Resources Planning Board, 56% of the average family's income is spent on retail goods of the type which will be available at the new center.

In order to arrive at the gross retail sales potential listed on the map opposite, this 56% has been applied to the gross income figures in each driving-time-distance belt. This rough estimate is combined with other rough calculations to arrive at the net retail sales potential. Research has shown that only 50% of shoppers are willing to drive 30 minutes to reach a complete, one-stop shopping center. 70% will drive 20 minutes, 80% 15 minutes, and 100% 5 minutes, to reach such a center.

Applied to the gross sales potential, in each time-distance belt, these percentages —with considerable reductions made for local competition by other store groups —give a net retail sales potential of approximately $200,000,000.

As a check on this figure the analysts have taken the present sales volume of competing centers: $141,000,000 in the downtown shopping district, $177,700,-000 in other competing shopping areas within the 30-minute Trading Area. Subtracting these from the $825,000,000 gross sales potential, gives a total of $506,000,000. Deducting 65% of this for escape buying, the final total, by this method of calculating net retail sales potential, is $176,000,000. This is not too far from the total of $200,000,000 already arrived at by the first (but equally arbitrary and tentative) method.

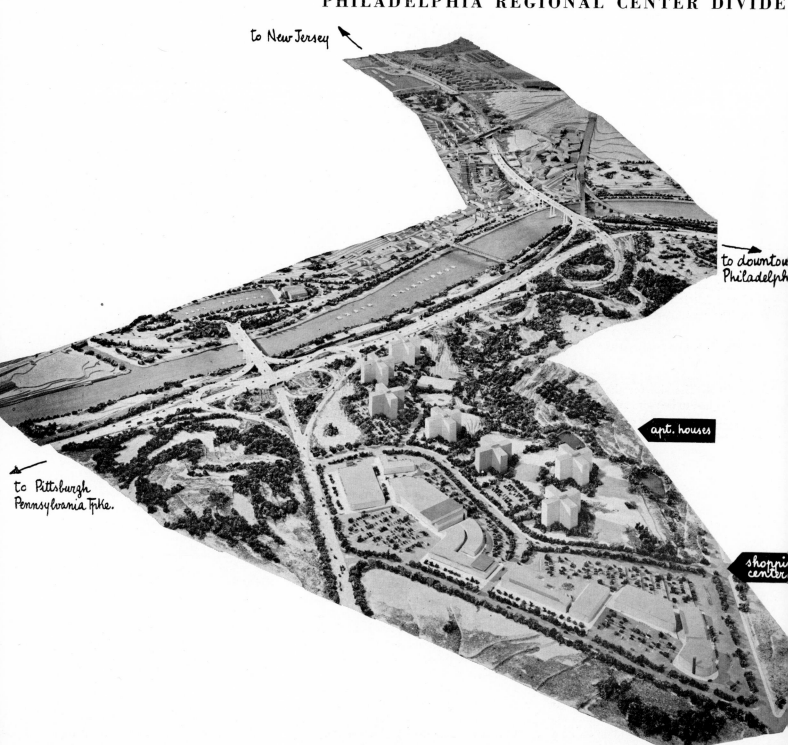

to New Jersey

to downtown
Philadelphia

apt. houses

shopping
center

to Pittsburgh
Pennsylvania Tpke.

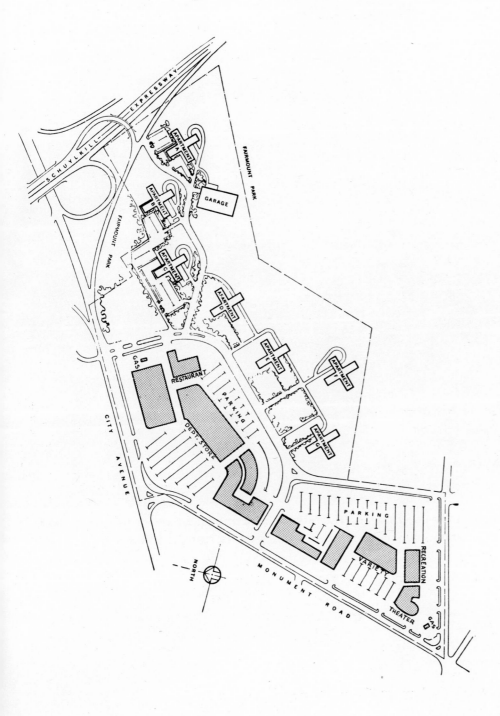

COUNTRY CLUB ESTATES, 15 minutes north of downtown Philadelphia, is near one of the main cloverleaf intersections on the Schuylkill Expressway. Easily accessible from the rich Main Line suburbs and from southern New Jersey, this proposed regional center should certainly attract those women who would otherwise have to brave the traffic congestion of downtown Philadelphia, in order to find a selection of fashion goods. The 90-acre site was formerly a golf course. No other site of comparable size and accessibility is likely to become available in this area, so the Country Club center should be protected from competition.

A five-year development plan envisages the 34 acres near Fairmount Park spotted with seven tall cruciform apartment houses. These eleven-story blocks would house a total of 2,000 families. The remaining 56 acres would be reserved for the shopping center. The Philadelphia Planning Commission has already given the scheme its blessing and supports the zoning changes required.

To give more intimacy, more shopping "excitement", than is generally found in a center of this size, the stores have been divided into two shopping courts. That to the north is dominated by a multi-story department store appealing primarily to the "carriage trade." Flanking this store are a number of specialty shops.

The southern shopping court is dominated by a variety store. Linking the two courts is a block of service stores, and shops carrying less expensive apparel. At the southern extremity of the center is a theater and recreation building. In the middle of the whole development, between the department store and the apartment houses, is a restaurant. This will have a large terrace dining room overlooking the river and the city stretching out in the distance beyond.

Judging by experience in other centers of similar type, the parking space will almost certainly prove to be too small when the store group is complete.

The planning of Country Club Estates was influenced to some extent by a committee of 26 experienced realtors organized by the Urban Land Institute (Seward H. Mott, director).

Owner: Country Club Estates Inc. *Archi*the "carriage trade". Flanking this store

Lake Merced

Metropolitan Life's Parkmerced

S. F. State College

A MODEL OF THE WHOLE STONESTOWN DEVELOPMENT — SHOPPING CENTER AND APARTMENTS—DUBBED INTO AN AIRVIEW OF ITS SURROUNDINGS. AT THE TOP EDGE OF THIS PICTURE IS THE PACIFIC; IMMEDIATELY IN FRONT OF THE SHOPPING CENTER IS 19TH AVENUE

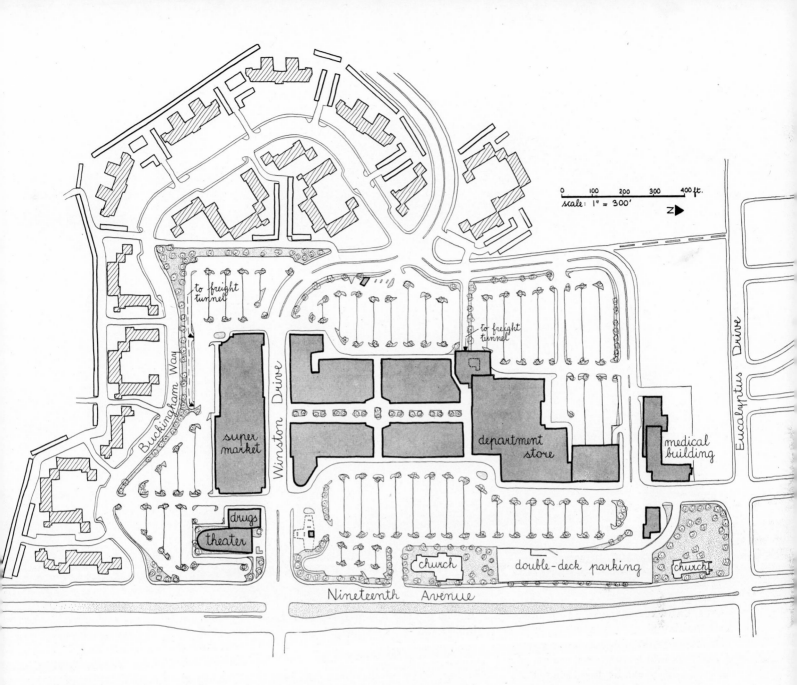

scale: 1" = 300'

SHOPPING CENTER SEPARATES APARTMENTS FROM HIGHWAY

STONESTOWN is a pioneer of the new shopping center type in San Francisco, Calif. Although some 5 miles from downtown, it is still within the city, on 19th Avenue, a heavily traveled north-south highway. Yet, significantly, the stores do not actually front on this road but are set back to provide parking in the front. The store group, surrounded by a belt of parking, has been intelligently planned as a buffer strip between 19th Avenue and the Stonestown apartments. The latter, like Metropolitan Life's towering Parkmerced blocks, are typical of the promising new growth in this section of the city in recent years.

Winston Drive, the main access to Stonestown apartments from 19th Avenue, cuts right through the store group. To the south of this road are neighborhood-type stores: a supermarket, a small department store, and a drug store next to the theater on the outer corner. This store group has its own parking area at the rear. To the north of Winston Drive are four blocks of stores fronting on a 60-ft. wide pedestrian mall with a major department store at its apex. All freight traffic is segregated in a tunnel.

This mall plan is becoming increasingly popular, as evidenced by many other centers shown in this book. It is most satisfactory when, as here, the central mall is narrow enough that shoppers are exposed to displays on both sides at once, like a city street for pedestrians only.

At the north end of the center, beyond the stores, is a medical building.

*Owner: Stoneson Development Corp.
Architects: Welton Becket, John A. Huberty & Angus McSweeney.*

CITY GROWTH is the cause of almost all the shopping centers shown in this book. As an exhibit of contemporary city growth Seattle is unsurpassed. It is still comparatively small: twentieth on the list of metropolitan areas in the 1950 census. Its population of 726,464 looks very small when compared with more than 4 million in Los Angeles, almost 13 million in New York, and 1½ million in Washington, D. C. Even Buffalo and Baltimore top the million mark.

The rate of population increase in Seattle, on the other hand, is impressive: 43.9% in the ten years from 1940 to 1950. In this respect it is inferior to only four of the nineteen metropolitan areas ahead of it in population count. Following the pattern of growth common to the majority of U.S. metropolitan areas in this decade, Seattle's population increase was much larger in the suburbs (92.8%) than within the city limits (25.7%). Sum-marized in these few figures are the conditions which cause shopping centers. And fortunately the analysis of Seattle's growth is simplified by geography.

Like so many of the great port cities, Seattle is hemmed in by water: Puget Sound to the west, Lake Washington to the east. San Francisco is at the end of a peninsula with the ocean on one side and the bay on the other. In New York the narrow island of Manhattan is hemmed in by water on three sides.

The easy way to expand in such conditions is along the narrow strip of land between the two water boundaries, until some new transportation link such as a road bridge, a railroad, a tunnel, or a subway, opens up the land beyond the water. In San Francisco two great bridges, joining the city to Oakland on the east and Marin Co. to the north, are stimulating a redistribution of the growing population throughout this area. In New York subway extensions and suburb-an railroads, bridges and tunnels, have disseminated the population through Long Island, New Jersey, Westchester County and Connecticut.

In Seattle it was the completion of a floating bridge across Lake Washington in 1940 which at last made it feasible for the city to expand eastward. But it was not until 1949, when this bridge was freed of tolls, that the dam really burst. The percentage increase of population on Mercer Island, in the center of the lake, and in all the burgeoning communities along the eastern shore, exceeded that in any other section of suburban Seattle by overwhelming numbers. Bellevue shopping center (see pages 222-231) was justifying the perspicacity of its promoters. Yet while, percentage-wise, the eastern suburbs were ahead, more people moved into the area beyond the city limits to the north, than moved across the bridge to

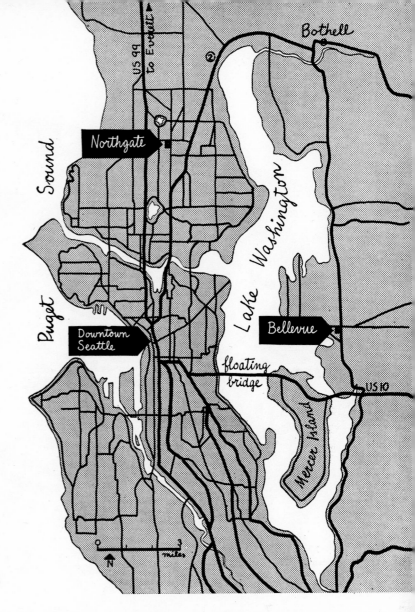

EW SHOPPING CENTER PLANNERS

the east. But these northern suburbs, being already quite heavily populated, showed a less impressive percentage gain in the census tables.

Seattle has been spreading north for many years, in spite of having to cross the Lake Washington Canal. The fastest and least congested highway out of the city in any direction, at the present time, is U.S. 99 going north, a six-lane road except for a few blocks in the downtown area. For automobile commuters and shoppers this is an important, enticing fact. Northgate shopping center *(see pages 214-221)* lies midway between U.S. 99 and State 2, another good road, but somewhat congested for the first five miles out of the city.

Driving out of Seattle to the east is less pleasant. There is an excellent six-lane highway at the far end of the bridge, but the approach to the bridge on the Seattle side is extremely congested.

While going east may be less easy than going north, going south is worse than either. The Duwanish River causes all the main roads and railroads to edge over toward the lake shore and the traffic congestion here is bad.

In all the residential areas on the edge of the city and beyond, development so far has been spotty. The immense amount of seashore and lake frontage, and the widespread love of the simple country life, have combined to leave large stretches of undeveloped land between relatively dense subdivisions. Of course as the city grows even the inland sections will eventually be built up.

At the present time there is not one of the developing residential areas on the outskirts of the city where the population exceeds 100,000. Only in the area to the north does the population even approach this figure. It stands to reason, therefore, that only in that section of suburban

Seattle could a shopping center as large as Northgate be successful.

If Northgate had not been established, some other center would have been built in that area. But a center as large as Northgate could not, at this time, be successful in Bellevue. On the other hand Bellevue itself is evidence enough that, when size is reasonably well matched with potentialities, success in a fast-growing neighborhood is assured. It may well be that growth on the southwestern fringe of the city, between the Duwanish River and Puget Sound, might soon justify one or two small community centers there, particularly if that growth were stimulated by improved accessibility.

The forces which guide and stimulate city growth such as this are also among the most potent of those which cause shopping centers to be born. Those forces must be identified, understood, anticipated by the shopping center promoter.

213

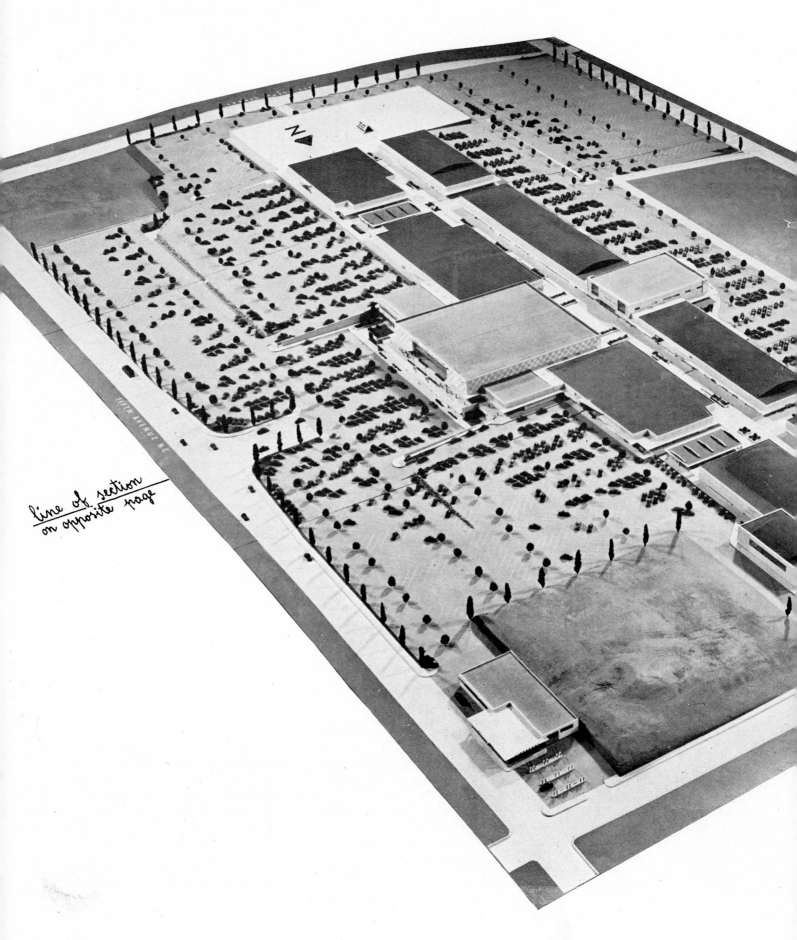

line of section
on opposite page

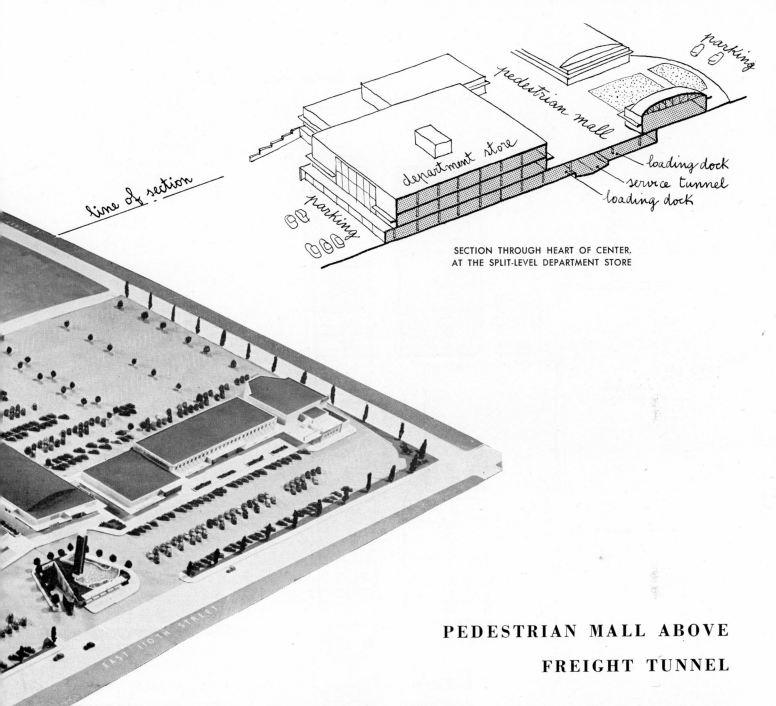

SECTION THROUGH HEART OF CENTER,
AT THE SPLIT-LEVEL DEPARTMENT STORE

PEDESTRIAN MALL ABOVE
FREIGHT TUNNEL

NORTHGATE, Seattle, Wash. has an eminently simple plan. A pedestrian mall 48 ft. wide and 1500 ft. long is the spine of the whole center. Beneath it is a freight tunnel, on each side are store fronts; beyond the store buildings is a band of parking for 4,000 cars.

To give variety of store depth, the blocks on the east of the mall are 150 ft. deep, those on the west 100 ft. deep. To allow for flexible space division with non-structural partitions, many of the roofs are supported by steel bow-string trusses with a clear span of 96 ft.

At the heart of this main group is the famous Bon Marché department store. To achieve a fashionable split-level plan, the ground on the parking side of this store was scooped out, so that facing the auto shopper there is a two-story front, and customers enter at what in all the other stores would be basement level. The upper floor is, of course, at the level of the pedestrian mall.

In a separate block to the south, along 110th Street, is a theater, a restaurant, and a four-story office building.

Owner: Northgate Co. *Architects and Engineers:* John Graham & Co.

MORE ABOUT NORTHGATE ON THE FOLLOWING SIX PAGES

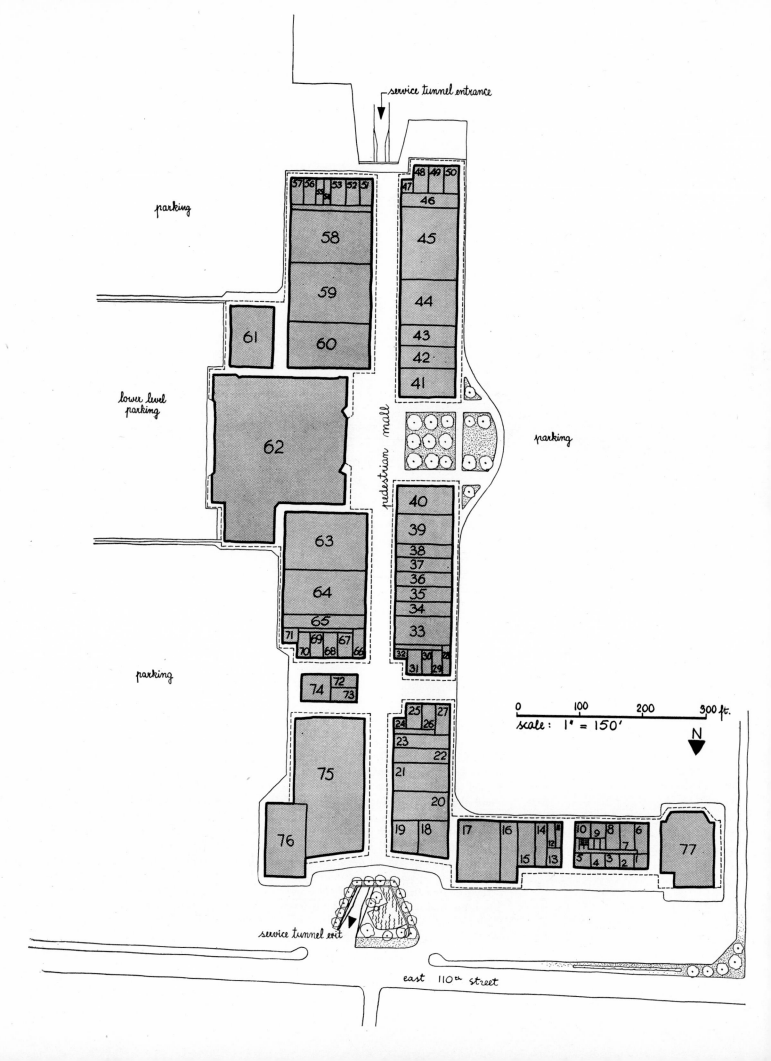

service tunnel entrance

parking

lower level parking

parking

pedestrian mall

parking

service tunnel exit

east 110th street

0   100   200   300 ft.

scale: 1" = 150'

N

NORTHGATE IS BIG ENOUGH FOR COMPARISON SHOPPING

	TYPE OF STORE	WIDTH, DEPTH	SQ. FT. AREA
1	Candy	24 x 24	576
2	Real Estate	24 x 24	576
3	Real Estate	24 x 24	576
4	Express Office	24 x 24	576
5	Pharmacy	24 x 24	576
6	Administration	24 x 48	1,152
7	Bank	24 x 42	1,008
8	Post Office	24 x 42	1,008
9	Gifts	24 x 24	576
10	Medical Supplies	24 x 24	576
11	Cigars	12 x 42	504
12	Barber	12 x 42	504
13	Coffee Shop	24 x 30	720
14	Delicatessen	18 x 72	1,296
15	Liquor	30 x 72	2,160
	Professional Offices (3 stories) above stores 1 through 15		
16	Restaurant	30 x 96	2,880
17	Drugs	72 x 96	6,912
18	Music	60 x 48	2,540
19	Men's Wear	48 x 54	2,375
20	Furniture	48 x 96	4,608
21	Fabrics	48 x 96	4,608
22	Sporting Goods	24 x 96	2,304
23	Florist	24 x 96	2,304
24	Nuts	18 x 24	432
25	Sportswear	24 x 42	1,008
26	Misses' Wear	24 x 42	1,008
27	Optician	24 x 48	1,152
28	Photographer	12 x 48	576
29	Cutlery	18 x 42	756
30	Beauty Shop	18 x 42	756
31	Women's Wear	24 x 42	1,008
32	Candy	18 x 24	432
33	Women's Wear	48 x 96	4,608
34	Women's Wear	24 x 96	2,304
35	Furs	24 x 96	2,304
36	Women's Wear	24 x 96	2,304
37	Jewelry	24 x 96	2,304
38	Women's Wear	24 x 96	2,304
39	Men's Wear	48 x 96	4,608
40	Shoes	48 x 96	4,608
41	Women's Wear	48 x 96	4,608
42	Household Appliances	36 x 96	3,456
43	Paint	36 x 96	3,456
44	Drugs	72 x 96	6,912
45	Supermarket	120 x 96	11,520
46	Meat	24 x 96	2,304
47	Malted Milk	24 x 24	576
48	Shoe Repair	24 x 48	1,152
49	Cleaners	24 x 48	1,152
50	Self-Service Laundry	24 x 48	1,152
51	Bakery	24 x 48	1,152
52	Health Food	24 x 48	1,152
53	Fish	24 x 48	1,152
54	Poultry	12 x 48	576
55	Florist	12 x 48	576
56	Delicatessen	24 x 48	1,152
57	Restaurant	24 x 48	1,152
58	Supermarket	84 x 144	12,096
59	Hardware	96 x 144	13,824
60	Variety	72 x 144	10,368
61	Restaurant	102 x 72	7,344
62	Department Store	210 x 228	53,424
63	Variety	96 x 144	13,824
64	Women's Wear	72 x 144	10,368
65	Women's Shoes	24 x 144	2,880
66	Women's Wear	48 x 24	1,152
67	Camera Shop	24 x 42	1,008
68	Women's Wear	24 x 42	1,008
69	Millinery	24 x 42	1,008
70	Lingerie	24 x 42	1,008
71	Gifts	24 x 24	576
72	Children's Shoes	24 x 48	1,152
73	Toys	24 x 48	1,152
74	Infants' Wear	48 x 48	2,304
75	Department Store	216 x 120	24,768
76	Bank	72 x 120	8,640
77	Theater	90 x 125	11,000
	TOTAL STORE AREA		299,991

NORTHGATE TRADE PROSPECTS
SURVEY BASED ON A SERIES OF CALCULATED ASSUMPTIONS

Northgate's position, relative to main highways and public transportation routes, is such that, for half the population of metropolitan Seattle, this new center will be more conveniently accessible than is the present downtown shopping district. So it was decided to develop Northgate into a "regional" center, with such a number and variety of high-class stores that it might become a potential competitor of downtown Seattle.

Moreover Northgate would have such additional advantages as abundant parking space, short walking distance between the various stores, covered sidewalks, etc. Obviously the success of this new center must depend upon its being able to provide the suburban shopper with a comprehensive group of carefully selected stores. A smaller or a less comprehensive group would probably be a failure.

An expert survey had already established the existence of a trade area with buying power enough to support such a large center. With 200,000 sq. ft. of selling space right in the heart of the new center already occupied by a branch of Bon Marché, well-known Seattle department store (one of the Allied Department Store chain), the *quality* of Northgate's appeal to shoppers would seem to be equally well established.

Surrounding Bon Marché will probably be as many as ninety individual stores (both chains and independents), service shops, restaurants, banks, offices for professional men, and a theater.

To build up a picture of the sales volume that might be anticipated by the various stores in Northgate, the developers hired Dr. Nathaniel Engle of the University of Washington, to make an economic survey. This was supplemented by later studies by Larry Smith & Co. Like all such surveys, this is based on a series of carefully calculated assumptions.

THE TRADING AREA is first mapped. From here the new shopping center will draw its Buying Power. The boundaries of this Trading Area will be set by the strength of the new center's field of attraction, when competing with the pull exerted by existing store groups.

Northgate, as envisioned by its promoters, will be so large and so comprehensive that its only serious competitor would be downtown Seattle. Thus it is the southern boundary of Northgate's Trading Area, where these two fields of attraction overlap, which is the most difficult to determine. Moreover an inaccurate assumption could cause large errors; for this is the most heavily populated part of the Northgate Trading Area, and a small shift in the boundary line would have a noticeable effect.

To minimize the possible margin of error, this economic survey has mapped two zones of "fading influence" at the southern end of Northgate's Trading Area. In the northerly of these two border zones only 60% of the buying power is attributed to Northgate, in the southerly one only 40%.

The boundary lines themselves are based on local conditions, primarily on the time taken to reach the shopping center, by private car and public transport. The Lake Washington Canal, which marks the southern boundary of the Northgate area's outermost zone, is approximately halfway between Northgate and downtown Seattle.

The northern boundary of the Trading Area has been set on the outskirts of Everett. It is based on a maximum driving time of 15 minutes. Its exact position is not too important, for the population in that area is comparatively sparse.

POPULATION. To bring the last census up to date has always been one of the analyst's most fundamental problems. In this case the 1940 figures could be supplemented to some extent by a 1946 survey made by the State Highway Department. Although this did not cover the whole of Northgate's assumed Trading Area, it did cover all of the vital 60% and 40% zones. It was also necessary to estimate the 1946 population of those areas not covered by this Highway Department survey, and finally to bring all the 1946 figures up to a 1949 estimate.

The various steps taken to arrive at the 1949 figures are shown in a table on the following page. The analysts feel that these figures, showing no population increase from 1946 to 1949 in the 60% and 40% zones, and an increase of only 12.4% in the 100% zone, must be deemed very conservative.

pedestrian mall

exit from
freight tunnel

Ben Maralie Dept. Store

entrance to freight tunnel

AIRVIEW OF NORTHGATE DURING CONSTRUCTION, 1950. DEPARTMENT STORE WITH SPLIT-LEVEL PLAN HAS SUNKEN PARKING. TWO STORY FRONT

BUYING POWER. Next these population figures have to be translated into dollars. How much do the people living in Northgate's Trading Area spend annually on each of the retail goods categories, such as food, general merchandise, apparel, furniture, etc.?

The analysts start from the per capita retail sales for this area in 1948, as listed in *Sales Management's* Survey of Buying Power: City of Seattle $1,740, King County $1,410, Snohomish County $897. These are *sales*, not *purchases* per capita. Many of the retail sales attributed to Seattle are purchases made by residents of King and Snohomish Counties, and indeed to a smaller extent the Seattle figures also include purchases by those living in more distant parts of the state who come to shop in this city. On the other hand it would not be sensible to assume that the residents of Seattle go shopping in rural Snohomish County. This explains why per capita sales in Snohomish are only a little over half those recorded in the city of Seattle.

It should also be borne in mind that part of King Co. and most of Snohomish is still rural; and rural families, being larger and more self-sufficient than those living in towns, spend less on retail goods, particularly on food.

Playing it safe, the Northgate analysts assume for their Trading Area a per capita retail sales figure of $1,153, halfway between that for King Co. and that for Snohomish Co. Multiplied by the estimated effective population of 150,000, this gives a total buying power of $172,950,000 in the Northgate area.

This total is broken down into the various retail goods categories according to what the analysts' experience has shown to be the prevailing pattern in the Puget Sound area. Then, finally, it must be decided what percentage of the sales expected in each category can be attracted to Northgate.

The pull of the new center will vary in strength between one type of goods and another. Shoppers will not go as far for grocery, for example, as they will for fashion goods. Northgate's grocery stores will be vieing with neighborhood groceries scattered throughout the trade area. Its apparel stores, on the other hand, should have no substantial competition within the same boundaries.

TRADING AREA ZONES	1940 CENSUS	1946	EFFECTIVE POPULATION (APPLYING ZONE %) 1946	1949 (ASSUMED)
100% Zone part covered by 1946 survey	38,175	62,553		
balance of zone	14,744	19,048 (assumed)		
100% Zone Total	52,919	81,601	81,601	89,400
60% Zone	57,212	66,066	39,640	39,600
40% Zone	45,006	52,605	21,042	21,000
TOTAL			142,283	150,000

POPULATION OF NORTHGATE TRADING AREA

TYPE OF STORE	*SALES PER CAPITA (IN DOLLARS)	TOTAL SALES FOR EFFECTIVE POPULATION OF 150,000	% OF TOTAL SALES LIKELY TO GO TO NORTHGATE	SALES VOLUME ANTICIPATED FOR NORTHGATE
Food	$ 300	$ 45,000,000	10	$ 4,500,000
Department Store	133	19,950,000	50	10,000,000
Variety Stores	34	5,100,000	55	2,525,000
Apparel	92	13,800,000	40	5,500,000
Furniture	47.50	7,090,000	30	2,130,000
Auto Agencies	179	26,855,500	None	—
Filling Stations	86.50	12,975,000	None	—
Lumber, Building Supply, Hardware	48	7,200,000	15	1,080,000
Eating & Drinking Places	92	13,800,000	15	2,070,000
Drug Stores	37.50	5,625,000	40	2,250,000
Other Stores	103.50	15,545,500	15	2,330,000
TOTAL	$1,153.00	$172,950,000		$32,385,000

ANTICIPATED SALES   *Based on prevailing pattern in the Puget Sound area.

ON PARKING (STREET) SIDE DEPARTMENT STORE FRONT IS HIGH AND OPEN

REUSE WELL-TRIED PLAZA LAYOUT

BELLEVUE is a community shopping center which serves a fast-growing suburban area just across Lake Washington from Seattle, Wash. *(see page 213).* It is the brain-child of two brothers, Kemper and Miller Freeman, who have been living in Bellevue ever since 1928. They were far-sighted enough to realize how fast this area would develop when the floating bridge across the Lake, completed in 1940, at last made it accessible for Seattle commuters. They bought 15 acres along the side of the main highway. In 1946 they started to build. The center has been expanding ever since.

For the general plan of their development the Freemans went to Highland Park *(see page 90).* Started 15 years earlier, its sound qualities had already been proven, though its architectural style had already been eclipsed. In Bellevue the plan remains, but the style has been changed, from Spanish to Modern. In both centers the store blocks are divided by wide parking streets with curb stalls down each side and a line of angle parking along the center strip. Unfortunately it is mathematically impossible for this plan to contain the amount of parking which modern conditions demand. As the now vacant lots are built up with stores, it will be essential to provide additional, and perhaps less conveniently located parking space.

In the central position on the highway front in Bellevue is a branch of Frederick & Nelson, Seattle department store. The buildings furthest from the highway (in the foreground of the picture at left) are given over to offices and a medical clinic *(page 230).* A supermarket and variety store dominate the block to the right of the picture, a theater, restaurant and drug store that to the left.

At present there are a number of small professional offices scattered through the stores. It is to be expected that, as the population builds up in this area, these will be gradually eliminated.

Owner: Bellevue Properties Inc. *Architect:* Bliss Moore Jr. and Associates.

MORE ABOUT BELLEVUE IN THE FOLLOWING NINE PAGES

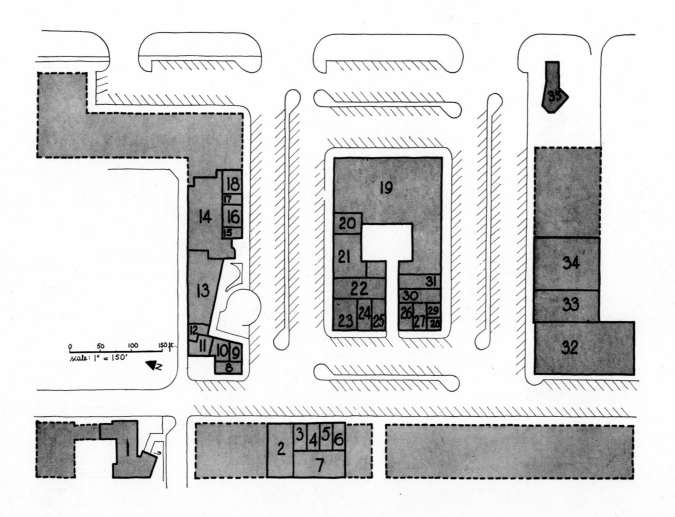

	TYPE OF STORE	WIDTH, DEPTH	SQ. FT. AREA
1	Medical Building	75 x 85	3,600
2	Bank	40 x 80	3,200
3	Newspaper Office	20 x 40	800
4	Shoes	20 x 40	800
5	Insurance & Law Office	20 x 40	800
6	Piano Studio	20 x 40	800
7	Printing Plant	40 x 80	3,200
8	Sporting Goods	20 x 40	800
9	Music	25 x 20	500
10	Stationery	25 x 30	750
11	Beauty Shop	40 x 30	1,200
12	Florist	20 x 30	600
13	Restaurant	100 x 45	4,500
14	Theater	120 x 60	7,200
15	Real Estate	15 x 30	450
16	Photographer	35 x 30	1,050
17	Barber	15 x 30	450
18	Soda Fountain, Lunch	35 x 30	1,050
19	Department Store	165 x 100	18,900

	TYPE OF STORE	WIDTH, DEPTH	SQ. FT. AREA
20	Jewelry	30 x 45	1,350
21	Drugs	60 x 45	2,700
22	Liquor	30 x 80	2,400
23	Men's Wear	45 x 40	1,800
24	Nursery	20 x 45	900
25	Radio	20 x 45	900
26	Bank	20 x 40	800
27	Woman's Exchange	20 x 40	800
28	Photographic Supplies	20 x 20	400
29	Law Office	20 x 20	400
30	Cleaners	20 x 60	1,200
31	Sewing Center	20 x 60	1,200
32	Supermarket	75 x 150	11,250
33	Hardware	45 x 100	4,500
34	Variety	75 x 100	7,500
35	Filling Station		
	TOTAL STORE AREA		88,750

A SUBURBAN BRANCH OF A SEATTLE DEPARTMENT STORE HOLDS THE CENTRAL SPOT ON THE MAIN HIGHWAY FRONT IN BELLEVUE SHOPPING CENTER

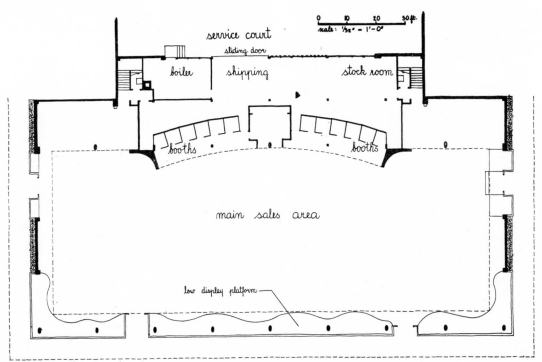

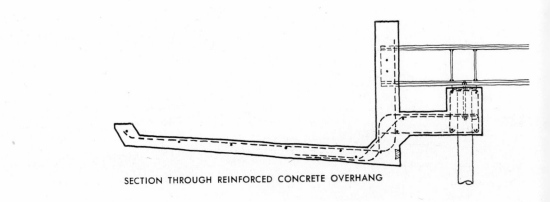

THE SALES ROOM, FREE OF ALL COLUMNS, CAN BE DIVIDED AT WILL WITH MOVABLE FIXTURES

SECTION THROUGH REINFORCED CONCRETE OVERHANG

LONG OPEN DISPLAY FRONT FACING THE HIGHWAY IS PARTICULARLY STRIKING AT NIGHT

THE DEPARTMENT STORE, a branch of Seattle's Frederick & Nelson, carries a limited selection of merchandise, mostly fashion goods. This is in essence a large, glass-sided box. It is particularly impressive as seen from the highway at night. The signs here, like all others in the center, are confined to a strip of corrugated Transite, which serves as a billboard above the show windows. At night the cut-out letters are back-lit.

The continuous, upward-sloping overhang, along the front of each store block, is cantilevered out about 8 ft. from the supporting columns. The latter are set inside the line of the show windows and are freestanding.

THE SMALLER STORES at Bellevue show an interesting variety of design and materials in the display fronts within the larger, uniform frame of the center itself. Particularly good use is made of textures, such as the horizontal courses of Roman brick and the vertically corrugated panels of Transite. Borrowed from modern home architecture is the free form of a planting pocket which continues through from inside to outside the show window. Many of these small store fronts are quite deeply recessed; and there is often an interesting contrast between the large open display windows and small, brightly lit display boxes prominently set at eye level.

PLANTING TROUGH PASSES THROUGH THE FLOOR-TO-CEILING GLASS FRONT

LARGE OPEN FRONT AND SMALL DISPLAY BOXES AT EYE LEVEL TOGETHER ACCOMMODATE A VARIETY OF MERCHANDISE

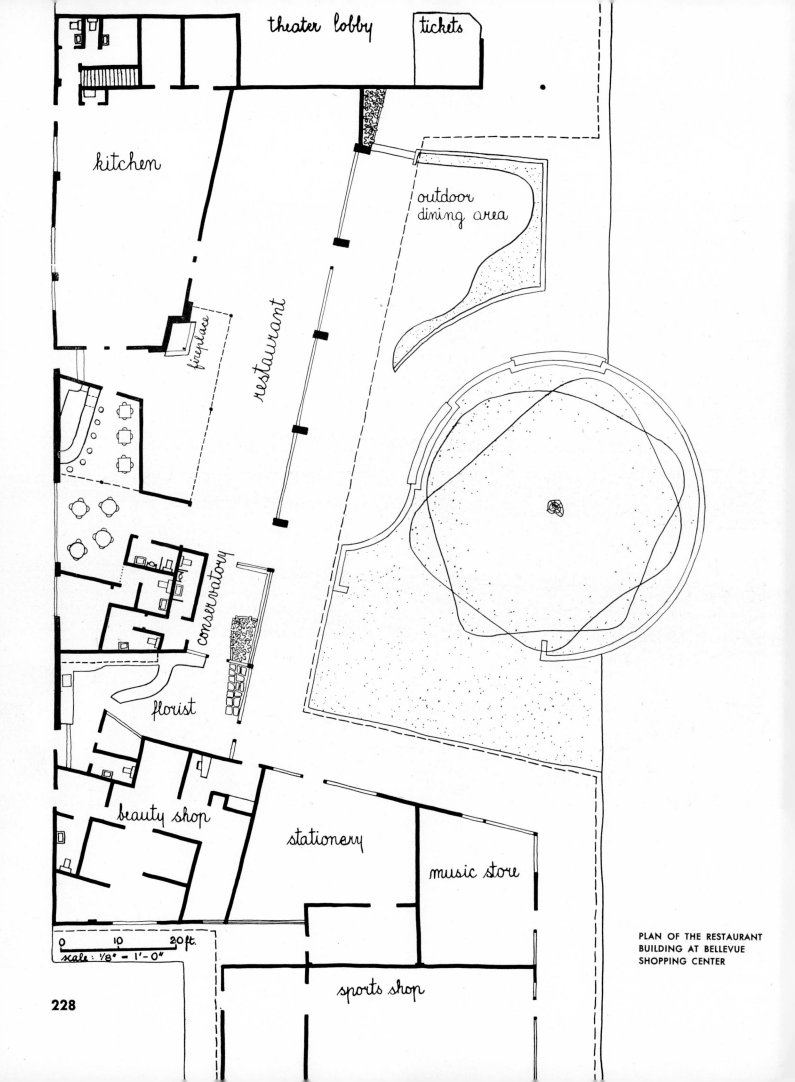

theater lobby

tickets

kitchen

outdoor dining area

fireplace

restaurant

conservatory

florist

beauty shop

stationery

music store

0   10   20 ft.

scale: 1/8" = 1'-0"

PLAN OF THE RESTAURANT
BUILDING AT BELLEVUE
SHOPPING CENTER

sports shop

THE RESTAURANT BUILDING AT BELLEVUE SHOPPING CENTER IS RECESSED BEHIND A GIANT MADRONA TREE *(SEE OVER PAGE)*

THE RESTAURANT *(for plan and picture turn back one page).* Recessed in a small courtyard behind a giant tree, the Crabapple Restaurant is well protected from noise and dust. Widely renowned for the high quality of its food, the restaurant draws many customers to Bellevue shopping center from far beyond what would normally be the center's calculated Trading Area.

At least half of the diners, seated in the long narrow dining room, and in summer at the sidewalk tables outside, can survey the passers-by in the street. The bar is set, on the other hand, in a secluded corner at the rear. A large corner fireplace contributes largely to the warm and home-like atmosphere of the room. An interesting detail of store arrangement in a shopping center is the position of the florist here next door to the restaurant. The flower display adds to the decoration of the restaurant, and the diners are tempted to buy flowers.

THE MEDICAL CLINIC at Bellevue shopping center is in the westernmost line of buildings (i.e. those furthest from the highway). While doctors are usually considered to be, in themselves, unprofitable tenants (particularly when one takes into account the special equipment which a clinic building requires), doctors' offices in a new suburban community such as this can be expected to bring new customers to the surrounding stores.

A one-story building, set on a lot large enough to permit windows opening on all sides, is usually more satisfactory for a medical clinic than the more commonly found second-story offices; provided, of course, that sufficient ground space can be afforded for a separate building. To be set off against this is the saving of cost on elevators, an essential item.

The Medical Clinic is divided into two sections. The clinic proper is located at one end, and the laboratory, with x-ray rooms and a small operating theater, is located at the other end. Each of these sections has a separate entrance. The doctors' offices in the clinic building receive daylight from high-set strip windows which are shaded by a roof overhang. These offices are situated along each side of a central corridor and the latter connects the reception room in the clinic with the laboratory building.

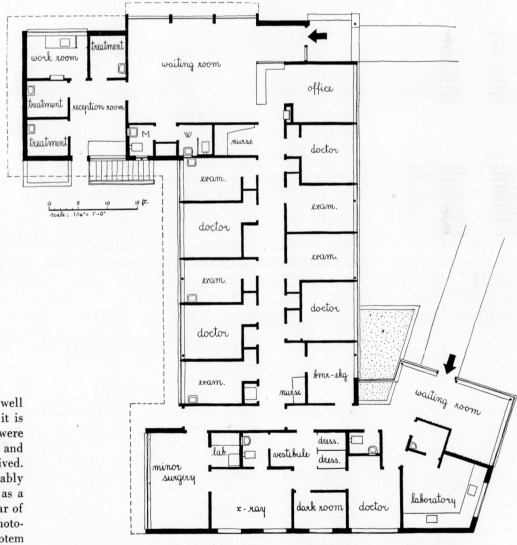

The medical building fits in very well with the store buildings by which it is surrounded. Contrasting textures were skillfully employed by its designers and the plan is extremely well conceived. The crisp efficiency which, suitably enough, characterizes the structure as a whole, is humanized by a thick pillar of carved redwood (visible in the photograph, opposite), reminiscent of totem poles in neighboring Indian villages.

PLAN OF THE MEDICAL CLINIC, BELLEVUE

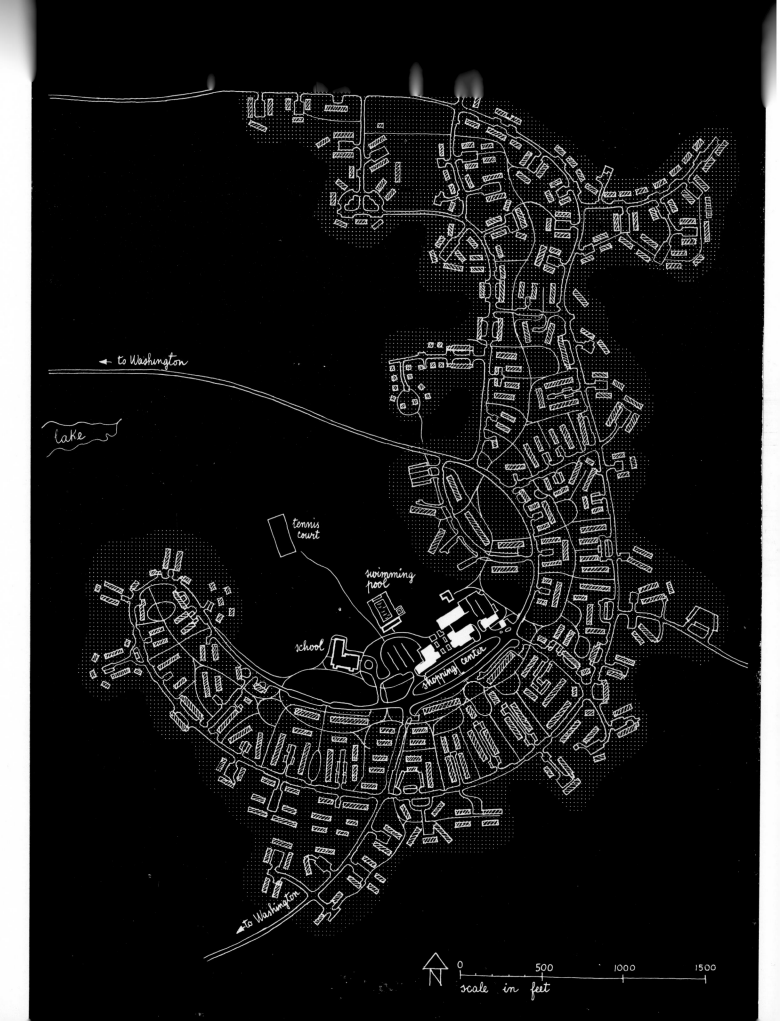

to Washington

lake

tennis
court

swimming
pool

school

shopping center

to Washington

N

| 0 | | 500 | | 1000 | | 1500 |

scale in feet

PLANNED COMMUNITY WRAPPED AROUND CENTER

GREENBELT, Md., 7 miles north of Washington, D. C., is the first and largest of the three Greenbelt towns planned by the Resettlement Administration during the Thirties. (The other two are Greenhills, outside Cincinnati, Ohio, and Greendale, near Milwaukee, Wis.)

The purpose of these new communities was stated in a basic program: "To obtain a large tract of land, and thus avoid the complications ordinarily due to diverse ownerships; in this tract to create a community, protected by an encircling green belt; the community to be designed primarily for families of modest income, and arranged and managed so as to encourage a family and community life which will be better than they now enjoy." Also, beyond the immediate economic advantage of giving work to large numbers of unemployed, it was hoped that the success of these communities would encourage private developers, and influence the design of subdivisions (cf. Park Forest, page 267).

Of the 3,371 acres belonging to Greenbelt, Md., only a few hundred have been developed. The original plan called for 885 dwelling units—row houses, single-family detached houses, and apartments —but streets, schools and public utilities were sized to accommodate three times as many. During World War II 1,000 new dwelling units were added.

The plan of Greenbelt is like a giant horseshoe of superblocks wrapped around the main community facilities, parks, a school, a swimming pool, and the shopping center, which includes the municipal offices.

In a community such as this, isolated from the encroachment of competitive store groups, with a population of limited size and controlled income, this central location of the main store group is just as logical as its co-operative ownership. As the town has extended to the north, the need for a subsidiary center in that area, or at least for a small food market, has become obvious; but its construction was delayed by wartime shortages. Meanwhile the existing supermarket, besides building for itself a new and much larger store (with bowling alleys in the basement), has been sponsoring a "house-to-house branch store" in the form of a motorized peddler's wagon.

The plan of the shopping center is a small and early version of the giant pedestrian malls that are currently so popular. The two parking pockets, on the outside edges of the center, added to the parallel parking allowed on the access road across the end of the pedestrian mall, together provide enough space except at peak shopping hours. This is partly explained by the large walk-in trade, which is encouraged by a widespreading network of footpaths. These are safe even for children, for they are carried in tunnels beneath all the principal through roads. As a result the central shopping mall, furnished with benches, adorned with bushes and statuary, and giving on to the central park at one end, has become a favorite meeting place for adults and children.

GREENBELT SHOPPING CENTER
PLANS AND PICTURES ON NEXT TWO PAGES

FOOTPATH APPROACH TO PEDESTRIAN MALL

AT THE HEART OF THE MALL IS A WIDE PAVED AREA

BOTH STATUARY AND BICYCLE STANDS ARE PROVIDED

THE NEW SUPERMARKET (AT REAR), WHERE THE MALL JOINS THE PARK

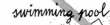

swimming pool

elementary school

parking

THE PEDESTRIAN MALL which forms the heart of Greenbelt's shopping center is one of the few so far actually built. It is, of course, on a very small scale; but it does show the possibilities of this plan. This central courtyard, with its benches and paved walks, encourages the old to

A SAFE PLACE TO BE, A SAFE FOOTPATH TO REACH IT

recreation bldg.

parking

supermarket

theater

statue

under pass

■ shopping center
▨ apartments

0   100   200   300

N

CENTRAL PEDESTRIAN MALL
PROVED IN USE AT GREENBELT

QUIET ACCESS ROAD ACROSS END OF MALL GIVES EXTRA PARKING SPACE

gossip and the young to play. Being withdrawn from roads and parking areas, it is quiet and free from dust.

The new supermarket (Ross & Walton, architects) may be matched with a similar unit on the opposite side, when further expansion of the center is necessary.

AT THE HUB OF LINDA VISTA LIES THE SHOPPING CENTER, A COMMUNITY SERVICE LIKE THE CHURCHES, SCHOOLS, FIRE HOUSE, AND MEETING HALL WHICH ADJOIN IT

stores
theater
community building

STORES SURROUND TREE-SHADED LAWN

LINDA VISTA, on the outskirts of San Diego, Calif., is a community built by the National Housing Agency during World War II to accommodate industrial workers. It is set in arid, semi-desert country, corrugated by scrubby hills and rock-strewn canyons. From a main highway, which runs through the middle of the community like a spine, dead-end roads branch off on each side. Each of these spur roads serves a group of houses set along the top of a mesa, which is separated by deep canyons from its neighbors on each side. Seldom has such an interesting and successful development plan been so completely dictated by topography.

There are 5,000 dwelling units in all, 2,000 of them prefabricated. Scattered through these houses are four small neighborhood store groups. At the hub of the community, on a 13-acre super-block alongside Linda Vista Road, is the main shopping center shown on these and the following four pages.

Turning their backs on the highways by which they are surrounded, these stores face inward on to a quiet lawn dotted with trees and benches. Parking space is in several sections between stores and highway. It is unfortunate that the passer-by on the road, and the arriving automobile shopper, are both presented with a sorry spectacle of service entrances and garbage cans. This is quite a heavy price to pay for the pleasant quiet charm which suffuses the pedestrian courtyard inside, with its elegantly curving walks marked by slatted sunshades. The uniform board-and-batten surface of the store buildings was originally painted gray-green; and slate blue tiles were used for the bulkheads below the show windows. All buildings are planned on a 14 ft. module grid, and many of the merchants would have been happier had circumstances allowed some form of construction with longer clear spans.

For identification of stores from the far side of the wide courtyard, there are large signs confined to a strip above the canopy. For shoppers walking beneath this canopy there are neatly lettered signs hung on the underside at right angles to This center was built during a period of wartime shortages, when many building materials were unobtainable, and many of the shoppers were without cars. By today's standards the parking space is insufficient, particularly if and when the vacant lots, now used for parking, are built up with stores. Already many of the merchants are pressing for the interior pedestrian courtyard to be converted into parking space. This would, of course, rob the center of its greatest and most distinctive charm.

Associated Architects: Earl F. Giberson and Whitney R. Smith.

LINDA VISTA SHOPPING CENTER PLANS AND PICTURES ON THE NEXT FOUR PAGES

SHELTERED PATHS FOR PEDESTRIAN SHOPPERS

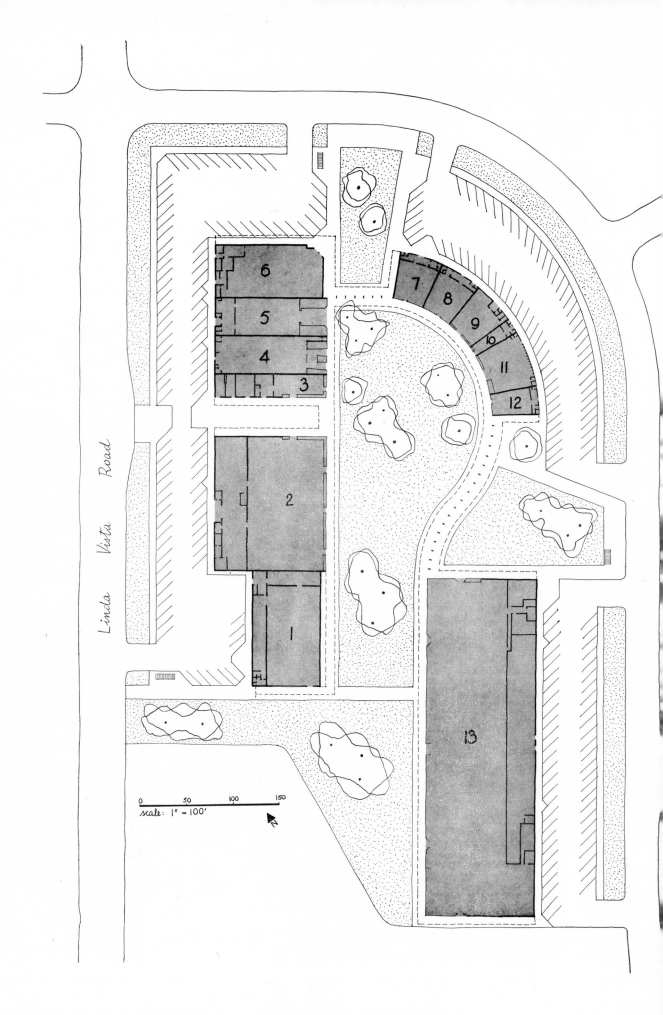

STORE SIGNS LARGE ENOUGH TO BE SEEN BY SHOPPERS ON THE FAR SIDE OF THE GRASSY COURTYARD

	TYPE OF STORE	WIDTH, DEPTH	SQ. FT. AREA
1	Supermarket	75 x 120	9,000
2	Variety	140 x 120	16,800
3	Bakery	25 x 75	1,900
4	Delicatessen	40 x 120	4,800
5	Shoes	40 x 120	4,800
6	Drugs	55 x 120	6,600
7	Barber	33 x 50	2,000
8	Beauty Shop	33 x 50	2,000
9	Cleaners	33 x 50	2,000
10	Liquor	10 x 50	550
11	Tavern	42 x 50	2,500
12	Utilities Office	22 x 50	1,300
13	Department Store	115 x 345	28,000
TOTAL STORE AREA			82,250

LINDA VISTA STORES ARE JOINED BY CANOPY

RESERVED FOR PEDESTRIANS. IN LINDA VISTA SHOPPERS DO NOT HAVE TO KEEP ALERT IN ORDER TO KEEP ALIVE

TALL AIRY COLONNADES CONNECT ALL THE BUILDINGS IN THE LOS ALAMOS CENTER, AND OPEN ON TO A GRASSY COURTYARD

COMBINATION OF COMMUNITY CENTER AND SHOPPING CENTER

Los Alamos, N. M., born urgently, secretly, during World War II, is now being gradually developed into a permanent industrial city. But the Townsite (as the non-industrial section of the community is called) is still more reminiscent of an army camp or a mining boom town, than of a planned community laid out by experts. The solidly constructed, $4 million shopping center, shown on this and the two following pages, is still surrounded by ramshackle barracks.

However, it does represent the first step in a five-year plan of expansion and improvement due to cost $100 million. By 1952 the population will have increased from 9,000 to 12,000; and the living accommodations should compare with this shopping center as to quality of construction. Almost all the population will, of course, be employees of the Atomic Energy Commission.

The cruciform plan of this center *(see next page)* divides it into four groups. At the south end, facing Central Avenue, is the variety store, the supermarket, and other food stores. The Post Office and a large cafeteria are set directly on the street, as they will derive most of their business from walk-in trade.

On the eastern side of the center are gathered those stores and entertainment buildings which will be most active in the evening. Here is the theater, bowling alleys, a drug store, and a luncheonette. Near these, but closer to the heart of the whole center, stands the town hall and the radio station building. For this is more than just a shopping center; it is the center of all community life.

Further to the north is a line of small service stores. And across the northern end of the whole center there will even-

FOR WALK-IN TRADE THE POST OFFICE AND CAFETERIA ARE PLACED ON STREET FRONT

PARKING AREA FORMED ON THE STREET SIDE OF THE SUPERMARKET-DRUG-STORE CORNER

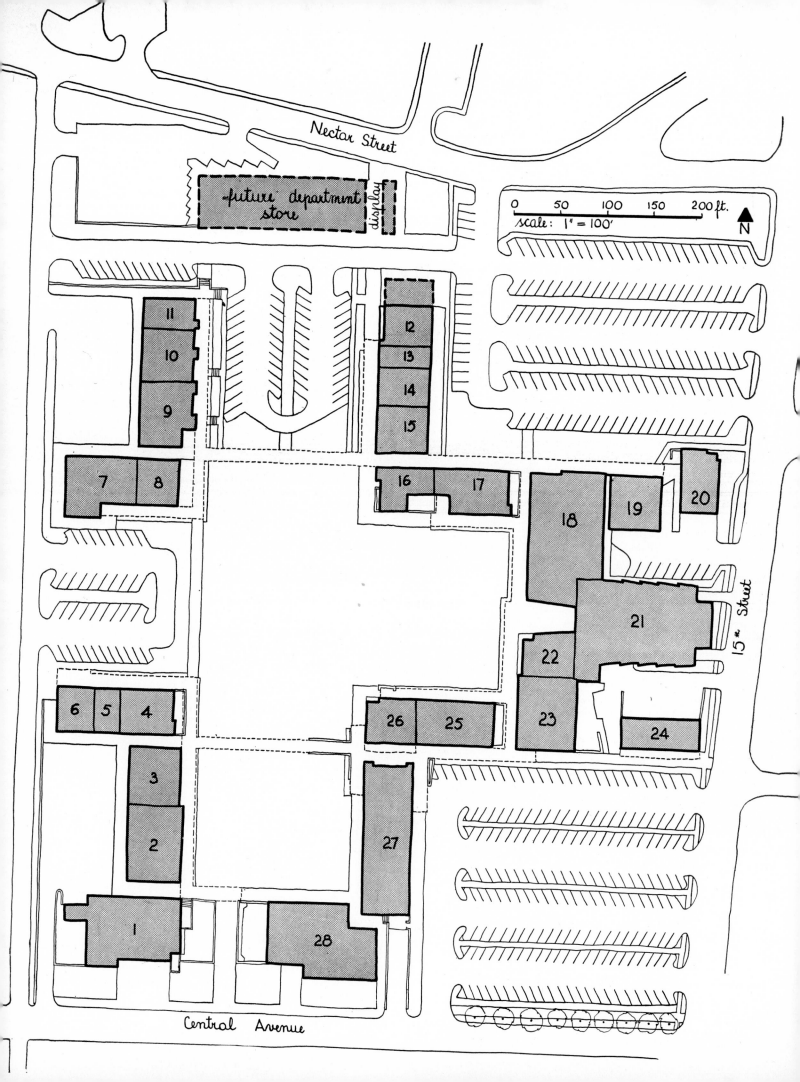

tually be a department store. Already built, to the west, are a number of smaller apparel and furniture stores. These, in conjunction with the department store, will offer a limited amount of comparison shopping for fashion goods.

This cruciform plan, by breaking the required total parking area into a number of smaller units, preserves the advantage of a pedestrian courtyard. At the same time stores and small parking areas are interlocked in such a way that the shopper can almost always find a parking space directly beside the store which she wants to visit. Like any pedestrian mall scheme this implies ample space, plenty of cheap land.

All the major stores are put in the outer blocks, near the surrounding streets, so that they have well-concealed service yards giving directly on to the street; and freight traffic does not pass through the customers' parking areas. Heating in all stores is from a central plant.

Owner: U.S. Atomic Energy Commission. *Architect:* W. C. Kruger & Assoc.

LOOKING NORTHWEST IN THE CENTRAL COURTYARD. AT RIGHT IS THE TOWN HALL

IN THE SNOW-COVERED CENTRAL COURTYARD, LOOKING EAST TOWARD THE THEATER

	TYPE OF STORE	WIDTH, DEPTH	SQ. FT. AREA
1	Post Office	100 x 70	7,000
2	Variety	80 x 60	4,800
3	Hardware	60 x 55	3,300
4	Bakery	60 x 48	2,880
5	Newsstand	25 x 48	1,200
6	Jewelry	40 x 48	1,920
7	Fabrics	75 x 65	4,120
8	Shoes	45 x 50	2,250
9	Clothing	70 x 57	4,000
10	Furniture	52 x 57	2,960
11	Music	32 x 57	1,820
12	Cleaners	40 x 55	2,200
13	Shoe Repair	25 x 60	1,500
14	Barber	40 x 60	2,400

	TYPE OF STORE	WIDTH, DEPTH	SQ. FT. AREA
15	Beauty Shop	50 x 60	3,000
16	Town Hall	65 x 45	2,300
17	Radio Station	80 x 45	3,200
18	Bowling	80 x 140	10,000
19	Offices	58 x 58	3,360
20	Power House	65 x 40	2,600
21	Theater	90 x 140	12,600
22	Luncheonette	55 x 45	2,500
23	Recreation Hall	75 x 65	4,900
24	Sporting Goods	85 x 32	2,700
25	Drugs	90 x 45	4,050
26	Bank	60 x 45	2,700
27	Supermarket	60 x 155	9,300
28	Cafeteria	120 x 80	8,300
TOTAL STORE AREA			113,860

ONE OF THE FOUR NEIGHBORHOOD CENTERS

SHOPPING CENTER FITTED
INTO MODIFIED CITY STREET PLAN

PARKCHESTER, New York. 12,272 families are housed in this 130-acre apartment house development in the Bronx, a half hour's subway ride from midtown Manhattan. The site is divided into quarters by two wide roads which cross diagonally, intersecting at a large central traffic oval.

The main shopping center spreads along the line of Metropolitan Avenue, which leads from the central oval to the subway station. It is therefore in the main stream of pedestrian traffic. In addition to this main center, with a branch of Macy's department store, a theater, and many chain stores, there are four smaller neighborhood centers scattered through the development. As most of the trade is walk-in, there is not as much parking space as other centers require.

These are all street-front stores which form a solid line one story high along the sidewalk, as in any other city street. But the apartment blocks are set back from the building line, and in many cases turned at right angles to the street.

Owner: Metropolitan Life Insurance Co. *Architects:* Board of Design, R. H. Shreve, chairman.

IN MAIN SHOPPING CENTER WIDE STREETS PARALLEL TO METROPOLITAN AVENUE ARE FOR PARKING

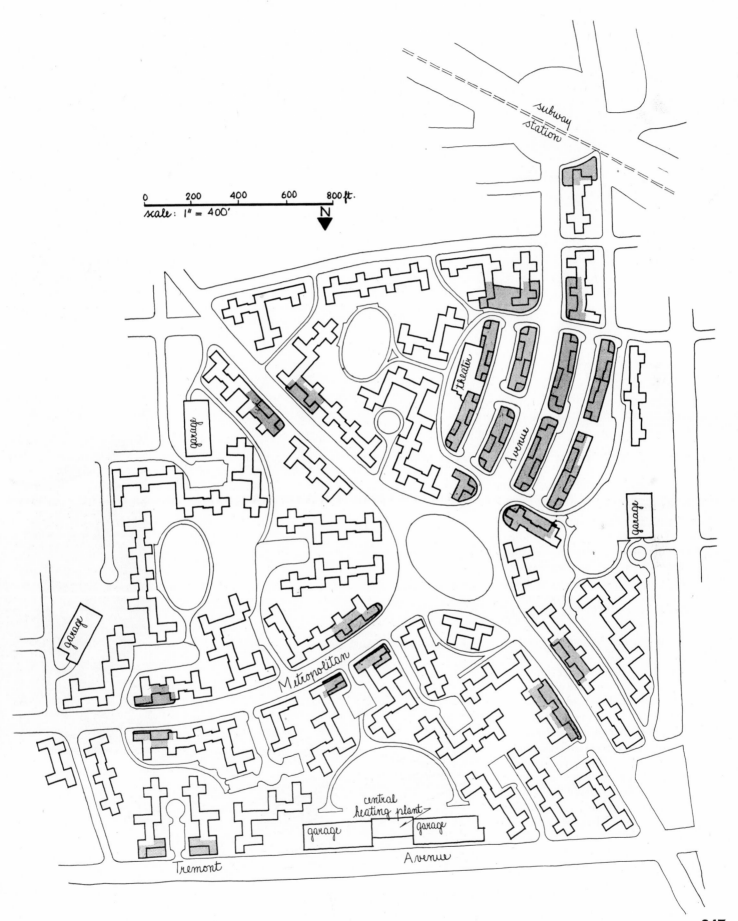

scale: 1" = 400'

0   200   400   600   800 ft.

N

subway station

garage

theatre

Avenue

garage

garage

Metropolitan

central heating plant

garage   garage

Tremont   Avenue

247

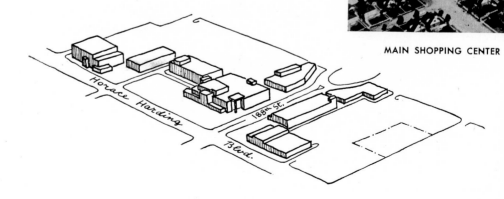

CENTER IN PLANNED COMMUNITY SEEKS
OUTSIDE TRADE ALSO

FRESH MEADOWS, a small town (pop. 11,000) built in a few months, is within the New York City limits, in the Flushing-Bayside district of Queens. During the last decade, population increase in this district was larger than in any other part of the city—46%, with the runner-up making only 29%. The New York Life Insurance Co., considering long-term investment values, has built these garden apartments to a density of only 17 families to the acre. Thanks largely to two 13-story blocks, the two- and three-story buildings have quite extensive lawns around them. The 174 acre site was formerly a country club, and the landscaping benefits from large trees left standing. More than 17 acres have been reserved for the main shopping center, another 3 acres for two neighborhood centers in opposite corners of the site. Unlike Greenbelt and Linda Vista, two self-contained and somewhat isolated new communities *shown on pages 232-241*, Fresh Meadows is surrounded by a competitive, built-up neighborhood. The main shop-

MAIN SHOPPING CENTER

248

secondary shopping center

secondary shopping center

main shopping center

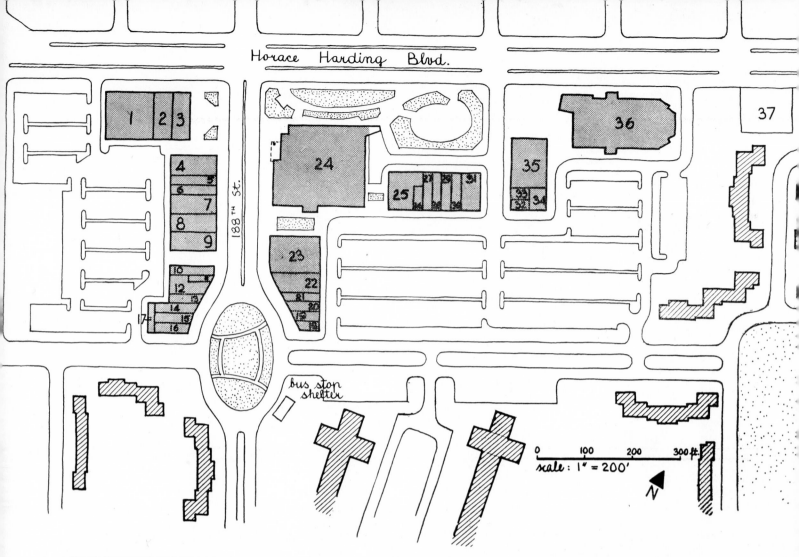

	TYPE OF STORE	WIDTH, DEPTH	SQ. FT. AREA
1	Supermarket	100 x 100	10,000
2	Bank	50 x 100	5,000
3	Drugs	35 x 100	3,500
4	Women's Wear	40 x 100	4,000
5	Shoes	20 x 100	2,000
6	Children's Shoes	20 x 100	2,000
7	Bank	40 x 100	4,000
8	Men's Wear	40 x 100	4,000
9	Women's Wear	40 x 100	4,000
	Doctors' Offices above stores 4-9		
10	Bakery & Delicatessen	20 x 96	1,940
11	Candy	15 x 50	1,000
12	Fabrics	30 x 80	2,480
13	Newsstand	20 x 75	1,500
14	Radio	20 x 80	1,560
15	Liquor	20 x 70	1,400
16	Florist	20 x 65	1,300
17	Delicatessen	17 x 65	1,140
18	Lingerie	20 x 40	770
19	Women's Shoes	20 x 45	908
20	Books	20 x 50	1,080
21	Luggage	20 x 60	1,254

	TYPE OF STORE	WIDTH, DEPTH	SQ. FT. AREA
22	Children's Wear	35 x 90	3,059
23	Variety	100 x 100	11,800
24	Department Store (2 stories and basement)	165 x 200	105,000
25	Post Office	60 x 80	5,400
26	Barber	20 x 60	1,000
27	Gifts	20 x 80	1,600
28	Cleaners	20 x 80	1,600
29	Children's Furniture, Toys	20 x 80	1,600
30	Beauty Shop	20 x 80	1,600
31	Tavern	40 x 80	3,200
	Bowling Alleys above stores 25-31		
32	Jewelry	20 x 40	867
33	Optometrist	20 x 40	853
34	Administration	40 x 40	1,600
35	Restaurant	80 x 100	7,700
	Administration Offices, Meeting and Banquet Rooms above stores 32-35		
36	Theater	100 x 220	22,000
37	Gas Station		
TOTAL STORE AREA			223,711

STORE GROUP IS SPLIT BY 188TH STREET. HORACE HARDING BOULEVARD IN BACKGROUND

ping center here is designed to serve about six times as many families as live in Fresh Meadows itself. So, for wider accessibility, it is placed at the northern edge of the community (on Horace Harding Boulevard, a main highway), rather than at its heart.

Preliminary surveys had shown the need for a department store, a theater, and a good restaurant, in addition to high-grade chain apparel stores formerly without representation in this neighborhood. Bloomingdale's was an almost inevitable choice for the department store. Thanks to their position on the Queens subway line at 59th Street, Manhattan, they are the most accessible New York department store for shoppers coming in from Long Island by subway or automobile. Consequently they already had

many customers in this area. Moreover they wanted to expand. They have been given a most prominent position in the middle of the store group on Horace Harding Boulevard.

It is interesting to find, however, that most of this important road frontage is occupied by a small park, which has been dedicated to the city. Perhaps this will prove an enticement for mothers and their children to cross the road from the houses on the far side of the Boulevard. The whole store group is split into two parts by 188th Street, the main entrance to Fresh Meadows apartments from Horace Harding Boulevard. This division by highway is somewhat out of line with most modern thinking on shopping center design. Moreover, the store group is further splayed at the south end by a

grand-plan oval at the street intersection. In addition the supermarket and the department store are both set on Horace Harding Boulevard, so they do nothing to pull outside traffic *through* the rest of the store group. In other words the planning of this center contributes little to increase the strength of that cumulative pull which we have previously stressed as one of the shopping center's most valuable extras for the merchant.

The theater, restaurant, and bowling alleys are all, reasonably enough, kept in a group at the east end of the Boulevard frontage, with a large parking area, in anticipation of peak evening trade.

Owner & Developer: New York Life Insurance Co. *Architects:* Voorhees, Walker, Foley & Smith.

OUTSIDE THE CORNER DRUGSTORE, SHADE TREES, BENCHES AND OPEN SPACE ENCOURAGE MOTHERS TO GOSSIP AND CHILDREN TO PLAY IN THE SUNSHINE

BY DAY SIGNS STAND OUT AGAINST WHITE-PAINTED BRICK OR MARBLE

AT NIGHT THE BACKGROUND STRIP IS BRIGHTLY LIT

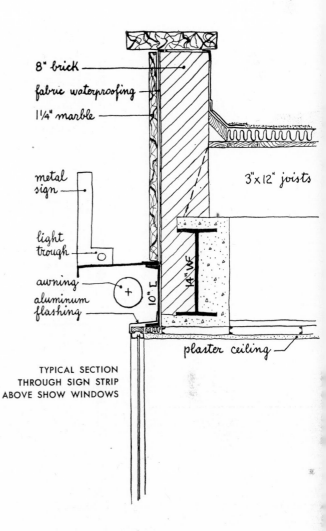

8" brick

fabric waterproofing

1¼" marble

metal sign

light trough

awning aluminum flashing

10" C

14" WF

3"×12" joists

plaster ceiling

TYPICAL SECTION
THROUGH SIGN STRIP
ABOVE SHOW WINDOWS

NAMEPLATES

Signs in Fresh Meadows are quite closely controlled by the landlords. As seen from Horace Harding Boulevard, the most prominent sign, especially when back-lit at night, is Bloomingdale's big trademark B on a tall panel of gray-white marble at the side of the store's tall main entrance.

Elsewhere in the center signs are confined to a strip of gray-white marble, or white-painted brick, above the show windows. At night this background strip is lit from the base of the sign letters, so that they stand out in silhouette. Everywhere through the shopping center there are trees, benches, flower beds, for the pleasure of shoppers and their children. It is the more surprising, therefore, that there is no continuous overhang along the face of the stores to protect shoppers from sun and rain.

253

FLEXIBILITY IN SECOND-FLOOR OFFICES

The Professional Building in Fresh Meadows is on the second floor, above the stores on the west side of 188th Street. The stores are 100 ft. deep, in five 20 ft. spans. This would make an awkward, too deep shape for division into offices, so the office floor is set back 20 ft. from the front. The corridor is then placed off-center, the office space on the street front being 40 ft. deep, that on the rear 30 ft. deep. This allows for a greater variety of size and shape. In the plan above is shown one part of the office space as divided at the present time. It is typical of the variety normally required in a professional building of this type. Another necessity for second floor doctors' offices is an elevator. Here it is housed in the southern of the two corner towers at the rear, as patients will normally come by automobile. Also in these towers are stairs and toilets.

SUPPLEMENTING THE MAIN STORE GROUP

Two secondary centers of neighborhood type supplement the shopping facilities of the main center at Fresh Meadows. They are placed on the two corners of the site most distant from the big store group, and contain the typical neighborhood center stores: supermarket, drug store and service stores. The two centers are similar both in size and plan. The store block is 80 ft. deep, increased to 100 ft. at one end for the supermarket. In a typical, time-tested pattern, the drug store is given the other corner position. In between are the service stores. One of the centers, opposite a public school, includes in its roster a branch of the Public Library. Most of the parking space is at the rear of the stores; but there are two lines in front also, for those using the centers for quick errands.

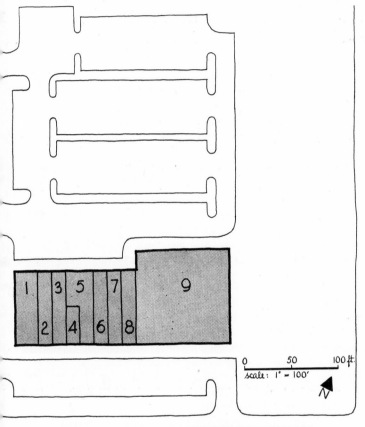

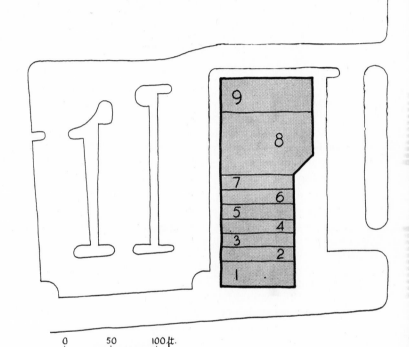

	TYPE OF STORE	WIDTH, DEPTH	SQ. FT. AREA
1	Drugs	32 x 75	2,320
2	Delicatessen	16 x 75	1,200
3	Shoe Repair	16 x 75	1,200
4	Barber	16 x 50	525
5	Public Library	16 x 75	1,875
6	Cleaners	16 x 75	1,200
7	Bakery	16 x 75	1,200
8	Newsstand	16 x 75	1,200
9	Supermarket	100 x 100	10,000
TOTAL STORE AREA			**20,720**

	TYPE OF STORE	WIDTH, DEPTH	SQ. FT. AREA
1	Drugs	28 x 75	2,160
2	Photographer	16 x 75	1,200
3	Newsstand	16 x 75	1,200
4	Delicatessen	16 x 75	1,200
5	Bakery	16 x 75	1,200
6		16 x 75	1,200
7	Liquor	16 x 75	1,200
8	Supermarket	66 x 100	6,600
9	Cleaners	33 x 100	3,300
TOTAL STORE AREA			**19,260**

METERED COOLING AND HEATING FROM CENTRAL PLANT

FRESH MEADOWS is probably the only large shopping center in which all the buildings are served by a central air-conditioning plant. The New York Life Insurance Co. had already decided upon a single large steam plant to heat the apartment houses and stores. In this carefully landscaped, and not too densely populated community, such a plant (furnished with elaborate control panels) was favored for appearance as well as cost.

Meanwhile the owners had also decided to supply the shopping center buildings with built-in air conditioning, rather than encourage each tenant to install his own equipment. They reasoned that, while the smaller stores could get along with individual units, the larger ones would require built-in equipment for cooling. The space needed to house such plants, the cost of service connections, and the added cost of operating and maintaining many separate plants—all these were obvious disadvantages of the method of air-conditioning each store separately.

If, on the other hand, a central cooling plant were set up alongside the central heating plant, the same crew could operate both. This saving in itself would almost if not quite offset the added cost of 2,000 ft. of insulated piping needed to connect the 26 stores, the bowling alleys, the professional building, and the theater with this central plant.

More important still in forcing a decision was the supply of cooling water for the compressors. Due to a recent alarming drop in the level of the water table in the western part of Long Island, New York State is now authorized by law to insist that any new well with a capacity of more than 69 gallons per minute, must return this water to the ground, after use, by means of diffusion wells.

Many buildings in the shopping center would have required a good deal more than this 69 gpm minimum for cooling their refrigeration equipment, so that there would have been a large number of supply and diffusion wells within a very limited area. This would gradually have raised the ground water temperature, reducing the efficiency of the whole system. To supply the central plant, two wells (600 ft. apart and 100 ft. deep) each give 500 gpm. This water is at a constant year-round temperature of 52°. The 1000 gpm flow will satisfy the cooling needs of refrigeration equipment with 1200 tons capacity. Two diffusion wells were sunk about 500 ft. away on the downstream side of the ground water flow, so that the heat added to the water by the equipment would be carried away from the two supply wells.

In accordance with the requirements of the New York State control commission, no water is allowed to escape from the system except into the diffusion wells. As a safeguard against loss, the lines out of the supply wells and into the diffusion wells are metered.

The temperature difference between the flow and return mains is designed to be 15° (45° as the chilled water leaves the plant, 60° on its return). Circulation is by three centrifugal pumps operating in parallel. Change in load changes the temperature difference; but this is immediately brought back to normal by changing the pump combination, which in turn changes the rate of flow.

Experience has shown that the total refrigeration load often drops to 400 tons or less for considerable periods during the summer. This small load could be handled by the ground water at 52°, with a 10° rise. Accordingly, connections have now been made so that ground water may be circulated through the system at such periods. The compressors are then shut down entirely, making for considerable economies in power costs.

The whole chilled water system is sensitively metered, partly as a check on its operation, partly for billing the two largest customers (theater and department store). The smaller stores are charged for air-conditioning at a flat rate. It was difficult to find a meter capable of measuring accurately the small temperature changes, and the sometimes low rate of flow, between the chilled water as it left the central plant and as it returned once again. The three meters now in use (one at the central plant, one at the theater, and one at the department store) read directly in therms (100,000 Btu) as a rate of flow indicated on a recording chart. At the same time the therms are totalized on a counter.

To compensate for variations in load, in peak hours, and in distance from the central plant, at each consumer's point of connection with the main supply lines there is a bypass from flow to return, with a three-way thermostatically operated flow valve. In each such bypass a balancing cock with indicating dial allows precise adjustment of the flow.

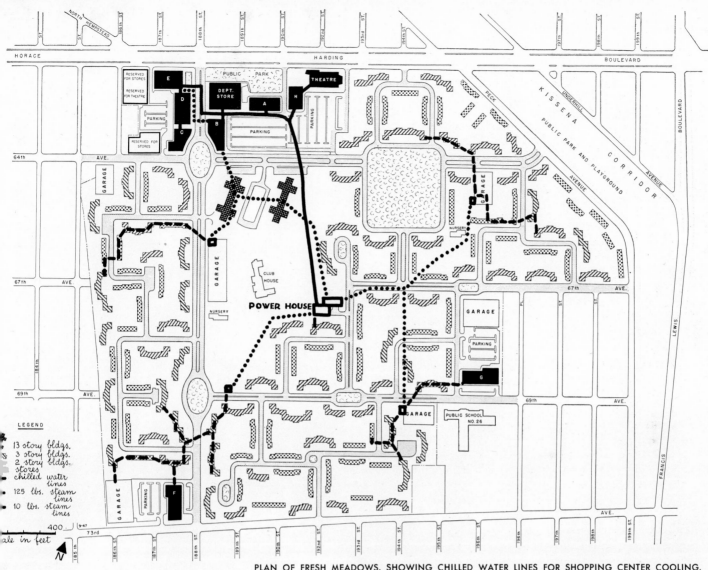

PLAN OF FRESH MEADOWS, SHOWING CHILLED WATER LINES FOR SHOPPING CENTER COOLING,
ALSO STEAM LINES (125 LB. PRESSURE, STEPPED DOWN TO 10 LB. AT LOCAL
CONTROL STATIONS) CONSULTING ENGINEERS: MEYER, STRONG & JONES

LEGEND

- 13 story bldgs.
- 3 story bldgs.
- 2 story bldgs.
- stores
- chilled water lines
- 125 lbs. steam lines
- 10 lbs. steam lines

400
Scale in feet

N

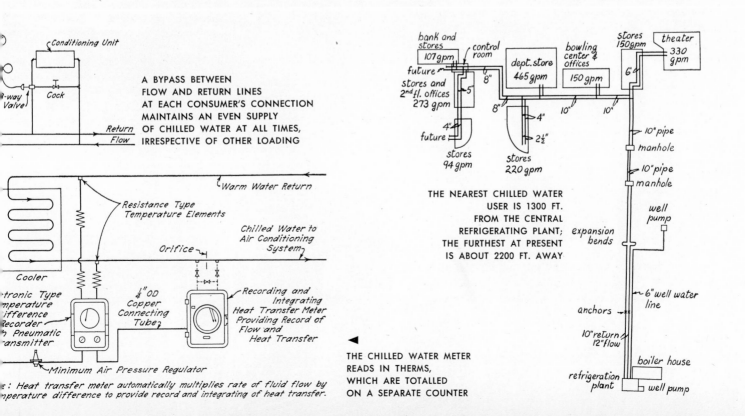

Conditioning Unit

3-way Valve

Cock

Return

Flow

A BYPASS BETWEEN
FLOW AND RETURN LINES
AT EACH CONSUMER'S CONNECTION
MAINTAINS AN EVEN SUPPLY
OF CHILLED WATER AT ALL TIMES,
IRRESPECTIVE OF OTHER LOADING

Warm Water Return

Resistance Type
Temperature Elements

Chilled Water to
Air Conditioning
System

Orifice

Cooler

Electronic Type
Temperature
Difference
Recorder
with Pneumatic
Transmitter

¼" OD
Copper
Connecting
Tube

Recording and
Integrating
Heat Transfer Meter
Providing Record of
Flow and
Heat Transfer

Minimum Air Pressure Regulator

Note: Heat transfer meter automatically multiplies rate of fluid flow by
temperature difference to provide record and integrating of heat transfer.

bank and
stores
107 gpm

control
room

future
stores and
2nd fl. offices
273 gpm

dept. store
465 gpm

bowling
center &
offices
150 gpm

Stores
150 gpm

theater
330
gpm

8"

6"

future

5"

8"

4"

4"

10"

10"

stores
94 gpm

stores
220 gpm

2½"

THE NEAREST CHILLED WATER
USER IS 1300 FT.
FROM THE CENTRAL
REFRIGERATING PLANT;
THE FURTHEST AT PRESENT
IS ABOUT 2200 FT. AWAY

THE CHILLED WATER METER
READS IN THERMS,
WHICH ARE TOTALLED
ON A SEPARATE COUNTER

10" pipe
manhole

10" pipe
manhole

well
pump

expansion
bends

6" well water
line

anchors

10" return
12" flow

boiler house

refrigeration
plant

well pump

MERCHANT BUILDER CREATES NEW TOWN

LEVITTOWN in less than three years has changed 4,500 acres of farmland into the largest town on Long Island, N. Y. It claims to have more free public swimming pools in proportion to its size than any other town in the U. S. It certainly has a smaller proportion of aged than any community of equal size, for it is populated almost exclusively by young veterans of World War II, who fall within a singularly narrow age group.

Levitt's houses have long been famous as the best value for money in any of the real estate developments in the New York area (in spite of the comparatively long and expensive commutation to work in New York City). Until recently they were sold only to veterans. All are single-family houses. What started as just another housing development has now blossomed out into a complete community, with new schools and shopping centers, as well as other facilities, strategically dotted among the 15,000 houses.

In such a community it becomes exceedingly important to satisfy the needs of young children. Sidewalks must be wide enough to accommodate bicycles and baby carriages, as well as pedestrian shoppers hauling their groceries home in a cart. The small neighborhood centers *(see next page)* have children's playgrounds, with swings and seesaws and sand piles, where mothers may leave their children while they go marketing. The larger shopping center, on Hempstead Turnpike *(see page 262)*, has a supervised nursery.

Going out in the evening becomes for these parents a somewhat complicated and expensive affair. And after all, when every house comes with a built-in television set, why should they want to go out looking for a half-way-good movie? It is perhaps significant that even the big central store group on Hempstead Turnpike does not include a movie theater.

Developer: Levitt & Sons.

**WIDE SHADY SIDEWALKS
FOR MOTHERS, CHILDREN, CARRIAGES**

community building

swimming pool

gas stn

stores

stores

stores

Childrens' playground

stores

stores

IN LEVITTOWN there are several small shopping centers for convenience goods strategically placed among the thousands of single-family houses which make up this community *(see airview, page 258)*. Each of these centers is of uniform type: four store blocks set on a shallow S curve, with the streets on each side widened to allow for angle parking at the curb. Alongside the stores and the gas station there is a swimming pool, a children's playground, and a community recreation building with bowling alleys and a restaurant. There are no large parking areas, merely widened streets, because much of the trade is walk-in.

The low, small-scale store buildings, of whitewashed brick, are the two-front type. Actually these independent merchants admit only one display and entrance front, that facing toward the swimming pool, for the parking street on the other front has to double as a service road. This plan is perhaps a little too simple to be satisfactory. But the short narrow blocks, widely spaced, give easy access from all sides.

EXTERIOR AND INTERIOR OF NURSERY AT MAIN SHOPPING CENTER

HAPPY CHILDREN, HAPPY SHOPPERS

CHILDREN'S PLAYGROUND AT NEIGHBORHOOD CENTER

MANY SHOPPING CENTERS have *planned* to include nurseries and playgrounds where children could play safely while their parents went shopping; but in centers so far built such accommodations are rare. Nurseries pay no high percentage rent; in fact taking care of other people's children may more easily lead to damage suits than gratitude. In Levittown, however, where the overwhelming majority of customers are young married couples with children, the need was imperative enough to produce a supervised nursery in the main shopping center, and playgrounds complete with swings and sandpiles in the small neighborhood centers.

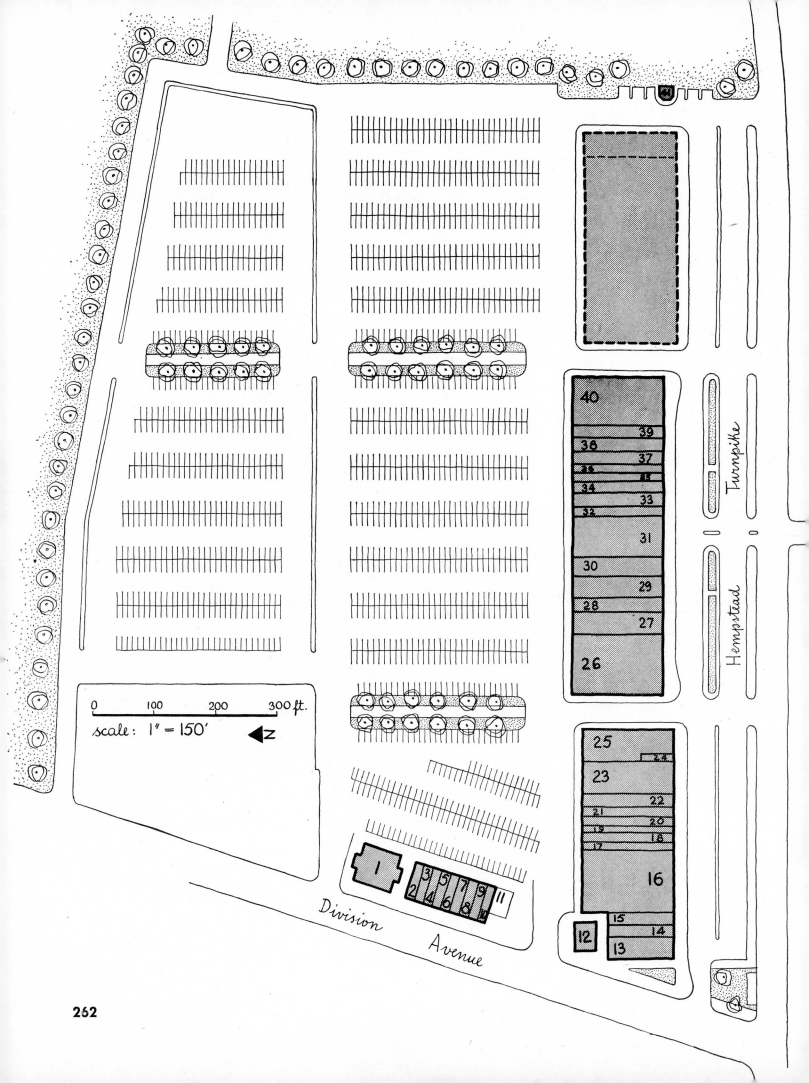

scale: 1" = 150'

N

Turnpike

Hempstead

Division

Avenue

40
39
38
37
36
35
34
33
32
31
30
29
28
27
26

25
24
23
22
21
20
19
18
17
16
15
14
13
12

1
3 5 7 9 11
2 4 6 8 10

0   100   200   300 ft.

	TYPE OF STORE	WIDTH, DEPTH	SQ. FT. AREA
1	Two story Office & Professional Building	80 x 70	5,600
2	Beauty Shop	15 x 60	900
3	Children's Shoes	15 x 60	900
4	Gifts	15 x 60	900
5	House Furnishings	15 x 60	900
6	Barber Shop	15 x 60	900
7	Finance Company	15 x 60	900
8	Cleaners	15 x 60	900
9	Shoe Repair	15 x 60	900
10	Optician	15 x 60	900
11	Gas Station		
12	Nursery	35 x 45	1,575
13	Drugs	32 x 100	3,200
14	Meat	18 x 100	1,800
15	Fruit & Vegetables	18 x 100	1,800
16	Supermarket	90 x 150	13,500
17	Cleaners	15 x 150	2,250
81	Liquor	14 x 150	2,100
19	Bakery	16 x 150	2,400
20	Bank	14 x 150	2,100
21	Children's Wear	14 x 150	2,100

	TYPE OF STORE	WIDTH, DEPTH	SQ. FT. AREA
22	Stationery	20 x 150	3,000
23	Supermarket	50 x 150	7,500
24	Interior Decorator	11 x 55	605
25	Men's & Women's Wear	40 x 150	7,050
26	Variety	100 x 150	15,000
27	Women's Wear	32 x 150	4,800
28	Women's Wear	19 x 150	2,850
29	Children's Wear	34 x 150	5,100
30	Women's Wear	34 x 150	5,100
31	Variety	65 x 150	9,750
32	Candy	15 x 150	2,250
33	Shoes	22 x 150	3,300
34	Jewelry	14 x 150	2,100
35		16 x 150	2,400
36	Haberdasher	16 x 150	2,400
37		14 x 150	2,100
38	Men's Shoes	16 x 150	2,400
39	Sewing Machines	20 x 150	3,000
40	Department Store	75 x 150	11,250
41	Gas Station		
TOTAL STORE AREA			138,480

COMPETITIVE STORE GROUPING

LEVITTOWN CENTER, though not owned or developed by Levitt Bros., is in the heart of Levittown, at the intersection of Division Avenue and the Hempstead Turnpike, which is a main through highway *(see page 258)*. Along this frontage there are three large store blocks, each 150 ft. deep. That at the corner, where there is a bus stop, houses food stores and a drug store. The center block contains two large variety stores and a number of smaller apparel stores.

The block at the eastern end is not yet completed. The aim throughout has been to group competitive stores, in order to offer comparison shopping equivalent to that found downtown. On Division Street, a less important highway, is a two-story block of professional offices (mostly doctors'), the nursery *(see page 261)*, a line of service stores, a gas station. There are four lines of front parking on Hempstead Turnpike, but the main parking area is in the rear, with access by roads cut between the store blocks. These roads are used both by pedestrians and autos. On the main front they are as much as 500 ft. apart, the length of the central store building. The rear parking area has been dedicated to the city, which maintains and polices it.

Developers: Hempstead Division Construction Corp. *Architect:* A. H. Salkowitz; Leo A. Novick, Willam Sambur, consultants.

TYPICAL LONG ISLAND MAJOR CENTER

GLEN OAKS shopping center, in Queens, is very typical of the larger store groups now springing up in this fast-growing section of New York City on Long Island. There are 3,000 people living in these garden apartments, and 20,000 more within two minutes drive. Yet there is no major store center within three miles.

In plan this center is reminiscent of Levittown Center, shown on the two preceding pages. But these two-front stores are not planned for front parking; only a wide sidewalk separates them from Union Turnpike, a much-traveled highway. And only pedestrian thruways connect the street front of the store blocks with the parking area in the rear. The automobile shopper must drive around one end of this 1,000 ft. long store block,

in order to reach the parking area. The pedestrian thruways, lined with service stores, continue as raised and landscaped pathways across the parking area, a safe route for mothers and children coming and going between the stores and the garden apartments in the rear.

The center store block is 150 ft. deep, with a two-story section at one end for the department store and apparel stores. The two flanking store blocks are only 75 ft. deep, except for a section at the inside end which is extended back to 150 ft. to provide for supermarkets or other high-volume stores.

Owner & Developer: Glen Oaks Shopping Center Inc. *Architect:* Leo V. Berger.

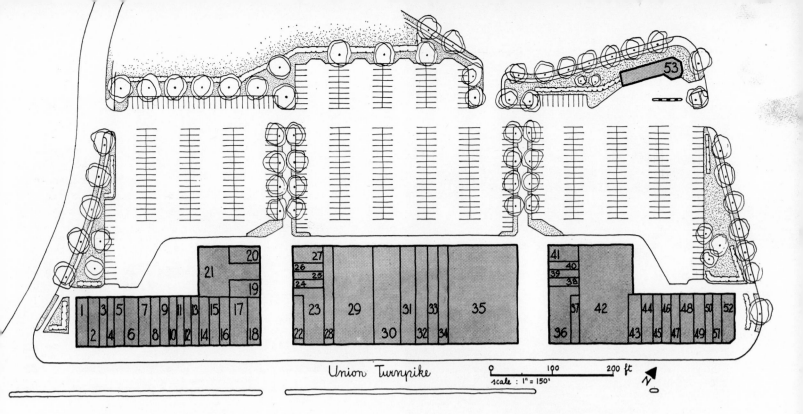

Union Turnpike

scale : 1" = 150'

	TYPE OF STORE	WIDTH, DEPTH	SQ. FT. AREA
1	Stationery	19 x 75	1,425
2	Luncheonette	17 x 75	1,275
3	Frozen Foods	11 x 75	825
4	Cleaners	11 x 75	825
5		16 x 75	1,200
6	Restaurant	22 x 75	1,650
7	Bakery	20 x 75	1,500
8		15 x 75	1,125
9	Children's Wear	15 x 75	1,125
10	Jewelry	11 x 75	825
11	Women's Wear	11 x 75	825
12	Florist	11 x 75	825
13	Children's Shoes	11 x 75	825
14	Furniture	16 x 75	1,200
15	Hardware	16 x 75	1,200
16	Fabrics	16 x 75	1,200
17		28 x 75	2,100
18	Cocktail Lounge	20 x 75	1,500
19	Public Library	27 x 50	1,350
20	Post Office	25 x 50	1,250
21	Administration Office	50 x 75	4,500
22	Men's & Boy's Wear	16 x 75	1,200
23	Radio	33 x 87	3,047
24	Beauty Shop	12 x 50	600
25	Photographer	12 x 50	600
26		12 x 50	600
27		25 x 50	1,250

	TYPE OF STORE	WIDTH, DEPTH	SQ. FT. AREA
28	Candy	15 x 150	2,250
29	Variety	65 x 150	9,750
30	Children's Wear	43 x 150	6,450
31	Shoes	22 x 150	3,300
32	Men's Wear	20 x 150	3,000
33	Specialty Shop	17 x 150	2,550
34	Women's Wear	17 x 150	2,550
35	Department Store	111 x 150	16,650
36	Drugs	35 x 90	3,750
37	Liquor	13 x 75	975
38	Beauty Shop	13 x 50	650
39	Barber	13 x 50	650
40		13 x 50	650
41	Shoe Repair	25 x 50	1,250
42	Supermarket	80 x 150	12,525
43	Interior Decorator	20 x 75	1,500
44	Luncheonette	18 x 75	1,350
45	Lingerie, Sportswear	15 x 75	1,125
46	Meats	15 x 75	1,125
47	Bakery	15 x 75	1,125
48	Fruit & Vegetables	20 x 75	1,500
49	Delicatessen	18 x 75	1,350
50	Cleaners	12 x 75	900
51	Children's Furniture	15 x 75	1,125
52	Stationery	20 x 75	1,500
53	Filling Station		
TOTAL STORE AREA			115,397

MORE PICTURES OF GLEN OAKS ON THE FOLLOWING PAGE

AT END OF STORE BLOCK, SIGN POINTS WAY TO REAR PARKING

SIGNS ON TOP EDGE OF OVERHANG BREAK SMOOTH LINE

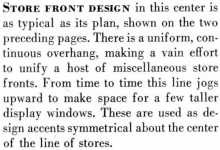

AGGRESSIVE INDIVIDUALITY IN SIGNS AND AWNINGS

GLEN OAKS SHOPPING CENTER, QUEENS, NEW YORK CITY

STORE FRONT DESIGN in this center is as typical as its plan, shown on the two preceding pages. There is a uniform, continuous overhang, making a vain effort to unify a host of miscellaneous store fronts. From time to time this line jogs upward to make space for a few taller display windows. These are used as design accents symmetrical about the center of the line of stores.

The overhang itself has shrunk to a narrow, vestigial feature. No longer capable of sheltering pedestrian shoppers from sun and rain, it serves merely as a continuous bracket for the lights which are set in the soffit. The supermarket, however, does have a deep vestibule to shelter baby carriages, children and housewives. The store signs have unfortunately been allowed to spread from the strip beneath the overhang and break out on its top edge. As for awnings, this center surely proves that individual choice is not advisable for improving appearance.

DEEP VESTIBULE OF SUPERMARKET SHELTERS CHILDREN AND MOTHERS

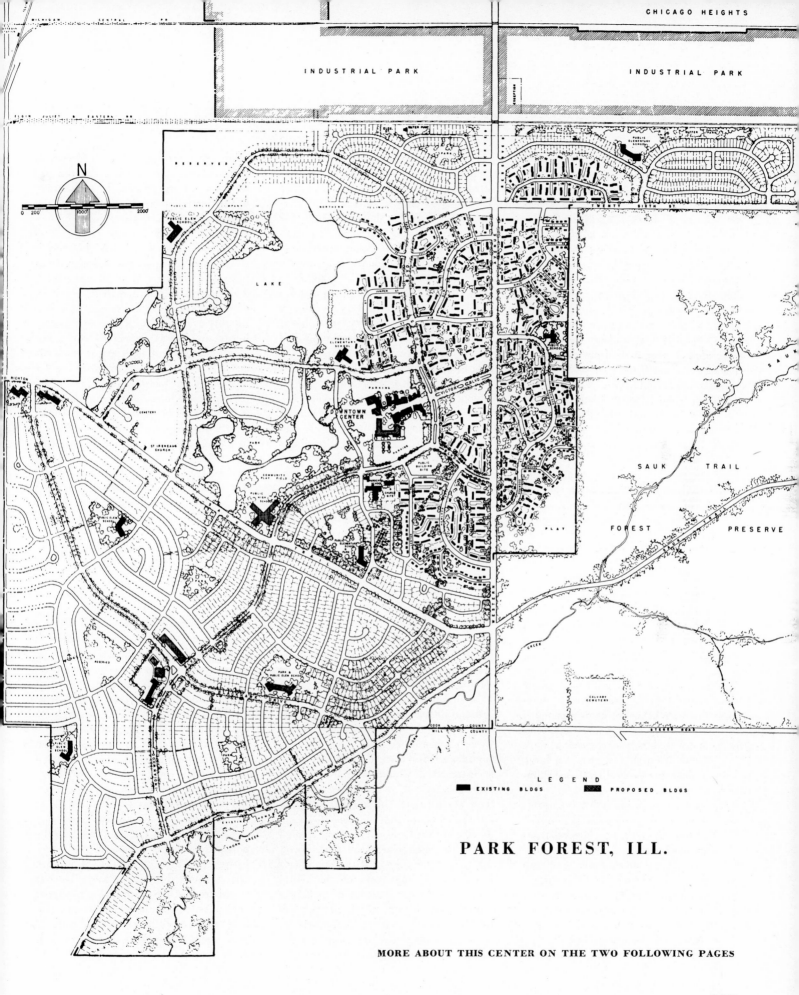

PARK FOREST, ILL.

MORE ABOUT THIS CENTER ON THE TWO FOLLOWING PAGES

267

PLANNED SUBURBAN COMMUNITY WITH REGIONAL-SIZE CENTER

PARK FOREST, Ill. is a newly created suburban community, 25 miles south of Chicago. Its layout is patterned upon the Greenbelt towns *(cf. the plan of Greenbelt shown on page 232)* built by the Resettlement Administration as relief projects (and also as working models for other planned communities) during the Depression years of the Thirties.

The Park Forest shopping center, like that in Greenbelt, is placed toward the center of the community, on the edge of a large public park and recreation area *(see plan on page 267)*. Immediately adjacent to the north and east are the 3,000 rental units already built. When the development plans are complete there will be 5,000 single-family homes stretching out south and west from the center.

According to a market analysis prepared by the Real Estate Research Corporation, the 8,000 families in the completed community will each have an average annual income of more than $5,300. All but $2,000 of this will, it is claimed, be spent in retail stores. 80% of the total (i.e. more than $21 million) will be spent at the Park Forest center.

However, the support of Park Forest residents will be less than half the new center's anticipated total. It hopes to draw trade from the whole South Chicago area. From 1940 to 1950 the wages of industrial workers in this area have increased by 124%. Since the end of World War II, a large number of new industrial plants have moved into the area. But the shopping facilities have not grown as much as the Buying Power. By exercising greater "suction" than any nearby center, Park Forest should be able to attract a large body of these presently dissatisfied shoppers on wheels.

To gauge the shopping habits and present dissatisfaction of those living outside Park Forest, Real Estate Research Corporation made three surveys. The first consisted of 2,121 on-the-spot interviews with women shoppers in five of the major shopping districts in the northern section of Park Forest's assumed Trading Area. The questions asked in this first survey were: Where do you live? How did you get here? Do you own a car? How many adults accompanied you? What merchandise did you come to buy? How often do you visit this shopping center? The answers showed that a large percentage of Saturday shoppers (48%, for example, of those interviewed in Chicago Heights) came from other communities. Many of them came by automobile (55% in Chicago Heights, 33% at the 63rd and Halsted shopping district, which is already within the Chicago city limits). Shoppers who are already in the habit of driving to other communities for major purchases could probably be drawn without too much difficulty to a new center such as Park Forest, which offered more convenience and value.

The second of the three surveys was by questionnaires mailed to 5,000 consumers outside the Chicago city limits (but still within the assumed Park Forest Trading Area), and distributed according to population density. The questions asked were: Where do you go for shopping goods (clothing, furniture, etc.)? How often? How do you reach the stores? What is your opinion of (a) the variety of stores, (b) parking facilities, (c) general accessibility, (d) merchandising and service, (e) general facilities?

The abnormally high response to this questionnaire (12% instead of a normal 3%) is considered by the analysts to be, in itself, a good index of the shoppers' general dissatisfaction. In addition the questionnaire confirmed the mobility of these shoppers: 40% always shopped by automobile, and only 26.4% did their shopping in the community where they lived. On the other hand (and of equal significance for Park Forest), few were accustomed to shopping in downtown Chicago; only 22% said they shopped there exclusively, with another 10% admitting an occasional trip downtown.

The last of the three surveys was limited to the present residents of Park Forest itself. With the help of data already collected by the managers of the rental units, the survey attempted to gauge family composition, place of employment, income, automobile ownership, previous residence, relationship of wage earners to rest of family.

In figuring the amount of trade which Park Forest should attract, and the size of store buildings which such trade would justify, these analysts follow the pattern already outlined on page 17. They assume that the new center will be of regional size, and that it will have such enticements as value, accessibility, comparison shopping and ample parking.

The analysts admit that their definition of the Park Forest Trading Area—a roughly oval shape with boundaries ranging from 24 to 42 miles from the center—is tentative and arbitrary. But this is actually not of major importance; for Trading Area boundaries and percentage discounts are interlocking computations. A large area with outer fringes drastically discounted can be the equivalent, in final figures, of a more confined area which has been less heavily discounted at the edges.

The 1,600,000 people included in what these analysts consider the Park Forest Trading Area spend $1,482,500,000 annually in retail stores. Dividing the Area into 33 sections, the analysts calculate for each the population, income, and retail expenditures in the various store classifications. Then they decide, mainly upon the basis of their own local knowledge and experience, what proportion of those expenditures will be attracted to Park Forest. To determine these discounts (or ratios of suction, as these analysts prefer to call them) account is taken of relative distance, accessibility, choice and price of goods, etc.

To each of the 33 sections of the Trading Area three different ratios are applied, one for shopping goods, one for convenience goods (food, drugs, liquor, hardware), one for miscellaneous stores. Ratios for shopping goods range from 1% at the edge of the Trading Area (that means that 1% of the total spent by the population of this section will in future be spent at Park Forest) to 80% in Park Forest itself. Ratios for miscellaneous stores are half those applied to shopping goods. As for convenience stores, no section except Park Forest, with a ratio of 80% (conservative), is given a ratio of more than 10%.

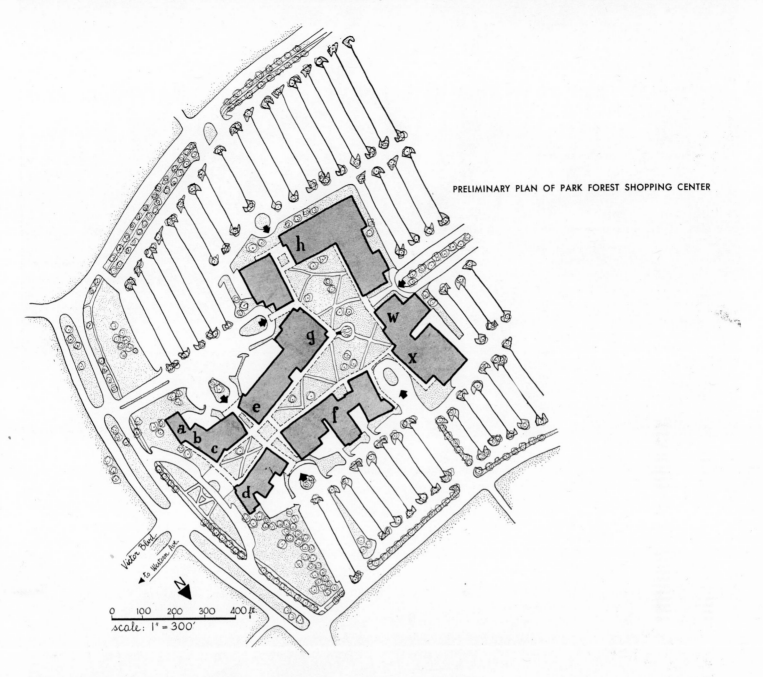

PRELIMINARY PLAN OF PARK FOREST SHOPPING CENTER

scale: 1" = 300'

0 100 200 300 400 ft.

N

Victor Blvd.
to Western Ave.

Having applied these ratios to the retail expenditures throughout the Trading Area, the analysts forecast annual gross sales at Park Forest of $43,934,600, actually no more than 2.3% of the total for the Trading Area. Only $10,513,000 would come from the residents of Park Forest itself.

As if acknowledging its dependence upon trade from outside the immediate community, the main axis of the pedestrian mall which runs through the center is a continuation of a four-lane divided highway branching off Western Avenue, the chief North-South artery which feeds the whole area south of Chicago.

The irregularly shaped buildings proposed for the center allow for a variety of store depths and easy, visually inviting access from the parking areas to the central grassed mall. The splayed siting of the building blocks helps to break the center into a number of more intimate courts, without sacrifice of spaciousness and continuity.

Each store block has a large, fenced service yard in the rear, shielded from the customer parking fields. This is an excellent feature in itself, but unfortunately it also increases the distance which customers must walk from the parking area to the stores and back again.

Owner & Developer: American Community Builders Inc. *Architects:* Loebl, Schlossman & Bennett.

KEY TO BUILDINGS IN PLAN ABOVE

a Medical Clinic
b Post Office
c Bank
d Administration Offices
e Drug Store
f Theater
g Supermarket
h Department Store
w Theater
x Bowling Alleys

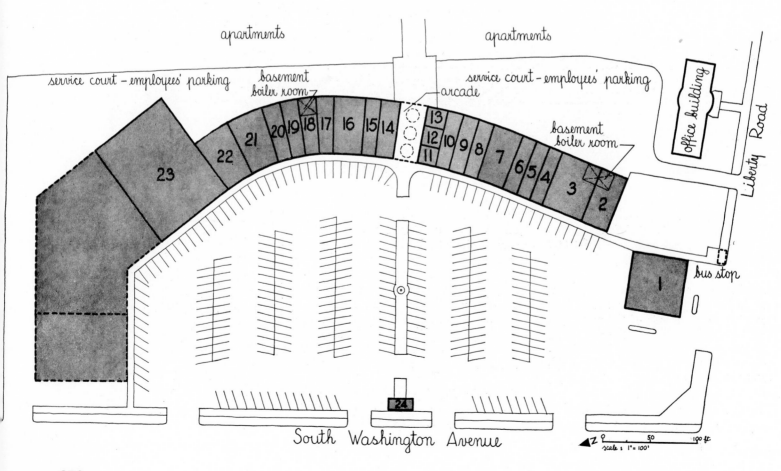

apartments   apartments

service court – employees' parking   basement boiler room   arcade   service court – employees' parking

office building

basement boiler room

Liberty Road

23   22   21   20   19   18   17   16   15   14   13   12   11   10   9   8   7   6   5   4   3   2

bus stop

1

South Washington Avenue

scale: 1" = 100'

CURVED PLAN WITH FRONT PARKING

FOSTER VILLAGE, Bergenfield, N. J. is a garden apartment development (636 families) in one of those New York suburbs which, since World War II, have outgrown their downtown shopping districts. This curving line of stores is on a 5-acre lot between South Washington Avenue and the apartments.

Adequate and free parking in this area has immense drawing power (Bergenfield's main shopping street, for example, has half-hour parking meters), so naturally enough it is all put out in front where it can be seen by passers-by. To encourage walk-in trade from the apartments at the rear, there is a connecting pathway through the central arcade.

The curved line of the store block puts this center halfway between the L and straight-line types. It avoids the L plan's dead space at the corner, and keeps more store fronts within the shopper's view. It also has a certain graciousness of form. On the other hand, the irregularly shaped service areas in the rear are wasteful of space; and construction costs are almost inevitably higher on a curved than on a straight building.

The standard store bay is 15 x 60 ft. Most are rented at a flat yearly rental which includes heating. Only the larger stores are on percentage leases. Ducts for air-conditioning are installed by the landlord, but tenants must pay for their own units.

Owner: Bergenfield Plaza Inc. *Architect:* Alan Wood Fraser.

	TYPE OF STORE	WIDTH, DEPTH	SQ. FT. AREA
1	Filling Station		
2	Restaurant	30 x 60	1,800
3	Hardware	45 x 60	2,700
4	Household Appliances	15 x 60	900
5	Children's Furniture	15 x 60	900
6	Upholstery	15 x 60	900
7	Women's Wear	30 x 60	1,800
8	Fabrics	15 x 60	900
9	Beauty Shop	15 x 60	900
10	Children's Wear	15 x 60	900
11	Gifts	20 x 20	400
12	Barber	20 x 20	400
13	Shoe Repair	20 x 20	400
14	Luncheonette	20 x 60	1,200
15	Drugs	15 x 60	900
16	Bakery	30 x 60	1,800
17	Delicatessen	15 x 60	900
18	Liquor	15 x 60	900
19	Stationery	15 x 60	900
20	Self-Service Laundry	15 x 60	900
21	Cleaners	30 x 60	1,800
22	Shoes	30 x 60	1,800
23	Supermarket	90 x 120	10,800
24	Frozen Custard	30 x 15	450
	TOTAL STORE AREA		35,250

PATHWAY THROUGH CENTRAL ARCADE TO APARTMENTS IN REAR

SUPERMARKET TOWER AT STREET END OF CURVE ANNOUNCES CENTER

ENTRANCE TO SECOND-FLOOR OFFICES

STONE FACING, SMALL-PANED WINDOWS
FIT STORES INTO RESIDENTIAL NEIGHBORHOOD

SPRINGWELLS PARK shopping center is on the outer edge of a subdivision near Detroit, Mich. This group of stores is designed primarily to supply the day-to-day needs of the subdivision residents. A large part of this trade is walk-in, and those who come in an automobile are usually on quick in-and-out errands. Consequently the parking space allowed is not as large here as in some other centers of equal size; but plenty of space has

been set aside for future expansion of stores or parking space.

There are a few professional offices (mostly doctors' and dentists') on the second floor. Entrance to these is from the central pedestrian mall between the two store blocks, which leads to the apartments and single-family houses in the subdivision at the rear.

The neatness and restraint of the store buildings is particularly commendable.

Store signs, in a uniform style of lettering, are all confined to a narrow band directly above the show windows. The latter, divided into small panes by white-painted muntins, help to maintain the small, domestic scale which characterizes the whole center, keeping it in harmony with its residential surroundings.

Owner: The Ford Foundation. *Architects:* R. Taylor (site), H. Colwell (bldg.).

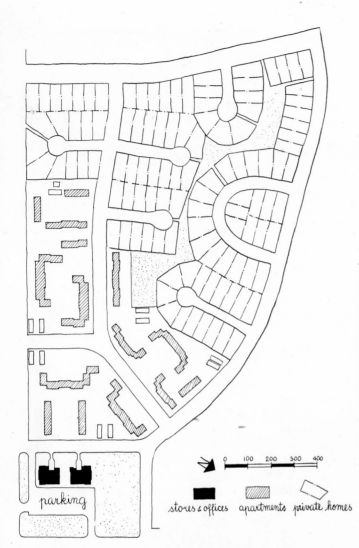

parking

stores & offices   apartments   private homes

THE STORES ARE AT ONE EDGE OF THE SUBDIVISION

SERVICE BAYS ARE SEPARATED FROM PEDESTRIAN TRAFFIC

PEDESTRIAN MALL BETWEEN THE TWO STORE BLOCKS

	TYPE OF STORE	WIDTH, DEPTH	SQ. FT. AREA
1	Drugs	25 x 80	2,240
2	Barber	20 x 75	1,500
3	Men's Wear	20 x 60	1,200
4	Women's Wear	25 x 70	1,750
5	Gifts	25 x 70	1,650
6	Church	25 x 60	1,500
7	Supermarket	40 x 80	3,200
TOTAL STORE AREA			13,040

Doctors' and Professional Offices on second floor

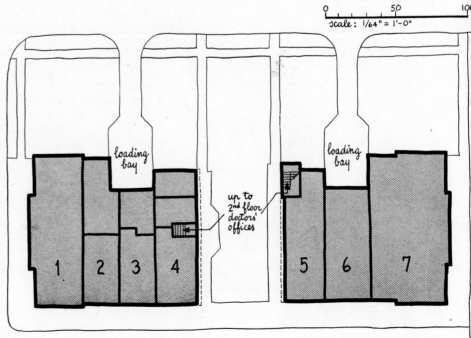

scale: 1/64" = 1'-0"

loading bay

loading bay

up to 2nd floor doctors' offices

CUSTOMERS ARRIVE AT LIDO SHOPS
BY BOAT, AS WELL AS BY AUTO AND ON FOOT

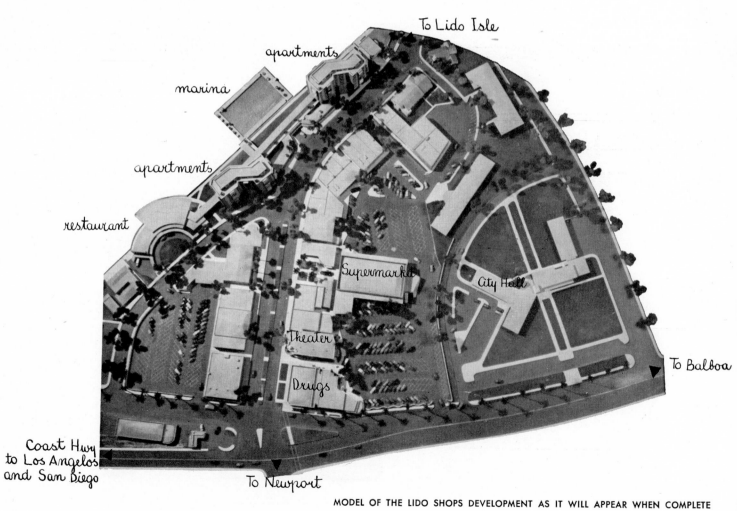

MODEL OF THE LIDO SHOPS DEVELOPMENT AS IT WILL APPEAR WHEN COMPLETE

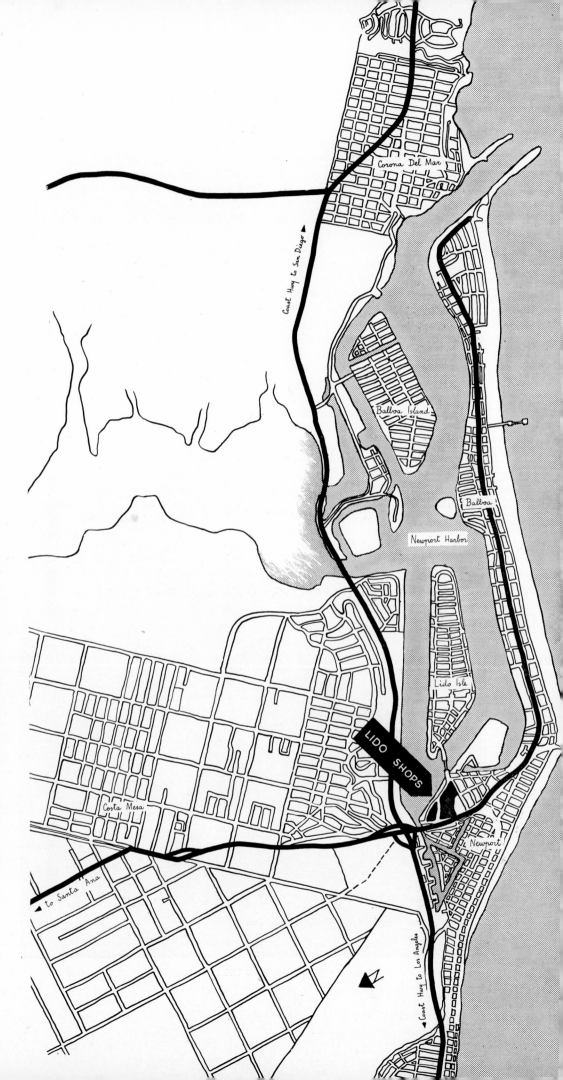

NEWPORT HARBOR, only 42 miles south of Los Angeles along the main Coast Highway, is the largest natural harbor between San Francisco and San Diego. It provides sheltered anchorage for more than 4,000 pleasure craft. During the last few years the harbor has become, indeed, so overcrowded that proposals are now being considered for extending it east of the Coast Highway by dredging the upper neck.

On the ocean side of the harbor, forming a gigantic breakwater, is the Balboa Peninsula, with Newport at its landward end. Projecting into the center of the harbor are Balboa Island and Lido Isle. On the far side of the harbor entrance, to the north, is Corona del Mar. Inland, beyond the Coast Highway, is Costa Mesa. It has a year-round population of 12,750. Access to Newport, the Balboa Peninsula, and Lido Isle is by wandering fingers of roadway which converge in Newport at a clover-leaf intersection with the Coast Highway. Dominating this bottleneck, next to Newport Town Hall, is the Lido Shops store group, owned by the Griffith Co., who also developed Lido Isle.

At present the main roadway passes right through the center; but traffic on this street will be eased when a new bypass road, at present under construction, is completed. So far Lido Shops contains only three units, a supermarket, a drug store, and a movie theater.

The completed center, however, is planned to include about 30 more stores. In addition the 1000 ft. of waterfront on Newport Harbor will be exploited with apartment houses, a hotel, and a large terraced restaurant overhanging the water. Of the 12.6 acre site 5 acres are reserved for parking, to accommodate those arriving by automobile. For those coming by boat there will be a spacious marina on the harbor front.

It has already been pointed out that any motorist who reaches Newport, Balboa, or Lido Isle must pass Lido Shops. The total population funneled through Lido Shops amounts to 3,193 families year-round, with a total purchasing power of $13,456,000. During the summer months there are 4,688 families with a total purchasing power of $19,485,800. These figures are taken from a market survey made by McConnell's Economic Surveys in 1949. The same firm made a survey in 1944, and comparison of the two gives a dramatic picture of the area's growth.

In 1944 Lido Isle had only 177 families; five years later there were 320. Purchasing power increased from $1,377,000 to $3,665,000. In 1944 the Balboa Peninsula had 418 families; in 1949 there were 700. With Balboa Island and Corona del Mar included, the total number of families in the Newport Harbor area rose from 4,741 in 1944 to 6,246 in 1949; and the total purchasing power jumped from $16,763,000 to $26,485,800.

Even more striking is the growth of Costa Mesa, inland across the Coast Highway. In 1944 its population was 1,425 families; in 1949 it was 3,400. In 1944 the purchasing power there was $3,140,000; in 1949 it had rocketed to $11,200,000. In order to forecast the purchasing power upon which Lido Shops may depend, McConnell's Economic Survey, covering all the communities in and around Newport Harbor except Costa Mesa, considers at first only the permanent residents: 15,453 people (or 4,351 families) with purchasing power of $18,086,000. From this is deducted $8,310,000 for expenditures outside retail stores: savings and insurance, for example, mortgages and rentals, taxes both Federal and local, automobile and boat upkeep and financing. This leaves a total of $9,776,000 "spendable commodity dollars", i.e. Buying Power. $2,500,000 was spent at Lido Shops. All but $366,000 of the rest was spent in competing centers, in Newport, on Balboa Island, on Balboa Peninsula, in Corona del Mar, along the Highway. So far, however, the analysts have not taken into account the added purchasing power during the 4- to 6-month summer season; also Costa Mesa has not yet been put into the ledger.

The summer residents' "spendable commodity dollars" are estimated at $1,762,000. For Costa Mesa, after subtracting expenditures outside retail stores ($6,005,000) from the total purchasing power of its 3,400 families, the "spendable commodity dollars," for a year, are estimated at $5,195,000. But Costa Mesa will pre-empt $3,350,000 of this, leaving $1,845,000 to be spent elsewhere.

The summer residents and Costa Mesa together offer a safety margin, therefore, of $3,607,000. The analysts estimate that one-third of this—$1,202,000—should be added to the Lido Shops take, so that gross sales there should be $3,702,000. A significant trend, which makes the long-term prospects for Lido Shops even more encouraging, is the number of families who start as summer visitors and then develop into year-round residents.

The design of the stores themselves is efficient as well as interesting. They are notable for high ceilings and restrained modern design, particularly in the fenestration. Both the supermarket and the drug store have extensive mezzanines and no basements. This mezzanine space is used for offices and storage.

In the supermarket incoming merchandise, delivered at the freight dock at the rear of the building, is lifted directly to the mezzanine by power conveyor. It is distributed in large storage piles according to the location of the various departments on the sales floor, and then moved into place by gravity chutes as required. Also on the mezzanine floor of the supermarket are rest rooms and the Ship's Galley, an order room for supplies to be delivered to ships in the harbor. It is anticipated that an increasing number of yachts will moor in the marina provided by Lido Shops on the harbor frontage, and then come to this supermarket to outfit their galleys for cruises which may range from three days to three weeks.

Throughout Lido Shops special attention is being paid to color and to landscaping. The supermarket front entrance, for example, is marked by a group of 70 ft. tall palm trees. Smaller trees and shrubs soften the outlines of the parking area in rear *(see page 279).*

Extremely conscious of the ugliness which can be created by uncontrolled combinations of color, but conscious also of the stimulating effect of carefully planned transitions from one color to another, the architect (Dwight Gibbs) has prepared a standard color chart. All exteriors will fit into this formula; it will also act as a guide for the decoration of interiors. Advertising signs must be approved by a three-man committee of owner, architect, and advertising counsel.

THE REAR (PARKING AREA) ENTRANCE TO THE SUPERMARKET IS RICHLY PLANTED

Pacific Ocean

Balboa

Lido Isle

Newport Harbor

Super Market

City Hall

Theater

Drugs

AT LEFT ARE THE FIRST THREE UNITS OF LIDO SHOPS. COMPARE WITH THE MODEL OF THE COMPLETED DEVELOPMENT ON PAGE 274

SUPERMARKET FRONT ENTRANCE SET BACK FROM ROAD

IN LIDO SHOPS, already described on the preceding pages, the supermarket and drug store (the only buildings except the theater so far constructed) each stand as large, independent buildings. They are unified by the same rhythm of fenestration and by the same sign script. The mezzanine is for offices and storage.

MODERN DESIGN, SIMPLE CLEAN LINES, ON PARKING AREA SIDE OF SUPERMARKET

BY NIGHT DRUG STORE CORNER FLAUNTS DISPLAY OF TALL OPEN FRONT. MEZZANINE STORAGE AT REAR

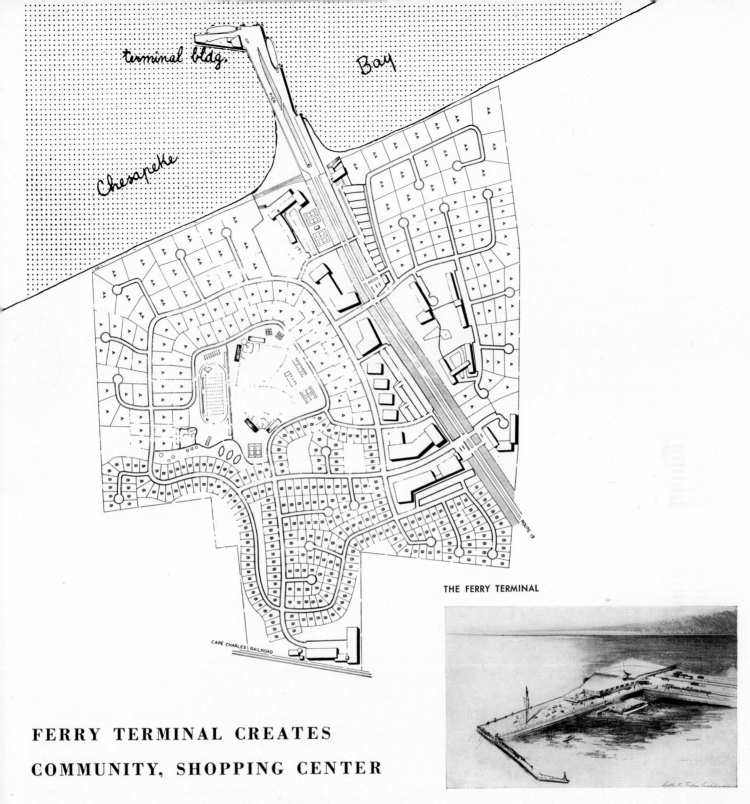

Map labels: terminal bldg. · Bay · Chesapeke Bay · PIER · ROUTE 13 · CAPE CHARLES RAILROAD

THE FERRY TERMINAL

FERRY TERMINAL CREATES
COMMUNITY, SHOPPING CENTER

KIPTOPEKE BEACH, Va. has now replaced Cape Charles as the northern terminal of the Norfolk-Cape Charles ferry. Being somewhat nearer the tip of the Delmarva peninsula this new terminal has enabled the ferry to cut 30 minutes from its crossing time. This is a vital link in U. S. Route 13, one of the most important north-south highways along the eastern seaboard. A new community to be built here will consist of single-family houses on lots ranging from one acre down to 75 x 125 ft. To isolate these from the heavy traffic to and from the ferry terminal on U. S. 13, this highway is channeled between two strips of parkland, and then further divided from the residential areas by a belt of non-residential building which will include the shopping center, a motor inn, and accommodation for trucks and their drivers. All of these are, of course, to a greater or lesser extent dependent upon highway trade. However, it is considered that as the community is built up the stores will draw an increasing amount of purely local trade.

Developer: Kiptopeke Beach Land Corp.
Architect: Lester C. Tichy.

TABLE OF STORE SIZES

The table on this and the following three pages lists stores by type and size in all of the shopping centers covered in this volume. The size is indicated in square feet of ground covered. A parenthetical number after a store area figure indicates that there is more than one store of the same type in that particular center. The list progresses from the smaller to the larger centers.

This table can be a valuable guide in preliminary shopping center planning. A word of caution is necessary, however. No two centers can have exactly the same store requirements nor can the fact that something has been done previously be used as an index to prove that it is entirely satisfactory. Market analysis *(see page 17)* is the only safe and accurate way for budgeting store size and type in a new shopping center.

SHOPPING CENTER / TYPE OF STORE	Springwell Park, Dearborn, Mich. page 272	Lake Shore Drive, Shreveport, La. page 144	Michigan Avenue, Washington, D. C. page 110	Fairlawn Shops, Stamford, Conn. page 104
FOOD STORES Groceries	3,200	15,200	7,810	2,240
Other Food Stores				
Delicatessens				1,120
Candy, Nuts, Confectionery				
Bakeries			1,420	1,615
GENERAL MERCHANDISE Department Stores				
Variety Stores		2,820		
Yard Goods				
APPAREL Men's & Boys' Clothing	1,200			
Women's & Misses' Clothing	1,750			
Infants' & Children's Wear		630		
Women's Accessories				
Shoes		620		
FURNITURE - HOUSEHOLD - RADIO Furniture				
Household Appliances				755
Radio, T.V., Music				
Drapery, Upholstery, Floor Coverings				
Housewares				
AUTOMOTIVE GROUP Auto Dealers				
Auto Accessories				
Gas Stations				
HARDWARE Incl. Paint & Seed Stores			2,485	
LIQUOR Package-Goods Stores				
DRUG STORES	2,240		3,900	2,240
EATING PLACES Restaurants, Luncheonettes		630		
Bars & Taverns				
OTHER RETAIL STORES Jewelry, Silverware		780		
Books, Stationery				1,120
Gift Shops	1,650		1,207	
Newspapers, Cigar Stores, etc.				
Florists			1,207	
Photo Supplies				
Opticians				
Sporting Goods				
Luggage & Leather Goods				
Pet Shops				
SERVICE STORES Cleaners & Laundries		630	1,207	
Self-Service Laundries				990
Barbers, Beauty Shops	1,500	620	1,207	910
Shoe Repair		630		
PROFESSIONAL OFFICES	c. 3,000			1,275
BANKS				
POST OFFICES				
THEATERS *				
COMMUNITY BUILDINGS, NURSERIES, ETC.	1,500			
VACANT & UNKNOWN				

ALL FIGURES ARE SQUARE FEET

Fresh Meadows, Long Island, N.Y. (Secondary Center) page 255	Fresh Meadows, Long Island, N.Y. (Secondary Center) page 255	Port Edwards, Wisconsin page 112	Naylor Road, Washington, D.C. page 114	Jefferson Village, San Antonio, Tex. page 122	Aero Acres, Middle River, Md. page 128	Linda Vista, San Diego, Calif. page 236	Broadway-Crenshaw, Los Angeles, Calif. page 174	Coral Hills, Washington, D.C. page 116	Fairway, Country Club District, Kansas City, Mo. page 86	Park Lane, Baltimore, Md. page 108	Broadmoor, Shreveport, La. page 142
6,600	10,000	5,900 (2)	7,500	10,170	4,500	9,000	22,000	8,960	8,368 (2)	7,200	16,500
									6,750	1,800 (2)	
1,200	1,200					4,800					
									1,020	1,700	540
1,200	1,200		1,050	2,250		1,900			868	1,700	
						39,675	58,000				
			2,100	6,750		16,800	22,500	4,100	3,108	8,000	3,400
				2,250			8,250				1,660
					1,680		11,250	1,230			
					1,800		11,200		868	1,700	1,800 (2)
			840				5,250	1,230	780	5,700 (2)	
							3,500				
						4,800	6,000	1,230		1,700	1,080
									1,980 (2)	1,700	1,120
				1,020						1,700	
											1,560
							Yes		Yes (2)	Yes	Yes (2)
		1,175		4,500				3,200	1,020		1,660
1,200		1,400			1,440	550		2,900			
2,160	2,320	1,800	3,000	8,500	2,100	6,600	20,250 (2)	7,550 (2)	2,450	4,800	2,960
		1,140	2,800		1,800		11,250	2,500	2,100	6,000	
						2,500					
				2,250							750
				1,020							
			1,050	2,250				800		900	
1,200	1,200										
				1,020						900	
				2,250							
3,000	1,200		1,050		1,560	2,000		2,560	868	850	2,160
											1,560
	525	1,400	1,050	3,270 (2)	2,520 (2)	4,000 (2)		1,870 (2)	1,302 (2)	900	2,910 (2)
	1,200							508	434	850	800
1,200		1,984				1,300	36,000		1,250		560
		3,125			1,950		7,500	600		2,100	
				1,020							
					6,000			8,000	6,250		7,000
	1,875	1,375			1,800					Yes	
1,200										900	

CONTINUED OVER PAGE ▶

SHOPPING CENTER / TYPE OF STORE	Cameron Village, Raleigh, N.C. page 147	Nob Hill, Albuquerque, N.M. page 126	Oakland Gardens, Queens, Long Island, N.Y. page 106	Foster Village, Bergenfield, N.J. page 270	City Line Center, Philadelphia, Pa. page 134	El Rancho Santa Anita, Arcadia, California page 140	Hampton Village, St. Louis, Mo. page 188	Los Alamos, New Mexico page 242	Edmondson Village, Baltimore, Md. page 138
FOOD STORES Groceries	15,750	4,900	14,040 (2)	10,800	15,500	17,200 (2)	30,000	9,300	15,000
Other Food Stores	2,580 (2)		3,760 (4)						1,200
Delicatessens			1,910 (2)	900					
Candy, Nuts, Confectionery			670		600				1,430
Bakeries	1,290	2,158	2,730 (2)	1,800	600			2,880	1,870
GENERAL MERCHANDISE Department Stores	7,500						21,700	4,000	15,000
Variety Stores	6,800	4,900				1,680	11,500	4,800	9,900
Yard Goods			490	900			1,100	4,120	2,200
APPAREL Men's & Boys' Clothing		1,320	1,125		1,200	1,020	1,100		3,750
Women's & Misses' Clothing	2,540	1,276	670	1,800	3,600 (2)	750	13,800 (4)		7,950 (2)
Infants' & Children's Wear	2,180	3,080	1,650 (2)	900	1,200	1,260	1,100		2,400
Women's Accessories		1,113	780 (2)		1,200	600			4,160 (2)
Shoes		2,158	1,980 (2)	1,800	2,400		2,200 (2)	2,250	2,200
FURNITURE - HOUSEHOLD - RADIO Furniture	12,000		3,485 (2)	900	5,610 (3)			2,960	
Household Appliances				900			1,100		
Radio, T.V., Music	6,000		2,575 (2)		1,200	1,000	1,100	1,820	3,630
Drapery, Upholstery, Floor Coverings				900	1,800		2,200 (2)		
Housewares									
AUTOMOTIVE GROUP Auto Dealers									
Auto Accessories									4,950
Gas Stations	Yes			Yes		Yes			Yes
HARDWARE Incl. Paint & Seed Stores		1,700	2,380 (2)	2,700	3,300	1,750	1,100	3,300	1,870
LIQUOR Package-Goods Stores			490	900		1,800			
DRUG STORES	2,540	3,320	4,120 (2)	900	4,080	3,000	6,900	4,050	7,500
EATING PLACES Restaurants, Luncheonettes	5,950		2,860 (2)	3,450 (3)			1,100	10,800 (2)	4,270 (2)
Bars & Taverns							1,100		
OTHER RETAIL STORES Jewelry, Silverware	2,540				900	500		1,920	910
Books, Stationery		3,400 (2)	980	900	2,400				
Gift Shops	1,290	1,386	1,000	400			2,200 (2)		2,200
Newspapers, Cigar Stores, etc.								1,200	
Florists					600	500	1,100		
Photo Supplies					600	1,080			1,870
Opticians			700						
Sporting Goods							1,250	2,700	1,400
Luggage & Leather Goods									
Pet Shops							320		
SERVICE STORES Cleaners & Laundries	4,890 (2)		1,670 (2)	1,800	900	1,500	2,750	2,200	1,400
Self-Service Laundries	1,290	1,612		900			1,100		
Barbers, Beauty Shops	2,580 (2)	1,991 (2)	1,630 (2)	1,300 (2)		2,490 (3)	1,100	5,400 (2)	
Shoe Repair		1,378	430	400		650		1,500	2,200
PROFESSIONAL OFFICES	1,290	7,106	2,425				44,000	3,360	
BANKS	2,080				1,800			2,700	3,750
POST OFFICES			4,120		480			7,000	
THEATERS					19,000			12,600	15,000
COMMUNITY BUILDINGS, NURSERIES, ETC.								20,400 (4)	2,400
VACANT & UNKNOWN			1,125				1,100		2,670 (2)

◄ CONTINUED FROM PRECEDING PAGE

Ridgeway, Stamford, Conn. page 130	Prairie Village Country Club Distr. Kansas City, Mo. page 88	Bellevue, Seattle, Wash. page 222	Fresh Meadows, Queens, Long Island, N.Y. page 248	Levittown, Long Island, N.Y. page 258	Suburban Square, Ardmore, Pa. page 191	Highland Park, Dallas, Texas page 90	Shirlington, Arlington Co., Va. page 180	Glen Oaks, Queens, Long Island, N.Y. page 264	Town & Country, Sacramento, Calif. page 98	Northgate, Seattle, Wash. page 214
7,510 (2)	7,250	11,250	10,000	21,000 (2)	12,944 (3)	12,500 (2)	13,750 (2)	12,525	7,550 (2)	23,616 (2)
				3,600 (2)	800	300		3,450 (3)	4,600	5,184 (4)
			3,080 (2)				2,500	1,350	850	2,448 (2)
			1,000	2,250	460	1,375	800	2,250	530 (2)	1,440 (3)
	720			2,400	533	1,400	1,600	2,625 (2)	1,800	1,152
6,250			105,000	18,300 (2)	28,385 (3)	8,100 (2)	16,500	16,650		78,192 (2)
10,080	2,870	7,500	11,800	24,750 (2)		2,800	10,000	9,750	1,800	24,192 (2)
	440		2,480					1,200	2,250 (2)	4,608
2,144	1,280	1,800	4,000	4,800	3,860	1,050	4,700 (2)	4,200 (2)	3,000 (3)	6,983 (2)
6,630 (4)	816		8,000 (2)	12,750 (3)	13,915 (4)	1,750	16,480 (5)	3,375 (2)	3,175	31,680 (11)
1,258	576		3,059	7,200 (2)			4,100 (2)	7,575 (2)	1,650	2,304
675		1,200	770	3,000	5,301 (3)	3,775 (4)	6,900 (4)	3,675 (2)	1,830 (2)	4,320 (3)
	960	800	4,908 (3)	6,600 (3)	2,920	2,400 (2)	5,540 (2)	4,125 (2)	2,995 (3)	8,640 (3)
1,900	3,712 (2)		1,600	1,505 (2)				3,825 (3)	900	4,608
2,340					2,625	3,000 (2)			5,500 (3)	3,456
		1,400 (2)	1,560		1,400	704		3,047	2,540	
					1,420	450	1,800			
					1,715 (2)					756
							Yes			
	Yes	Yes	Yes	Yes (2)	Yes	Yes (2)	Yes	Yes		
	1,860 (2)	4,500			1,100	1,400	6,400 (2)	1,200	2,400 (2)	17,280 (2)
1,470		2,400	1,400	2,100				2,800	975	900	2,160
3,360	2,880	2,700	3,500	3,200	2,200	3,600	5,000	4,125 (2)	2,250	14,976 (4)
2,970	660	5,550 (2)	7,700		3,450	8,400 (2)	2,440 (3)	4,275 (3)	6,700 (3)	12,672 (5)
			3,200					1,500		
1,040	1,200 (2)	1,350	867	2,100	533	1,925 (3)	1,000	825	900	2,304
675	576	750	1,080	3,000	1,125	810		2,925 (2)	630 (2)	
2,400	420	800	1,600	900	5,570 (3)	675	1,900 (2)		4,030 (5)	2,304 (3)
			1,500							504
626	900	600	1,300		615	1,050	1,400	825	375	2,880 (2)
	720	400			1,660	1,050			825	1,008
			853	900	533	700	1,600			1,152
		800				1,500			800	2,304
			1,254		615				330	
									900	
2,400 (8)	990 (2)	1,200	1,600	3,150 (2)	850			4,000 (2)	1,725 (2)	675	1,152
310	720									1,152
970	2,264 (3)	1,650 (2)	2,600 (2)	1,800 (2)	861	4,500 (3)	3,150 (3)	1,900 (3)	1,425 (2)	1,260 (2)
	360			900				1,250	450	1,152
	3,180	11,100	17,600	6,500	8,110	11,860	21,154	5,100	4,325	3,456
5,032	2,856	4,000 (2)	9,000 (2)	2,100		3,600	3,200		2,700	9,648 (2)
2,560	1,920		5,400			3,300	2,800	1,250	450	1,008
9,500		7,200	22,000		10,800	7,000	13,000			11,000
		900	28,000	1,575				1,350		
7,720 (4)	1,450			4,500 (2)	1,921	2,800		5,725 (5)	3,525 (5)	

ALL FIGURES ARE SQUARE FEET

ACKNOWLEDGMENTS

The McKim Fellowship, which was awarded to Bruno Funaro, has been responsible for the basic research in this book. The authors wish to express their gratitude to every individual and organization that contributed material for this volume including those whose names appear herein. Homer Hoyt, Larry Smith and Kenneth G. Welch were most cooperative in supplying information on economic surveys. Howard T. Fisher & Associates, Clarence Stein, and the Urban Land Institute were most helpful in having made their extensive files available to the authors as were the editors of *Architectural Forum the Magazine of Building, Architectural Record,* and *Progressive Architecture.*

The work of the following photographers is included in *Shopping Centers:* Aerial Photo Service 90, Apex Photo 119, Bob Bailey 44 (top), 50 (bottom right), Chas. Baptie Studios 181, Barnes & Caplin 127, Harry H. Baskerville 200, Brant Studios 222, 230 (bottom), Kenneth S. Brown 70 (bottom), 214-215, Louis Checkerman 30, Marjory Collins 235, Copy Craft 205 (2), Gil Culver 100 (bottom right), Delmer L. Curtis 90, Dearborn-Massar 225, 227 (2), 229, 230 (top), F. M. Demarest 64, George Dorrill 190 (2), Louis Dreyer 25, 123, Wm. Eccles 169, Ernst Studio Co. 184, Fairchild Aerial Survey 27, Lionel Freedman, Pictor 195, 199, Lee Frenzel 94 (bottom right), Alexander Georges 72 (top right), Gottscho-Schleisner 56, 167, Ben Greenhaus 163 (top), Kent Hitchcock 277, W. H. Hoedt Studios, Inc. 208, Floyd Hopkins 278 (bottom), Hylite, Inc. 45, 80, 84, Dorothea Lange 71 (top right), J. Alex Langley 261 (top 2), C. "Pop" Laval 97, Russell Lee 7 (top left), 72 (top left), Manning Bros. 57 (bottom right), McAnally Studios 93, Moulin Studios 210, Pacific Aerial Surveys 218, Pacific Air Industries 47, 166, 174, 218, Pacific Northwest Photo Pool 220, Elwood M. Payne 129, Paul Peters 50, Photo Bureau, M.L.I. Co. 246 (top), Photograph House 202, Pilch 242, Edward Ratcliffe 76 (bottom), Floyd Ray 72 (bottom left), 179 (right), Otto Rothschild 73 (top right), 177 (top), Frederick C. Ruhl 121, Jerry Salsberg & Assoc., 253 (2), 254, Ben Schnall 133 (bottom right), 161 (right), Julius Shulman 48, 49 (2), 69 (right), 77 (top and bottom right), 102, 103, 164, 165, 168, 170, Skelton Studios 75 (left), 99, 100 (top and bottom left), 101, Skyviews, N. Y., 264, Studna-Millard 79, 85, 86, 88, Dean Stone & Hugo Steccati 54 (top left), 68 (top right), 72 (bottom right), Thomas Airviews 162-163 (center spread), 249, 258, 260, John Vachon 7 (center), 68 (center right), Nowell Ward Photo 63, 105, Lewis P. Watson 155 (2), Dick Whittington 33 (top center), 58 (bottom), 76 (top left), 95, 178, M. Wilson 72 (center), 75 (right), 186, 187 (3), H. O. Wiseman 145, T. D. Wood 191.

The authors also wish to give their thanks to William W. Atkin for nursing the book through from manuscript to finished product, to Marion LaFollette for page layouts, Ralph Meyer for drawings, and to Mr. and Mrs. William McRostie of the Architectural Book Publishing Company for their help in collecting material.